THE
SUCCESSFUL
THERAPIST

THE
SUCCESSFUL
THERAPIST

*Your Guide to
Building the Career
You've Always Wanted*

Larina Kase

WILEY

John Wiley & Sons, Inc.

Published by John Wiley & Sons, Inc., Hoboken, New Jersey.
Published simultaneously in Canada.

Library of Congress Cataloging-in-Publication Data:

ISBN-13 978-0-471-72197-0
ISBN-10 0-471-72197-2

Printed in the United States of America.

10 9 8 7 6 5 4 3 2 1

Contents

CONTENTS

Acknowledgments

To all of my educators, mentors, colleagues, and supervisors who have helped me to become a successful therapist and writer and a connoisseur of knowledge.

To my editor at John Wiley & Sons, Inc., David Bernstein, for all of his excellent suggestions.

To my father for serving as a role model of a shrewd, ethical, self-made businessperson throughout my life.

To my mother for the support which has shaped me into who I am.

To my grandparents for teaching me some of life's most important lessons.

To my sister, Nicole, for endless encouragement over the years.

And to John for believing in me and sharing in my joys and accomplishments.

CHAPTER 1

Be the CEO of Your Career

"If you don't know where you are going, you might wind up someplace else."

Yogi Berra

In the long run, we only hit what we aim at.

Henry David Thoreau

YOU DESERVE TO HAVE THE CAREER YOU REALLY WANT

As therapists and mental health professionals, we have the opportunity to experience wonderfully rewarding and exciting careers that make a real difference in people's lives, communities, and organizations. You already know this—it may even be the reason you entered this field.

The practice of mental health is, however, one of the more difficult and challenging vocations. Having undergone years of training, unpaid practicum placements, seemingly endless tests and evaluations, long nights of writing dissertations or theses, and thousands of dollars of student loans, we finally obtain internships that pay around $15,000 a year, or postdoctoral fellowships or jobs that pay around $25,000 or $30,000 a year, and we have to take licensing exams that can cost from $1,000 to $3,000 when you include study materials and fees. Ultimately we get jobs that can be emotionally exhausting and that may not provide the compensation we deserve.

This sounds like a pretty dismal situation on some levels, but it does not have to be. The solution to these frustrations is to begin to approach your career as if you were the chief executive officer (CEO) of a major corporation. You can take the leadership role in your own career, forge a direction for yourself, and follow your passion. There is no reason that you cannot do what you love *and* earn a comfortable living doing it. As a CEO/therapist, you can start to create a more rewarding career by being proactive in designing opportunities for yourself.

CEOs are all about profit. Their success and the ranking of their company hinges largely on the profit they earn for their shareholders. But profit can be defined in many ways, not only numbers and money. A career can provide many profitable rewards, including the following:

- Monetary compensation
- Personal fulfillment
- Helping clients make major life changes
- Collaborating with expert colleagues
- Creating exciting new programs
- Exploring different avenues such as teaching or writing
- Contributing to and disseminating psychological research
- Having your dream office in the place you want to live
- A healthy balance between your work and family life

Profit Follows Value

Regardless of what is in your portfolio of desired profits, you deserve to be profitable. Your profit follows your vision. When you decide what is most meaningful and important to you, and pursue that, your career becomes more rewarding on several levels. Profit is also a close companion of value. Profit results when you deliver something of value. *Value* refers to the monetary, material, or personal worth that creates profit, utility, merit, meaning, or importance. Another definition of *value* is a principle, standard, moral, or quality that is significant to you.

As psychologists, we often ask our clients to engage in self-assessment, but we do little of it ourselves as it relates to our careers. Take some time now to think about what you most value and how you can create value in your career. Think about how you can provide for yourself and become happy, fulfilled, and wealthy in different areas of your life. Ask yourself, what do I really value? To help answer this question, complete the following assessment of your career values. Rank-order the list of core career values in terms of what is most important to you. Add your other values to this list.

Core Career Values Worksheet

Career Value	Ranking
Stability of position and income	_____
Feeling relaxed, calm, and stress-free	_____
Intellectually stimulating work	_____
Working with enjoyable and interesting colleagues	_____
Room for spontaneity and change	_____
Attainment of a powerful leadership position	_____
Financial wealth	_____
Limited hours—time for family and socializing	_____
Client population (presenting problems, etc.)	_____
Flexibility in work schedule	_____
Opportunity to work within a high-powered team	_____
Working with a reputable organization or university	_____
Independence of decision-making	_____
Convenience of work's geographical location	_____
Entrepreneurial opportunities	_____
Recognition for successes	_____
Creativity involved with the type of work	_____

Once you know your primary career and life values, you can begin to think about how you can create value in your career. First and foremost, you can create value for yourself by adhering to your fundamental career values from the preceding list. Recognizing your values will help you create a vision for your career (discussed in Chapter 2) that will guide you in making decisions consistent with what is truly important to you.

For career success, you also need to understand what other key people value. What does your employer value? Employers and agencies differ in terms of what they look for in employees. Some want employees who will accept a low salary. Some value therapists who do excellent work with their clients. Other employers prioritize efficiency and seek clinicians who can see a certain number of clients each week. Some organizations look for people who will be excellent researchers and contribute to the body of knowledge on a subject. Other agencies want employees who will be great teachers and supervisors.

The more specifically you can define what your employer values, the better you will be able to achieve it. You will then know how you can provide real added value. Ask yourself about the values of many layers in your work system: the organization as a whole, your department, your team or group, and your supervisor. Think about how you can add value on each of these levels. You can use this process to keep you focused and best advance your career.

If you are applying for a job, a great question to ask is, what does this prospective employer value? When you know the answer to this question, you can highlight the aspects of your training, experiences, and interests that are in line with what the employer values. I have found this practice very useful when I have applied for positions. When you are asked questions in an interview, you can likely think of several examples and answers that you could give. When you understand the values of the people asking the questions, you can pick the response most in line with those values. This is not to say that you should answer in a way that is not completely honest, but when you have many possible answers, you can use these ideas to help guide you in making the best response possible.

Another important value system to understand is that of your clients. Just as there are differences between various employers' value systems, there may be similarities and differences in what your clients place worth on. Think about how you have created value for your clients in the past and what they have been most pleased with or have most appreciated. When you understand clearly what your clients value then you can find ways to improve your ability to offer those things to them. If your clients have really appreciated your focused, time-limited approach to treatment, you can take continuing education seminars on time-limited and empirically supported treatments. If you find that your clients note how your office feels like a soothing oasis for them, you can focus your energies on continually refining your office interior and atmosphere.

In summary, understanding what you and others value is important because it allows you to create real value—for your own career and for those you work for or help through your treatments.

IT'S WIN-WIN

Behavioral health specialists have much to offer the world. From groundbreaking research data to stellar clinical skills that help people dramatically change their lives, to abilities to unite different groups of people, we have the potential to make a significant impact. In order for this impact to be greatest, two factors need to exist. First, accurate information needs to be widely disseminated to the public. Second, psychologists should be adequately compensated, in terms of both fulfillment and profit, so they can best perform in their careers and best help their clients.

You may be thinking, "My mission is to help other people—why is it so important to think about myself and profit?" This is a good point, and you certainly want to integrate your ideals about helping people and populations into your career mission statement. It is possible, however, to help people *and* earn a great living. In most cases, you are in the best position to truly help others once *your* needs are met and you have helped yourself. We know that financial concerns are some of life's greatest stresses. When you are worrying about how you will pay your car insurance, your children's college tuition, or your mortgage payment, are you really able to be fully present with your client? You can best help your clients if you are in a financially stress-free mind-set, not worrying about your own financial difficulties.

I remember a client session during graduate school, when my client was telling me about her student loan problems, and I could not seem to focus on what she was saying. Ironically, prior to the session, I had gone to the bank to withdraw $10, leaving only $8 in my account, and my student loan disbursement was not coming through for another couple of weeks. Some of my friends in other industries who were earning fantastic salaries enjoyed making fun of me and my 79-cent meals of boxed macaroni and cheese. (I was proud that I could make a box last for two meals—just 40 cents per meal!)

I eventually learned that I was able to do my best clinical work when I was well nourished (not just mac and cheese), not worrying about my rent, and feeling inspired and enthusiastic about the direction my career was heading. I could then take this inspiration and begin to think bigger and dedicate myself to helping as many clients as possible.

Financial stress can impact your career in another way. You may be a skilled therapist who has a lot to offer to clients. If you do not market your services, however, you will not be able to help many people who could very much benefit from your expertise—they cannot become clients if they do not know about you. You do not want to be the world's best-kept secret—you won't be helping anyone that way.

If you want to market your services to a larger audience, then you know that you will need to spend some money. Marketing takes money. To be able to market your psychological services to large audiences, you need some capital to fund your public relations, marketing materials, and so on. When you have a profitable career, you can easily do this. Not only will your career profitability help you and your family, but it will allow you to expand your services and help more clients.

INTEGRATE BUSINESS INTO YOUR PROFESSIONAL CAREER

You do not need to become a business psychologist to integrate business into your career. Many psychotherapists think of business as antithetical to psychotherapy, believing that if they are concerned about profit they are selling out or sacrificing the clinical work they know and love. This is not true—at least, it does not have to be, if you understand what you are doing and strictly adhere to your professional code of ethics and career values.

Business principles and projects can help you expand on your career no matter what your area of specialty. The first half of this book explores these principles and projects in detail. In the second half we explore various areas of career specialty that may suit you, such as forensics, teaching, administration, and consulting.

You can also maintain the clinical piece of your work and integrate some part-time projects (like writing, speaking, or consulting) into your career portfolio. Or you may decide to fully pursue business-related aspects of psychology or social work, such as executive coaching or small business consultation. There are many options for therapists who want to use business in their professional careers to boost income, improve their abilities to differentiate themselves from other therapists, reach a wider audience, and keep their careers continuously evolving and interesting.

Throughout this book, we explore different ways that therapists create value for themselves and others. But to start, here are a few examples:

- Maintain a position at a community agency and offer workshops on diversity to local businesses or large corporations.
- Work at a college counseling center 40 hours per week and see five private practice therapy clients per week.
- Obtain a position as a corporate psychology consultant with a major consulting firm.
- Develop and maintain a successful full-time private practice.
- Work part-time at a hospital and give workshops one or two days per week on stress management and time management to businesses.
- See 10 families per week in a private practice and provide consultation to six family businesses per week.
- Serve as a faculty member at a university and earn additional income by writing books on your areas of research.
- Work in a cognitive-behavioral therapy (CBT) practice or clinic and earn extra income by selling CDs and e-books on self-help CBT techniques.

This book will help you learn how to do any of these things or use any number of other ways that you choose to diversify your career.

A BIG PROMOTION

From therapist to CEO—that is a major promotion in terms of compensation and visibility. To be a successful CEO, you must develop some critical skills. An effective CEO is visionary, knows where the company and his or her career are heading, and is able to integrate the big picture with specific action steps and strategies to meet goals and objectives. Such a person understands the relationship between profit and value. The top CEOs have great leadership ability and the power to influence and motivate people. Behavioral health care professionals, too, have leadership skills and the ability to influence and motivate people. This book will help you develop the other skills of the CEO.

You may be thinking that it would certainly be nice to receive the compensation of a CEO, but that you came into the mental health field for a reason, and part of that reason is to *not* be a businessperson! Can you, however, entertain the idea of starting to approach your career as a CEO would approach her Fortune 500 company? This means beginning to think about a vision, business principles, a plan, and specific goals for your career.

Such a process need not seem foreign to a psychologist. In fact, it is similar to conducting a psychological assessment. When you conduct an assessment, you must first figure out what question needs to be addressed and how that fits into the bigger picture of the client's functioning. This is like the process of creating a business vision or mission for your career. Second, you conduct the evaluation, a step similar to learning specific business planning principles. The last step of a psychological assessment is to make specific recommendations for the client you assessed. This is analogous to the process of setting and achieving specific goals and action steps in various career arenas.

AN MBA FOR THOSE WHO DON'T REALLY WANT ONE

Many psychologists and psychology graduate students recognize that their careers would benefit if they knew more about business, but most have little interest in enrolling in an MBA program. However, it can be difficult to teach yourself about business, because business books are often written by specialists and filled with jargon. It is like being dropped off a plane in a foreign country, where everything is unfamiliar and you cannot understand the language. That is not to say that you should not try to read these resources, but reading a book like this one first will help put business concepts into a language therapists understand. You can then branch out and read the *Wall Street Journal* and *Fortune* magazine every morning if you like.

Some mental health professionals and graduate students in psychology take MBA classes in the evenings to learn more about business. While this can be a great way to learn about things like marketing, management, or finance, for many people it is not practical. Imagine working or going to class all day, only to go into the classroom for three hours at night. There is no time to see your family, have a social life, exercise, and do errands.

I sacrificed all these things and completed an MBA concurrently with my PsyD. It was a very difficult couple of years, and I continue to have a mixed view of my decision to sacrifice a social life. . . . Having survived that period, and having gone on to create and grow a corporation, I appreciate and use ideas from the MBA program every day, so I feel that overall it was worth it for me.

During my MBA program, I learned a great deal about business and businesspeople. Approximately 75 percent of what I learned will not be directly relevant for my career in psychology. For someone who is not inherently interested in business, completing an MBA in order to get the useful 25 percent may not be practical. Because this knowledge can greatly benefit you in your professional career, I include in this book the most helpful 25 percent. More important, I include many interviews and ideas from other therapists who have tried these ideas and found that they work.

Rather than present these principles in an abstract way, I offer them in the context of a business plan for your career. You will learn how to create a business plan, both to help you understand fundamental business principles *and* to help you to take the approach of a CEO so that you can develop your ideal career.

A BUSINESS PLAN

The idea of creating a business plan for your career may sound like a foreign concept or may sound uninteresting to you. But learning how to develop a business plan can help you do the following:

- Clarify what you really want to accomplish in your profession.
- Plan for the various areas that lead to career success (i.e., finances, marketing, etc.).
- Understand how to turn your calling and your goals into your occupation and daily practices.
- Create numerous strategies and methods for accomplishing what you want.
- Write a business plan for your private practice or company, your program or workshops, or products you sell.

Instead of teaching business planning principles textbook style, I present them in the context of professional development. You may not have a business for which to create a plan at this point, but you definitely have a career to develop. The business plan process is divided into five steps:

1. Description of the business/your career
2. Vision and mission statement
3. Marketing plan
4. Financial plan
5. Management and operational plan

The second through fifth steps will be explained in detail over the next several chapters. Because marketing is such an integral component and there is so much to say about it, I have devoted both Chapters 3 and 4 to that topic.

To get started, let us first consider step one the description of your career. This is not the same as the vision and mission statement that we will cover in the next chapter; rather, it is a series of statements describing what your career is all about. We will use this information later to develop your vision and your mission statement.

Fill in the following lines with descriptions of the type of work that you currently do. Include factors such as where you work; who your clients are; the type of work that you do; the colleagues, supervisors, or other people with whom you work; and how you spend most of your work time.

Write Down Your Current Career Description

_____

_____

_____

SAMPLE CURRENT CAREER DESCRIPTION

Samantha graduated three years ago with a master's degree in social work. Here is how she describes her current career:

I am working in a community mental health center as a therapist. I see about 25 individual therapy clients per week and run several dialectical

10

behavioral therapy (DBT) groups, some for older adolescents and some for adults. I enjoy working with my colleagues because overall they are very nice and clinically astute. I like the diversity of the clients that I see in terms of socioeconomic status, ethnicity, and age. The location of my work is ideal because it is only a 10-minute drive from my house, and I am settled in this area with my family and have no interest in moving.

I do not like the pressure that is placed on the therapists in my setting to see 30 client-hours per week and run groups. I sometimes feel that the number of clients I see is the way that I am valued and evaluated, and that my strong clinical skills are overlooked or of lesser importance to the supervisors and administrators at my center. The other problem I have is that of independence—I am a very independent person and I do not like the sense of being watched over to make sure that I see all the clients I am expected to see. Some of the administrators do not appear to be very interested in my professional development or ideas for organizational improvement. I would also like some more creative outlets in my job because it can start to feel very routine.

After you have completed your description of your current work life, take some time to think about where you *want* your career to be. It is fine if you have no idea how to get there at this point. Think about the aspects that are crucial for you to find your career profitable and fulfilling. Again, do not worry about whether you know *how* to do them. This is the time to dream and think about what you would really enjoy and want from your career.

Look over the values that you selected and be sure to include your top three to five values. Consider factors such as the number of clients you will see; the types of clients with whom you will work; your weekly, monthly, and yearly income; the amount of space for creativity; issues of diversity and multiculturalism; the other professionals in your work environment; the type of office and setting; your work-life balance; where you will live; the combination of various types of activities (assessment; workshops and seminars; individual, group, couples, or family therapy; consulting; coaching; etc.); and active versus passive income. (Active income comes from ongoing work, like conducting therapy, assessment, or consultation; passive income includes revenue streams that keep paying after you have done the initial work—things like books, products, CDs, and videos).

Description of Future Career

_____

_____

_____

_____

_____

SAMPLE DESCRIPTION OF FUTURE CAREER

Now look at how Samantha envisions her future career:

> My future career will be one that fosters a greater sense of independence and entrepreneurship, while allowing for a good deal of collaboration with interesting and inspiring colleagues. I will be in a group practice with about four other colleagues. I will see both adolescents and adults. My average week will consist of seeing about 18 clients and running two groups—one support group for people with chronic pain, and one DBT group. My practice will be located within 20 minutes of my house and will be in a nice, professional complex of offices. I will be on a few insurance panels (those with the better reimbursement rates in my area), and clients with other insurance providers can submit their claims out of network.
>
> To supplement my private practice income and fulfill my need for creativity, I will write a column for my local newspaper and begin working on a nonfiction book, inspired by my work with therapy clients. I have always been told that I am a good writer, so I definitely want to include writing in my ideal career description. I will limit my hours to 40 or 45 per week so I have time to spend with my children before they go off to college.

You can see from this example that Samantha was able to utilize her career values to create some ideas for how she can get the most profit out of her career. When you have a good sense of what is most important to you, you can begin to determine how your optimal career will look.

Now you have the first piece in your business plan completed: the description of your career/business, including current position and future prospects. You also have a good idea for some of the opportunities that you want to work toward. Keep these in mind as you learn business concepts over the next several chapters. You are now on your way from therapist to CEO.

The United States Small Business Administration (www.sba.gov) recommends the following elements of a business plan.

Elements of a Business Plan

Cover sheet, Statement of purpose, Table of contents

I.   *The Business*
Description of business
Marketing and competition
Operating procedures
Personnel
Business insurance

II.   *Financial Data*
Loan applications
Capital equipment and supply list
Balance sheet and breakeven analysis
Pro forma income projections (profit and loss statements)
- Three-year summary
- Detail by month, first year
- Detail by quarters, second and third years
- Assumptions upon which projections were based
Pro forma cash flow

III.   *Supporting Documents*
Tax returns of principals for last three years
Personal financial statement (all banks have these forms)
For franchised businesses, a copy of franchise contract and all supporting
        documents provided by the franchisor
Copy of proposed lease or purchase agreement for building space
Copy of licenses, resumes of all principals, and other legal documents
Copies of letters of intent from suppliers, etc.

Interview with Lee Lister, CEO of Biz Guru LLC

Lee Lister's company, Biz Guru, focuses on helping companies create business plans. They can be reached at www.bizguru.us, telephone (866) 537-7575.

Who needs a business plan?
Many people think that they will need a business plan only if they are going to look for investors. This is not necessarily true. A business plan is actually the foundation of your business or career. If you were building a house, the investment would be the mortgage, but you need a good structure. You should not create a business plan just to get loans, but to plan who you want to sell to, what you want to sell, how you can differentiate yourself from others, and who your alliances will be (such as hospitals). If you have reached the point that you want to develop your own practice, consultants can help you decide how to develop a business plan.

What are some of the mistakes you have seen when professionals create a plan for their careers and businesses?
One of the major problems is not realizing how important your plan is. People download a template that everyone else has used. It is the difference between going to a job interview in a handmade suit versus one you purchased at discount store. Spending the quality time creating your plan can help you get familiar with what it is that you want to do.

What initial ideas do you recommend that your clients consider?
First, think about how you'll structure your business or career and how you want it to be perceived by your clients and peers. Second, understand what your market is and what your potential clients are looking for. Third, financials are important—be sure that you are not overstretching yourself. Know that most people do not make a profit in the first year. Do not try to turn a hobby into a business. Consider where to position your services. If you are working with agoraphobics, you should not locate your practice off the beaten path where it would take them two hours to access you. It is also nice to have other medical professionals nearby for professional development.

What are the challenges that professionals face when creating a business plan for themselves, their companies, or their careers?
Professional services face a uniform environment. It can be difficult to differentiate yourself from other professionals. You can do it by how you de-

scribe yourself and what demographics and target clientele you address. I recommend that people trust themselves to do their jobs properly, and if business planning is not your thing or your core competency, get help by reading a book like this or hiring an informed professional.

RESOURCES

BOOKS

Burton, J. E. (1999). *Total business planning: A step-by-step guide with forms* (3rd ed.). New York: Wiley.

Bangs, D. H. (2002). *The business planning guide*. Chicago, IL: Dearborn Trade.

Coomber, S., Crainer, S., & Dearlove, D. (2002). *The career adventurer's fieldbook: Your guide to career success*. New York: Wiley/Capstone.

Leuin, B. A. (2003). *Planning with a heart: A business planning book for women only*. West Conshohocken, PA: Infinity Publishing.

Middleton, J. (2002). *Smart things to know about your career*. New York: Wiley/Capstone.

WEB SITES

The United States Small Business Administration's business plan:

www.sba.gov/starting_business/planning/basic.html

For general business information:

www.business.com

Business Planning web sites:

www.businessplans.org

www.bplans.com

Biz Guru:

www.bizguru.us

TERMINOLOGY

CEO   Chief executive officer who heads a corporation.

business plan   A written description of the scope and goals of a business, including elements such as statement of purpose, financials, and marketing plan.

profitable (defined by Word Net 2.0, © Princeton University)   1. yielding material gain or profit: "profitable speculation on the stock market." 2. promoting benefit or gain: "a profitable meeting to resolve difficulties." 3. providing profit: "a profitable conversation." 4. productive of profit: "a profitable enterprise," "a fruitful meeting." Note that *profitable* does not solely refer to monetary gain.

SBA   The United States Small Business Administration.

shareholder   An individual who has a stake (usually monetarily) in a company in the form of shares; also called a stockholder. In your career these can be conceived of as those who are invested in your career progression.

value   1. monetary or material worth that creates profit. 2. worth in usefulness, utility, merit, meaning, or importance to the possessor. 3. a principle, standard, moral, or quality considered worthwhile or desirable.

value added   A term used in many business settings to describe the additional value or worth that an employee or work team brings to a project, scenario, or the place of employment. The value may be measured by multiple variables, such as financial, social, creative, innovative, or efficiency aspects.

CHAPTER 2

Your Vision and Mission Statement

Vision is the art of seeing things invisible.

Jonathan Swift

Good business leaders create a vision, articulate the vision, passionately own the vision, and relentlessly drive it to completion.

Jack Welch, Chairman, General Electric

WHAT IS A VISION?

Having a vision will enable you to say, "I know exactly where I want my career to go. I can see the purpose of my career so clearly it is tangible. This feeling is incredible because it helps to gear and guide me as I move along my career path. My decisions are clear and easy to make, I know precisely what I want. I am able to clearly communicate my career objectives to anyone who asks."

Does this sound nice to you? Wouldn't it be wonderful to know exactly what your career is all about, where it is heading, and where you currently are along the path to your destination?

WHY YOU NEED A VISION

The prominent business person, Jack Welch, stated that great leaders have a strong vision. Most people would agree that a key factor in any CEO's effectiveness is having a strong vision for their company and career. This strong vision is what enables them to motivate and positively influence others. Because of their great vision, people want to hear what they have to say, and the message is communicated in a powerful and inspirational matter.

In a business setting, the vision is the purpose or overall meaning of the company's existence. Effective and highly successful CEOs have the unique ability to foresee future trends, market factors, growth opportunities, setbacks, and challenges. They are able to rely on information gleaned from past experience and utilize it to plan for the future. A strong CEO has one foot standing solidly on the past and always has an eye toward the future.

A vision is also a crucial component of a business plan. When you begin a new company, you need to be able to articulate the purpose and the goals of the business. The vision is the backbone that supports and dictates the development of the business's goals, objectives, and daily operations. It is what enables the small business owner to obtain loans and funding, attract the best employers, effectively market to target customers or clients, sell successfully, and become profitable in an extremely competitive market in which most small businesses fail.

Just as a CEO and a small business owner need a strong vision, you need a vision for your career. You can work without one, but having a clear vision can help you achieve success not otherwise possible. Your vision for your career motivates you, and decision making becomes much easier.

Let's illustrate this with an example of one of my favorite things to do: travel. Say you are going on a vacation. What is one of the first things you need to think about for your trip? The purpose or your vision for the trip, right? You may actually picture yourself on the trip: hiking, reading a book in the country, exploring sites, visiting art museums, swimming in the ocean, and so on. You can see it so clearly, it is as if you are temporarily transported to the log cabin in the Alps. Of course this image is going to be very motivating as you sit in your office next to a pile of paperwork. The vision propels you to start making plans and taking action to turn the vision into a reality.

When you create your vision of your trip, you ask yourself, why am I going on this trip? Is it to relax and unwind? To spend quality time with family and friends? To do some adventure activities and try something new and wild? To lie on the beach and get a tan? To see some historic sites or learn about a new city? Your answer to this question forms the vision for your trip.

Lacking a vision for your trip, you may try to do it all and get overwhelmed and exhausted. I recently had such an experience on a trip to Europe. I didn't think much about the vision for my trip before I left. When I arrived there, I got excited about all the great things to do in nearby cities, and I spent every waking moment of my trip sightseeing and traveling around. Later I realized that what I had really wanted to do was to relax in a beautiful lakeside Italian town and eat as much pasta and gelato as possible. I don't deny that those day trips and sightseeing activities were great things to do. But during my flight home, I realized that I was completely exhausted and not rejuvenated like I had hoped to be when I had to return to a busy schedule. Vision helps you to keep a long-term perspective. I got caught up in the short-term view and my long-term functioning and fulfillment suffered.

As in this vacation example, a vision creates a long-term perspective for your career. After all, our careers in the mental health field are a long journey. For some, the journey started at a young age—we knew we wanted to be therapists or involved with health care and helping people heal. For others, interest in a psychology class in college sparked a desire to enter the field. Still others may have tried a different career first but felt a strong need to help people, which wasn't being fulfilled in that field, so they switched careers and came into psychology or psychotherapy via another route. Others began the process and then took a break due to life factors that arose, returning later to psychology.

The journey has been different for each of us, at times perhaps rocky and uncertain. Remember all those exams, writing a thesis or dissertation, grueling supervision sessions discussing incredibly difficult cases, sacrificing your social life, missing your children while sitting in a long class, wondering if you were really cut out to be in the mental health field, writing never-ending reports and case summaries, hours of preparation to teach one class, client crises . . . The list could go on and on.

Of course, the journey also presents numerous rewards: the joy of helping people make major life changes; the fascination of learning new theories and methods of therapy; feeling that you are truly following your dreams and doing what you love; meeting wonderful classmates, colleagues, and professors; jumping through the last hoop and getting licensed or certified . . . There are certainly many great moments.

The glue that holds all of these experiences together is your vision. Your vision takes all the puzzle pieces and puts them together to create a clear picture of what you really want out of your career. Without the glue, the puzzle could break at any time. You could lose track of certain key pieces; you could become frustrated that you did all that work only to have things fall apart; or you could feel unmotivated to figure out the challenging parts because you don't know what the picture will turn out to be or how it will stay together.

Imagine that you are preparing for a long flight, such as to Asia or Australia from the east coast of the United States. Now imagine that you don't know how long the flight is going to be, what is going to happen along the way, or where exactly you are going to end up. Do you think this would be a relaxing and enjoyable flight? Naturally, this scenario would be a lot more difficult to cope with than if you knew exactly where you were going, why you wanted to get there, and how long you could expect to take to get there. For instance, a useful vision would be, "I am traveling to Sydney, Australia, and it will take about 14 hours to get there. I will be there for two weeks to relax, visit friends, and rejuvenate before embarking on a major project when I return. I need to pack casual clothing with a couple nice outfits for going out to dinner with my friends." This trip sounds much more productive and less stressful than traveling without a vision and just getting on a plane.

The vision keeps your sense of purpose as clear as freshly Windexed glass. Going through your career without a vision can be like driving a car with a dirty windshield and mirrors. You can miss important signs and turns, feel easily frustrated, and not enjoy some of the beauty around you. Have you ever noticed how different the world looks from your car when you first come out of a car wash and the windshield is sparkling clean?

Just as knowledge about the flight to Australia makes the trip more enjoyable and endurable, and the spotless glass improves your driving abilities and experience, your career vision propels you ahead. It keeps you going in the best direction for you during the difficult times. It motivates you to pass those exams, work those long hours, write those tedious treatment plans, and get those progress notes done on time. For this reason, it is best to create your career vision as early as possible. If you are still in graduate school, now is a great time to begin formulating your vision. If you are a professional in practice, you may already have a vision for your career. If you have already been in practice several years and have not yet created your vision, it is never too late to do so. Just remember that the vision is always a work in progress, so reevaluate it regularly to make sure it is still exactly what you want.

Your Vision Can Help You Get a Job (or an Internship, a Practicum Placement, a Promotion, or a Raise)

If those many analogies about having a career vision have not yet convinced you, maybe I now have your attention. The market for great jobs is extremely competitive these days, and you need something to set you apart from all the other applicants who have the requisite skills and experiences. We go into this idea in Chapter 3, but basically, a strong career vision is what makes you as competitive as possible for job placements and career advancement. In order to effectively market yourself for a new position, or make a case for being promoted or given a raise, you must be able to clearly and concisely communicate your professional strengths and how they fit into your overall goals for your career.

When I served as a hiring manager at a major company, I would ask myself two fundamental questions when reviewing applicants: (1) What do they have to offer that would be a great fit for the company? and (2) Why are they interested in this position?

The first question is, of course, important because whoever is doing the hiring needs to know not only what experience and strengths you have but also why those are a good match for the position and for the organization. You may have incredible assessment skills, but if the company does not provide assessment services, that skill is not so relevant. The second question is important because it reveals what is motivating the potential employee. This helps the hiring manager discern whether the position will meet the applicant's needs, which would increase the likelihood of good performance and loyalty to the company.

With your vision in the back of your mind, you can easily describe why you want the position and how it fits in with your career aspirations. More important, you will be able to convey your passion for the position. Passion directly follows purpose, and when someone is passionate it is both obvious and contagious. Not only would you want to hire such a person, but you would want to work with them as well, which is critically important in service industries.

Compare the following two responses to this interview question: "Describe your experience working with children with attention deficit/hyperactivity disorder."

1. "I have worked as a practicum student at three community mental health centers and two schools. I have done many evaluations, diag-

nosing children with ADHD or the applicable disorders, such as conduct disorder, oppositional defiant disorder, or an anxiety disorder. I have treated about 20 kids, and collaborated with the treatment team to help create the best treatment plans, which typically included medications, education, and psychotherapy. I also have a good deal of experience working with family members and teachers."

2. "After exploring many clinical areas, about two years into graduate school, I decided to dedicate my career to furthering the appropriate diagnosis and optimal treatment of children with ADHD. I then sought out practicum placements at community agencies to gain experience in the assessment and treatment of these children. Since I learned that teachers and family members can significantly improve the functioning of children with ADHD, I pursued practicum placements in two schools and furthered my interest and experience in training parents and teachers."

Can you tell which is the vision-based response? Which is more compelling? Which conveys a strong sense of purpose and passion? Which person would you want to hire to work with you? Which person would you want to treat your child? The vision response is the second one. Essentially the same information is conveyed, but it is done from the standpoint of the person's career vision.

Once you know your vision, you can combine it with your mission (outlined next) and be able to say not only what your career purpose is but also exactly how you plan to get there. Without this information, people making hiring decisions may make assumptions about you and your purpose in pursuing that position, and these assumptions may not be to your benefit. The same is true for decisions regarding promotions and raises. When the deciding parties can see how the promotion or raise fits with your career vision—and is, therefore, in the organization's best interest, since they will be more able to optimally utilize you—they are much more likely to consider the change.

YOUR VISION CAN HELP YOU BE MORE INTERESTING, LIKABLE, AND ATTRACTIVE

Okay, maybe I went overboard on this section title, but I stand by the idea that your vision can make you more interesting and likable. What happens when you go to a cocktail party or a get-together and someone

22

asks you, "What do you do?" Do you respond with, "I'm a psychologist" or "I'm a social worker"? Many if not most mental health professionals respond this way. Unfortunately, these responses are not the most interesting or the best conversation starters. This is a shame, because we have such interesting careers to discuss.

What if, on the other hand, you say, "I help children who have learning disabilities to improve their school performance" or "I help couples with relationship difficulties figure out and get to the next step in their relationships"? Now you sound more interesting, and the people you have just met become curious and want to ask a follow-up question and get to know more about what you do. They may think of some good referrals for you, some great job opportunities they have heard about, or you simply may end up having an interesting and enjoyable conversation with them.

Revealing a bit of your career purpose makes you more likable. We know that people like others who are interesting, passionate, ambitious, and confident. We like to surround ourselves with people who can inspire us with their go-getter attitudes and behaviors. We want to know more about how they found a path that is right for them and how they are pursuing it. It is human nature to be curious about others once we are fed a little information to peak our curiosity. A response that demonstrates your vision will help you come across as much more self-assured and dedicated to your career's purpose than one that does not. It also generates referrals because people will know what you do and assume that you are good at it, seeing that you are so resolute in your career plan.

You Can Be Creative with Your Vision

The last thing that you want to do is rigidly adhere to your idea of what makes a perfect career. A vision is more of a general guiding principle than a set-in-stone snapshot of your dream destination. It can be used negatively if you begin following it in an inflexible way.

Sometimes opportunities come up that we never expected. You do not want to disregard these potentially excellent avenues just because they are seemingly not in direct line with your vision. Instead, before ruling them out, get creative and ask yourself how these situations may tie in to the overarching purpose of your career. Consider how an opportunity may lead you down a circuitous route to where you want to go. Think about how the situation could help you fulfill your core career values. Stopping to smell the roses and picking up some great information, skills, and contacts along the way is never a bad idea—unless that is all that you are doing.

Because serendipitous occasions are some of life's most enjoyable, rewarding, and interesting situations, use your vision to guide you but do not put on blinders and ignore different prospects. Thinking outside the box and looking for new ways to turn your hopes into reality are excellent ways to utilize your vision.

YOU MAY BE DISREGARDING SOME ASPECTS OF YOUR IDEAL VISION

Many mental health professionals have ideas about what they should *not* have in their vision. It is important to explore these, because you may be ruling out aspects that can actually fit in and add to your vision and purpose.

In working with many therapists on business planning, I have seen a couple of themes emerge. One is sacrifice and the other is compromise. Many therapists feel (or think they *should* feel) that helping others is so rewarding that they do not need financial wealth or significant compensation. Many also feel willing to compromise—since the work is meaningful, they can work for less income.

These ideas are neither good nor bad. They certainly make sense. At times, however, they come not from what people really believe or desire, but what they are trying to tell themselves. This is like the cognitive dissonance theory of Festinger, which states that we resolve dissonance by changing a negative or distressing belief. According to this theory, individuals seek congruence in their thoughts, beliefs, attitudes, and opinions. If there is dissonance between an attitude and a behavior, something needs to change. Typically the attitude will change to accommodate the behavior.

For instance, if the dissonance is, "I have seven years of advanced education, but I am making only $36,000" the resolution may not be to change your behavior and quit the job, but to change your beliefs or your attitude about this situation. Instead of changing careers or jobs, you could change the thought by saying, "It's okay that I am not earning much income, because I really enjoy the work."

But what if I told you that you could really enjoy the work *and* enjoy the satisfaction and freedom of a lucrative career? It is a *both/and* proposition, not *either/or*.

24

I am not saying that you *must* include a financial aspect in your vision. For many, it is not relevant—they may already be financially well off, or they may have sufficient cash flow for their basic needs and not want more. For many of us, however, the ideal scenario would be to do what we absolutely love *and* be well compensated for it.

WHAT IF YOU CAN HAVE IT ALL?

Maybe if you incorporate in your vision monetary compensation or other aspects that you previously thought should not be included, you can truly have it all. If these things are not part of your career vision and purpose, it logically follows that you will not achieve them as well as you could. We are all familiar with the concept of self-fulfilling prophecy, and it applies to career vision quite well.

First, it is important to figure out what you may have ruled out of your vision. I gave the example of income, but it could be any number of things: flexibility, independence, diversity, certain patient populations, particular types of student bodies, geography, hours you want to work, colleagues you want to work with, and so on. Take a few minutes now to think about whether you have excluded something from your career purpose that may in fact be important to you either now or down the line.

Whenever you find yourself thinking that you *should* include something in your vision, it may be an indication that you are neglecting something else. Some therapists, for instance, feel they *should* work with underprivileged clients, and they overlook their desire to work with very high-functioning individuals. Others feel they *should* start a private practice because it could be lucrative and they could better support their families, but they would actually *prefer* to work for an agency because of the steady client load and the types of clients they would get to see in a community setting.

Think about the things you may have ruled out of your vision. Why did you rule them out? Did you think they were things that you do not need or should not desire? If you can think of anything else that you may have ruled out of your vision, add it to your list above.

Next, consider what to include in your vision. You probably already have a vision at this point, although you may not really know it. Now is the time to work on clearly articulating it. You have probably helped many people explore their inner wants, needs, goals, and desires. You can use the same process with yourself to create your dream for your career.

You may be thinking, "Yeah, I've heard this stuff before, but what I want is practical, hands-on, how-to advice on how to turn the vision into a reality." Good point, but rest assured, you will get a lot of hands-on pointers throughout the rest of this book. None of those pointers will be helpful, though, if you are not headed in the right direction by creating your purpose or vision early on. Jumping to the strategies without determining your career vision is like starting a clinical treatment program with no evaluation, diagnosis, or case conceptualization. You would have nothing to guide you.

So take some time and complete the lists and worksheets I offer, to formulate your career's purpose. See this as a work in progress that can change over time, and revisit your vision periodically as you move through your career. I recommend revisiting it biannually and making applicable changes.

YOU ALREADY KNOW THE PROCESS OF CREATING A VISION

As we discussed in Chapter 1, the best visions are those that are closely aligned with your most important values. Again, creating value for your career and for the lives of your clients stems from understanding your own values. You use your values to construct your career vision.

As a therapist, you are trained in how to help clients examine themselves and explore their inner goals and drives. You can use a similar process in creating your own career vision. Developing a vision is something you know how to do but may not have done yet. We may know that it would be a good idea to go to the gym three days a week, but we may not actually go. If we were to go, however, we would know what to do when we got there. Creating a career vision is similar—you actually know how to do this process because you use a similar process in therapy.

Different theoretical orientations have different methods for helping clients learn about themselves and discover their own values and goals. For example, from a humanistic psychotherapy perspective, you help your clients by developing a relationship of unconditional positive regard with you, the therapist. Your clients create a sense of purpose in their lives and further their processes of becoming self-actualized in ways that are personally meaningful to them. In doing this, you help them to determine their values and purpose and then use these ideals to further their process of becoming what they want to be.

Similarly, in creating a vision for yourself, you use your career values to develop a sense of what you want out of your career. You take a non-judgmental stance on your values and incorporate your fundamental values into your plan for the purpose of your career. Your vision fuses together the ideas regarding what is most important to you and where you want to go with it.

From a cognitive-behavioral perspective, you help a client identify maladaptive thought and behavioral patterns that lead to anxiety, depression, or other distress. You create specific goals and homework assignments to assist the client to reach those goals. You help the client to begin thinking about things differently and changing behavioral patterns to result in a different outcome. As the therapist, you continuously help your clients to take steps toward meeting their goals and to assess their progress toward achieving those goals.

You can use a similar technique when you use the vision creation process with yourself. While the focus is not on eliminating pathology but on clarity of goals, the process is similar. First, identify what values you really have versus which values you think you *should* have. Explore how your belief systems affect your career values. During this process, you can identify how maladaptive thoughts can get in the way of creating and achieving your vision. For instance, the thought, "I should build a successful private practice" may get in the way of realizing your *true* vision, which may be something very different. You then begin challenging the thoughts that are getting in the way of your vision until your vision is a clear, distilled version of your most important values.

The same process will work for any theoretical orientation from which you practice. Because you have helped so many clients to explore their self-images, goals, and direction in life, you know how to do this process.

Think about some of the techniques or methods you have used to help your therapy clients understand and achieve their goals. Then try to use these processes to create your own career purpose and vision using the Career Vision Worksheet.

Career Vision Worksheet

Complete as many of these questions as you are able to. Depending on the way you think, you may choose to answer some of the questions out of order. Begin with the ones that are easier for you to answer.

What is your current job and how satisfied are you with it? _____

_____

What specifically inspires and satisfies you about your current job? _____

_____

_____

Your reason for doing what you're doing now is: _____

_____

_____

What are the underlying qualities or values from your current position that you know you want in your career? Into what types of positions do you see those qualities leading you in the next few years? _____

_____

_____

Your greatest hopes for your career include: _____

_____

_____

The reason you entered the field of mental health is: _____

_____

_____

The overarching purpose of your career is to: _____

_____

_____

The passions within your career include: _____

_____

_____

You will know that your career is turning out ideally when: _____

_____

_____

Your greatest personal and professional values include: _____

_____

_____

Career Vision Statement (summary of the above points in 1 to 5 sentences):

_____

_____

_____

_____

_____

_____

CREATE A MISSION STATEMENT FOR YOUR CAREER

Once you have an overall vision or sense of purpose, you can start to develop it into more action-oriented steps. A mission statement is fueled by your purpose/vision, principles, beliefs, values, and business practices. The mission is the actual business practices, but it is not enough just to describe the business practices without including the driving force behind these practices, your vision.

Returning to the travel metaphor: I created a trip to Mexico for a week for the purpose of relaxing and spending time with my partner, John. That was my vision or purpose. Once I knew that, I could start to create my mission statement. It would incorporate that purpose and then provide some objectives and general steps. For example, I would say that my mission for the trip was to relax by going to the spa, reading a book on the beach, or taking long naps in the afternoon.

Let's take a look at some examples of how mental health practitioners can create mission statements that incorporate their vision. The first example is Maria, a private practitioner working with traumatized children. Her mission statement is as follows:

Vision/Purpose: To help children and adolescents overcome childhood trauma in order to increase their chances of flourishing throughout life, and to create an emotionally and financially rewarding career to support myself and my own children.

Values: Helping others, positive change, advocacy against violence and sexual trauma, ending crimes against children, furthering education and growth, diversity, personal fulfillment, helping my own family.

Business Practices: Providing therapy, advocacy, counseling, education to parents and schools.

The second example is Don, an academician in a school of medicine, researcher, teacher, supervisor. Here is his mission statement:

Purposes: To spread knowledge of sound psychological theories to students; to train residents to better understand empirically supported therapies; to gain personal and professional fulfillment by providing diversified services; to be financially stable and ease the stress of unstable income experienced earlier in my career.

Values: Spreading knowledge, research, scientific discovery, variety, education, stability, security for the future (for retirement).

Business Practices: Conducting clinical research, designing and implementing studies, writing grants, supervising interns and practicum students, providing education to psychiatry residents, presenting data in grand rounds and other conferences, lecturing.

YOUR MISSION STATEMENT

Now you can work to create your individualized career mission. On the following worksheet, write down all things you are currently doing. Then think about them and see which ones align best with your vision. Include three or four business/career practices in your final mission statement.

Career Mission Statement Worksheet

My primary purposes, values, and career vision can be summarized as: _____

_____

_____

The above factors translate into my business practices in the following ways (check all that apply):

- ❑ Therapy with children and adolescents
- ❑ Therapy with adults
- ❑ Therapy with couples or families
- ❑ Therapy with a specific clinical population
- ❑ Therapy with groups
- ❑ Supervision of students, interns or advanced trainees
- ❑ Supervision of other providers (residents, nurses, etc.)
- ❑ Supervision of therapists or licensed professionals
- ❑ Peer group supervision
- ❑ Teaching large lecture courses
- ❑ Teaching small graduate courses
- ❑ Teaching other professionals
- ❑ Teaching or providing education to clients via classes
- ❑ Advocating for important issues
- ❑ Volunteering or providing pro bono work
- ❑ Consultation to mental health centers
- ❑ Consultation to physicians

❑ Consultation to schools

❑ Consultation to businesses

❑ Consultation to government agencies

❑ Providing workshops and seminars

❑ Writing books and articles

❑ Creating products, such as CDs

❑ Writing newsletters and brochures

❑ Providing life coaching

❑ Providing executive coaching

❑ Other services: _____

DIVERSIFYING YOUR BUSINESS PRACTICES

As you went through the preceding list of services and business practices, you may have noticed some things that you do not currently do but would like to do. If so, great! Put a mark next to the ones you are not currently doing but would like to do.

One of the primary missions of this book (see, it's important to have a mission!) is to help therapists enjoy and excel in their careers by diversifying their career areas. For instance, if you are currently working at a community mental health center and would like to begin seeing some therapy clients in private practice or conducting assessments part-time to supplement your income, that may be an effective way to address the various aspects of your vision. In the following chapters, you will learn how to diversify your career and pursue other avenues that are in line with your vision, so you can include these additional business practices in your mission statement.

A MISSION TO SHARE WITH YOUR CLIENTS

You may not wish to share all the personal aspects of your career vision and mission statements with your therapy clients. I recommend creating a separate mission statement to share with your referral partners and prospective clients. Being up-front and genuine with your clients in this way will greatly assist in your marketing. It also sets the best stage for therapy because clients will know whether you offer what they are looking for and whether working with you is likely to be a good match. Your mission statement conveys your passion and purpose and helps people to feel like they know you and want to work with you. If your mission does not involve working directly with clients, you may still want to include that on your marketing materials for potential consultation projects, teaching opportunities, speaking engagements, and so on.

When creating a mission statement that deals directly with providing therapeutic, assessment, or coaching services, the following elements should be included:

- Your theoretical orientation or approach to treatment
- Your view of change
- The process of treatment or consultation that you use

Take a look at the following example of a mission statement, created by Jytte Vikkelsoe, Ph.D., a private practitioner in Portland, Oregon. Jytte works with clients from a predominantly process-oriented standpoint and lectures around the world. Note how this mission statement reflects pieces of her professional philosophy and theory, the types of clients she works with, her belief about how people change, and how she helps people to change.

Imagine if dealing with change, uncertainty, and trouble was like reading a well-written suspense thriller. Imagine that exploring who you are in the midst of troubling experiences meant you were embarking on a daring adventure and lifestyle of ever-expanding horizons.

Each one of us has the right to a life of happiness and fulfillment. And though the human journey also includes the meeting with obstacles, change, uncertainty, loss, and trouble, problems can be seen as attempted solutions. Problematic moments usually mean we are stuck in a struggle between the new and the old, where we attempt to meet the new and unknown with habitual reactions. If we understand that a problem is nothing but a meeting with an experience that does not fit with who we know ourselves to be, we understand why change can't happen. From such a viewpoint, problems can be seen as possible meetings with new and unknown parts of ourselves.

Using a process-oriented approach combined with my own research, I work with individuals, relationships, and groups to help them modify their view of change.

Shifting attitudes about change, clients begin to see and experience problems as expressions of the unconscious mind. They see that change must first appear as a problem if it is to ever get their attention. Clients who develop this kind of attention become more curious about themselves. This curiosity is the first step inside their experience. Once inside, things that were problems become valuable information giving them a direct encounter with their creativity, potential and power. Through this process, clients gain awareness and control over issues about which they were most hopeless and begin to view themselves as the authors of their lives.

Here is another example of a mission statement, this time from the professional services marketing division of my business coaching practice, Performance and Success Coaching LLC:

If you are a professional who has a high level of training and experience helping people make significant changes in their lives, then I want to put those clients in front of you. I realize that you cannot help clients that you do not have. My mission is to help professionals to gain more clients, build their companies, market their professional services, and find the greatest benefit possible out of their careers.

By providing direct consultation and ongoing coaching and support, my clients are able to turn their business and career goals into reality. My coaching clients learn and utilize the most effective low-cost marketing strategies to attract new clients and create highly profitable practices. They are challenged to push themselves to new heights and they are able to greatly enjoy helping others without the stress of wondering how to build a thriving business.

FROM A MISSION TO GOALS

After defining the mission statement for a business, the company uses it to create very specific objectives or goals. You may have heard of a short-term plan or a long-term plan. It is a good idea to think of goals in terms of a time frame. I recommend time frames of 1 year, 3 years, 5 years, 7 years, 10 years, 15 years, and on up to 20-year-plans.

Goals that are well stated are considered to be SMART goals. An unknown goal-setting or marketing guru came up with this idea. To be a SMART goal, it must be:

Specific

Measurable

Action-oriented

Realistic

Timed

A good goal is set in very *specific* terms so that the results can be *measured* and quantified. It should be behavioral or *action-oriented* and should be achievable and *realistic* for you in the given environment or economy. Good goals are also *time-limited* so you know when to plan to achieve them.

Here is an example of a good goal: "Obtain professional licensure by completing all requirements, studying for and passing the state and national exams, and receiving notification of approval of application for licensure within the next year and a half, by March 2006."

Now that you have your vision to guide you, your mission to add your objectives, and your specific career goals, you are ready to begin marketing yourself and expanding your career.

Interview with Joan Borysenko, Ph.D.

Joan is a professional speaker and author of the 1987 classic *New York Times* best-seller *Minding the Body, Mending the Mind*. Her organization, Mind-Body Health Sciences, Inc., offering new dimensions in health and healing, can be contacted at (303) 440-8460, or on the Web at www.joanborysenko.com.

You are someone who has consistently relied on your career vision and found great success. What are some ways in which your vision has guided you?

I gave up an about-to-be-tenured position at Tufts University in 1978 to follow my career vision. Academically, people thought I was crazy. I went to Harvard to work with Herbert Benson with his work on meditation, which meant being an instructor on soft money. I did it because it was my vision. In 1988 I decided to leave the Harvard academic position. I was the director of research in behavioral medicine and was seeing a lot of patients, supervising, and administrating. I was so interested in the spiritual aspect and wasn't able to do it there, so I decided to leave. People thought, "She is a nut—why would she leave a dream job like that?"

When I was first talking with my lawyer about creating my own company, the lawyer asked about my vision for the business. I thought of being a conduit for information to go to people, as I have nurtured along other people's careers. Being a scientist in the area of mind-body, which is a big field, I created a niche market in which I took a scientific look on things that people consider spiritual or psychological.

Is it important to communicate your vision in your marketing?
Yes. I do so right on my web site. My bio states it: "Joan Borysenko, Ph.D. has a powerfully clear personal vision—to bring science, medicine, psychology and spirituality together in the service of healing." And it's spelled out on my home page like this:

> Hello and welcome to my web site. If you are already familiar with my work, then you know that I am a former Harvard medical scientist and psychologist whose vision it is to weave together science, psychology and spirituality in the service of wholeness. That's what this site is all about. Each one of us has the right to happiness and peace. As we move toward these qualities within ourselves, we become more joyful, creative and healthy. The attitudes of patience, kindness, gratitude, understanding and compassion naturally evolve, and we become generators of peace in our homes and workplaces. That is my highest vision for myself, and my wish for you. I hope that the information already posted here and the information that you can receive by subscribing to my monthly e-mail newsletter broadcast will help you take simple, practical steps toward wholeness in our busy world.

RESOURCE LIST

BOOKS

Abrahams, J. (1999). *The mission statement book: 301 corporate mission statements from America's top companies.* Berkeley, CA: Ten Speed Press.

Brinckerhoff, P. C. (2000). *Social entrepreneurship: The art of mission-based venture development.* New York: John Wiley & Sons, Inc.

Blanchard, K., & Stoner, J. (2003). *Full speed ahead! Unleash the power of vision in your company and your life.* San Francisco: Berrett-Koehler Publishers, Inc.

Hesselbein, F., & Rob J. (Eds.). (2002). *On mission and leadership: A leader to leader guide.* San Francisco: Jossey-Bass.

Jones, L. B. (1998). *The path: Creating your mission statement for work and for life.* New York, NY: Hyperion.

O'Hallaron, R., & O'Hallaron, D. (2000). *The mission primer: Four steps to an effective mission statement.* Richmond, VA: Mission Incorporated.

WEB SITES

Biz Guru—Create Your Mission:

www.bizguru.us

Business, vision, and mission planning:

www.bplans.com

Vision and mission creation:

www.missionexpert.com

Web site of Dr. Borysenko, which gives a great example of vision:

www.joanborysenko.com

TERMINOLOGY

business practices   A company's operational goals or methods for achieving its values and vision on a daily basis.

mission statement   An organization's (or individual's) declaration of its principles, purposes, and objectives. A mission statement contains the vision and adds to it the means of creating or achieving that vision—the objectives.

objective   A goal or something to be worked toward, striven for, and achieved. Objectives are best stated in behavioral and realistic terms so one can know when the goals are met.

principles   The fundamental values, rules, and standards on which a company or one's career is based. A statement of principles includes ethically, morally, personally, and professionally meaningful characteristics and is incorporated into the company's vision.

SMART   An acronym created by an unknown goal-setting and marketing genius, describing the method for creating the most motivating and effective goals: specific, measurable, achievable (or, as I say, action-oriented), realistic, and timed.

values   The core principles of importance or worth from which a vision is created.

vision   A picture, image, or idea which encapsulates the essence and purpose of an organization or company. The vision states why the company is in business, both at present and into the future, and forms the essence or foundation of a business plan.

CHAPTER 3

Marketing 101

Half the money I spend on advertising is wasted; the trouble is I don't know which half.

John Wanamaker, American merchant (1838–1922)

Service is the heart of service marketing. But the heart alone cannot keep the service alive. Marketing is the brains of service marketing. If the brain fails, the heart soon will fail.

Harry Beckwith, author

WHY YOU NEED TO MARKET

What is marketing and why do you need to do it? Marketing is not just for businesses. You can significantly benefit from using marketing in various aspects of your career. Even if you do not have a private practice and never intend to, you can create great advantage for your career by learning about marketing. Whether you plan to teach, do research, be an administrator, work in a community agency, work in a counseling center, or go into different avenues such as coaching or consulting, knowledge of what marketing is and how it can help you achieve your mission will be extremely valuable.

Marketing is fundamental to all businesses today, and yet it used to be thought of as an expense and as an inconsequential part of an organization. Thirty or forty years ago, companies viewed marketing as something that cost money and had unknown returns or value. Today, marketing departments receive a large part of a company's budget, and the returns from marketing are measurable and quantifiable. Coca Cola, for example, conducted a study that showed they could define their target market as including anyone who drinks liquids. Their goal then became marketing to every human being who consumes beverages! To reach this target market, they have developed extensive marketing campaigns and invested millions of dollars.

The traditional notion of marketing relates to promoting something specific or tangible, such as a product. If you want to gain more private practice clients, promote and sell your book or CD, get more attendees at your seminars, or change the focus of your clinical practice, marketing will help you.

You can also learn how to market yourself. If you want to move up in your organization and become a director, you can do so by marketing your achievements within the organization. Letting people know who you are, what you do, and why they can trust you can lead to achieving your goal. If you want to be in the best position to receive an offer for your dream job or receive a raise, marketing can help you. If you want to be considered for exciting new projects or jobs, marketing can be of great assistance.

To be successful and differentiate yourself from your competitors, you must become sophisticated at marketing. Whether you are marketing your services, yourself to move up in your field, your books, or your potential for a new position, a large investment of your time and energy in this area will prove rewarding.

Marketing is Psychology

Mental health practitioners have the potential to be very strong at marketing. This is because we already know much more about marketing than 80 percent of businesspeople do. This may sound strange, because when people think "marketing," people probably think "business," and many therapists are not experts in business. Marketing is business but successful marketing is also psychology. After a marketing class in my MBA program, I was talking with the professor, who proclaimed, "If you are in a doctorate of psychology program, you already know marketing. Marketing is all about psychology. You could be teaching this class."

We are experts in much of marketing because it fundamentally rests on psychological principles. Effective marketing depends on understanding how people think, behave, and buy. In fact, I have built the small business marketing division of my coaching business on the principle that to effectively attract customers and have them buy from you, you must understand their psychology, including what motivates them to purchase your product.

One goal of marketing is to influence others. Marketers work to understand how their prospects think and what their wants and needs are. They then seek to influence the decision processes of those people. The goal is to create a perceived value to the individuals who are prospective or current clients. This is similar to the process of therapy: You assess the situation, values, background, and goals of your client; you then serve to positively influence them to assist them in developing their abilities to meet their goals.

From a cognitive psychology or neuropsychology perspective, marketing makes a lot of sense. A fundamental goal of marketing is to create a heuristic or mental shortcut to make something memorable. Having visual or auditory cues greatly assists in our recognition memory. My neuropsychology professor and dissertation chair, Jeffery Allen, PhD, ABPP, taught my class how the human brain responds to and remembers various stimuli. The brain strives for efficiency because it can only attend to and deal with a certain amount of information at a time, typically between five and nine pieces of information. Information must first be attended to in order to be remembered. When information is encoded through elaborative rehearsal or through repetitive presentations, it has a greater chance of being remembered.

One way marketing serves to accomplish the task of drawing attention and triggering remembrance is through brand recognition. Think about a brand that you know well. Sometimes just seeing certain colors or designs or hearing certain sounds can make you think of this brand. Because we are so bombarded with information in our culture, brands are useful to help us make decisions and save time. If we had to go through every type of soda in the supermarket before deciding what to buy every time we bought soda, we could spend a lot of time walking up and down the soda aisle. A brand, however, provides us with a recognition cue and helps us make our decision more easily and efficiently.

From a social psychology standpoint, heuristics are also used to provide us with mental shortcuts. Rather than making our brains perform an algorithm to explore every possible piece of information, we often rely on labels and groups of information. This is partially how stereotypes develop regarding specific groups of people. We cannot know all of the individuals who compose those groups. While stereotypes and biases about people are often thought of as negative and resulting in prejudices, marketers rely on the similar brain mechanism of mental heuristics to create an impression of their brand. Marketing seeks to create a positive stereotype or a favorable bias toward a given product.

While you may have no idea how to do marketing yet, it is important to recognize that you have the *potential* to be very effective at marketing. As a mental health professional, you already know a great deal about it, probably more than you previously realized.

SOME BASIC MARKETING PRINCIPLES

What exactly is marketing? In short, marketing means showing potential clients or interested parties the services or benefits that you can offer to them. It means making yourself and your products visible to prospective buyers.

According to Jay Conrad Levinson, author of the classic book *Guerrilla Marketing*, marketing is "everything you do to promote your business from the moment you conceive of it to the point at which customers buy your product or service and begin to patronize your business on a regular basis." He goes on to define what marketing encompasses: "Marketing includes the name of your business, the determination of whether you will be selling a product or a service, the methods of manufacture or serving, the colors, size, and shape of your product, the packaging, the location of your business, the advertising, the public relations, the sales training, the sales presentation, the telephone inquiries, the problem solving, the growth plan, the referral plan, and the follow-up. If you gather from this that marketing is a complex process, you're right." (Levinson, 1998, p.8).

I give you this long definition, not to overwhelm you or make you think there is just too much to do, but rather to illustrate the point that marketing is not just taking out an ad. Marketing is commonly confused with advertising. Advertising is one component of marketing, but there are many other components to effective marketing, most of which Levinson describes in the preceding quote.

CLEAR, CREDIBLE, VISIBLE

According to Robert Middleton, owner of Action Plan Marketing (www.actionplan.com), there are three major areas of marketing. If you do not focus on all three, your marketing efforts are unlikely to work. These three components are:

1. Clear message
2. Credibility
3. Visibility

The first of these, creating and communicating a clear message, will allow you to tell others clearly and distinctly what you can do. Without this clear message, you will look like everyone else. The market is currently flooded with therapists, so it is important to differentiate yourself from others. In developing your message, it is important to look at factors such as clients' problems, concerns, issues, pains, and challenges, as well as effective solutions and results.

Middleton says, "Nobody cares what you do or what the process is." This is an important point, because many if not most therapists describe their process to others, but what people really want to know is the results. For instance, when describing your cognitive-behavioral treatments, a client is less likely to care that you will develop an activity schedule of pleasure and mastery activities than that you can help her overcome her struggles with depression. To this end, Middleton recommends, when someone asks you what you do, that you don't say, "I'm a therapist." Instead, focus on conveying your fundamental message, which describes your vision and the client's potential benefits.

The second important point is conveying credibility. You can show your credibility through your marketing materials, such as a high-quality web site with a lot of relevant resources and information. You can also build credibility through your written articles, publications, research results, reports, and newsletters, and through speaking engagements. We will talk about writing and speaking strategies in greater detail in later chapters.

Visibility, the third component described by Middleton, involves how to get the word out about your services. Therapists and other medical professionals work mostly on the basis of referrals as a means to increase visibility. Specializing in some way can increase your visibility because people will know where to find you. For instance, if you specialize in cognitive-behavioral therapy for anxiety disorders and are a member of the Anxiety Disorders Association of America (ADAA), people can find you by looking at ADAA materials. Many other activities can boost visibility, and you need to find out which are best for the product or service that you are selling. Some combination of networking, writing, sending newsletters, and speaking engagements is typically ideal.

To choose appropriate marketing methods for your situation, go back to your vision and think about what the point of your career is. Do you want to work one-on-one with people and have a laid-back lifestyle? Do you want to be out in front of the media sharing your research and ideas? Do you want to work with the government and the military? Do you want to collaborate with multidisciplinary teams and work with children? The answers to your vision questions will help determine your marketing strategy. For instance, as Middleton states, "If you want to be well known, sell books."

A CREATIVE PROCESS

The "guerrilla marketing" guru, Jay Conrad Levinson, describes marketing as a creative process. He couches this idea, however, in the fact that "marketing is not creative unless it sells" (Levinson, 1998, p. 50). While you certainly want to use your creativity to develop effective marketing, you do not want to lose sight of the most important reason to market: to generate clients.

Levinson advises that there are seven steps in the creative process of developing a marketing campaign:

1. Find the inherent drama in the services that you offer.
2. Translate the inherent drama into a description of meaningful benefits.
3. State the benefits in a believable way that people will understand.
4. Get people's attention (by using steps 1 through 3 above).
5. Motivate your audience to get involved.
6. Be sure that you are communicating clearly.
7. Measure the results of your marketing efforts.

AIDA

In his book *Streetwise Low-Cost Marketing*, Mark Landsbaum (2004) describes the four fundamental phases of effective marketing:

1. Attention
2. Interest

3. Desire
4. Action

Attention relates to capturing the focus of your prospect. It is estimated that the average individual in the United States is bombarded with 20,000 messages per day. Since it is impossible to attend to all of this information, we learn how to tune things out. When you want to market something to someone, you must first compete for their attention. One of the best ways to gain the attention of a prospect is by making sure that your marketing message is pertinent and relevant for those in your target market. If you can connect with people's value systems, you can create a marketing message worth attending to.

Interest is created after you have gained people's attention and engendered a sense of curiosity. A great marketing message is one that makes someone think about it, makes them stop and say, "Hmm . . ." This makes your message more memorable and therefore more effective.

Desire develops when someone has become interested and curious and then wants to know more. You can create a desire by illustrating the benefits of your services. Rather than focusing on the features of a service, a focus on its potential benefits creates a desire in the minds of prospects. They wonder how they, too, can achieve those benefits.

The last stage is *action*. This is the point when you close the sale—you sign up a new client, you get a job or a promotion, you sell one of your books or articles, you get hired as a workshop presenter. The sale is the goal. However, while the last stage of marketing is to inspire action or make sales, marketing and sales are actually separate concepts.

THE DIFFERENCE BETWEEN MARKETING AND SALES

Marketing can be thought of as bringing potential clients or prospects to you by making your services or products visible, capturing people's attention, communicating your clear message of value, securing their interest and desire, and inspiring them to take action. Sales refers to the process of closing a deal or exchanging a good or service for payment.

Ron Willingham (2003) describes *selling* as "a process of identifying and filling people's wants or needs that creates mutual value for customers, salespeople and their organizations." He defines *integrity selling* as "a win-win customer-focused process driven by honesty and sincerity, creating mutual value for sellers and buyers."

These definitions are important to carefully read and think about because many people, particularly mental health professionals, have an unpleasant reaction to the word *sales*. They feel the word *selling* has a negative connotation and that the process of selling involves manipulative tactics or deceptive practices. The idea of selling our services can put a bad taste in our mouths, but when you begin to think of sales as coming from a place of integrity and mutual benefit, it begins to taste different. Clients pay you for your services because your services are worth it to them.

Recall our discussion in Chapter 1 of the creation of value as a driving factor in your career. According to Willingham's definition, the goal of selling is to create mutual value for you and your client. When you begin to recognize the value that you are creating in the lives of your clients, their families, and your community, you will become increasingly comfortable with the process of selling and charging what you are worth.

Willingham also describes six steps of the selling process:

1. *Approach*: Meet and develop rapport with the client.
2. *Interview*: Conduct an interview to identify the client's needs.
3. *Demonstrate*: Explain the features and benefits of the product or service.
4. *Validate*: Prove your claims.
5. *Negotiate*: Work out problems or scheduling.
6. *Close*: Ask the client for a decision.

Many therapists say that they have no idea how to sell, but perhaps you know more than you think. What does the above process resemble? Isn't it very similar to conducting an intake interview?

During the beginning of an intake, you focus on developing rapport with your client (selling stage one: approach). You then move into the diagnostic or information-gathering interview (selling stage two: interview). If it appears that your services would be appropriate for the client, you might then talk a bit about the process of therapy. You may ask them whether they have been in therapy before and what they expect from the process of therapy (selling stage three: demonstrate). You can answer their questions and describe some ways you have helped clients overcome similar issues in the past (selling stage four: validate). You could then work out scheduling or payment issues (selling stage five: negotiate). Finally, you would agree to work together and set your first therapy session appointment (selling stage six: close).

The best selling techniques are those that focus on the client or customer. This type of selling is *not* traditional product selling. Product selling generally entails going in and giving a sales presentation or speech to tell your prospect why they need your product or service. Dialogue-based selling, on the other hand, focuses on your client, not on what you are trying to sell. The goal is to engage the client in a conversation rather than give a sales pitch or what Linda Richardson (1998) calls a "product dump." Dialogue selling, she says, focuses on truly understanding whether and how you can benefit the customer. It involves asking a series of questions in order to understand what the customer needs and to determine whether you can provide that for them.

Willingham says that highly effective salespeople display four common traits:

1. Strong goal clarity
2. High achievement desire
3. Healthy emotional intelligence
4. Excellent social skills

Again, these are qualities that most mental health professionals excel in. Many therapists understand how to set clear goals and are achievement oriented. To get through all the education, training, and credentialing necessary in psychology and social work, you need to have an achievement desire. Therapists understand emotional intelligence and self-awareness better than almost anyone, and most successful therapists have strong interpersonal skills.

THE MARKETING PLAN

A marketing plan describes how you will market your services. As the name implies, it is a written plan that is updated frequently. According to Leexan Hong, President of X-Marketing Consulting LLC (www .x-marketingconsulting.com), every marketing plan should have the following six parts:

1. Situation analysis
2. Marketing goals
3. A marketing strategy
4. Specific marketing tactics to support the marketing strategy

5. An implementation plan (including budget)
6. A method or methods to track progress of marketing plan

This chapter discusses the situation analysis, marketing goals, and general principles of marketing strategy. Chapter 4 explores specific strategies to implement and track your successful marketing plan.

SITUATION ANALYSIS USING THE "SWOT"

The situation analysis is the most important part of the marketing plan and the part on which, unfortunately, many businesses and people spend the least amount of time. Many of us are familiar with conducting a situation analysis for a clinical case or a psychological assessment. You analyze the client's environmental, cultural, and familial situations, as well as their personal difficulties, problems, and strengths.

One of the most important parts of the situation analysis is the "SWOT analysis." The acronym stands for strengths, weaknesses, opportunities, and threats. You can conduct a SWOT analysis on yourself, your career, your industry, or your products and services. The SWOT analysis is one of the most discussed and utilized concepts in marketing. I learned about the SWOT about 10 different times in my MBA program. I will summarize it for you here as simply as possible.

THE INTERNAL ANALYSIS

The S and the W refer to *internal* strengths and weaknesses—inherent characteristics of the individual, her company or practice, or her product that she would consider to be either strengths or weaknesses. Some of the factors you want to look at in the *internal analysis* include the following (extrapolated from Aaker, 1998):

Your Own Performance
- Client satisfaction and new clients
- Profitability and costs (education, books, trainings, supervision, etc.)
- Diversification of services
- Time frames (for clients, for finishing theses or dissertation)
- Student performance or quality of teaching

Determinants of Strategic Options

- Success of past and current strategies
- Financial resources and constraints
- Personal life considerations
- Geography and location
- Personal and professional strengths and weaknesses
- Strategic problems or market needs

It is important to note that a characteristic could be considered both a strength *and* a weakness. For example, for someone in the service industry, being young or at least appearing young could be perceived as a lack of experience and therefore classified as a weakness. However, being young could also be perceived as being energetic and dedicated and therefore be classified as a strength.

The manner in which you market yourself is a huge factor in how clients and colleagues will perceive you. You can try to overcompensate for your perceived weakness or you can market your strengths. In the example of appearing young, if you try to act more mature or professional and do not act like yourself, you may come across as artificial or as trying too hard. If you market yourself as energetic, enthusiastic, and eager to implement all of your great education, you will come across very differently. It is likely that your colleagues, supervisors, and clients will treat you differently based on how you market your internal strengths and weaknesses.

The External Analysis

The O and the T refer to *external* opportunities and threats, or factors outside of an organization's services and products that other businesses may be able to take advantage of or that may pose a threat to the company. Some of the factors you want to look at in the *external analysis* include the following (extrapolated from Aaker, 1998):

Client Analysis

- Different segments or target markets
- Motivations, unmet needs, problems, concerns, and issues

Competitor Analysis

- Performance and profitability
- Strategies and objectives

- Culture and organizational effectiveness
- Strengths and weaknesses

Market Analysis

- Size and segments
- Projected growth and trends
- Entry barriers (education, training, certification, licensure)
- Key success factors
- Demographic factors, geography

Environmental Analysis

- Technological
- Governmental
- Economic
- Cultural and demographic
- Information-need areas

Threats and opportunities could be cultural trends, legislation, or competitors. An example of an opportunity is the current trend in the United States with the Atkins diet and the whole low-carb craze. You might have noticed that a number of companies, such as Subway and GNC, have taken advantage of this opportunity by offering new low-carb products.

Therapists should also research the market, or their potential clients. What type of person buys the services that they sell? What factors influence the buying decision? Where do people go for services or to purchase products? Where do they go to get information about the products and services? These are all questions that should be answered when doing the situation analysis for a marketing plan.

Another important facet to look at in situation analysis is the competition. Which organizations or practices are considered to be the leaders in the area? If you are going for a job interview, who are your competitors? If you are going into a private practice treating depression, who else is doing that in your area and where? If possible, you should perform a SWOT analysis for those practices or businesses that you feel are your biggest competitors. This helps you to position yourself in relation to your competitors.

What are some trends in the marketplace? Many therapists have successfully identified trends as they are beginning. They are able to get ahead of the curve and find a great deal of profitability. Making projections in the marketplace requires looking at large demographic trends as well as trends in the specific field. For instance, a large demographic trend is the aging of the population. Many forward-thinking therapists anticipating this trend began to specialize in geriatrics, and even in more specific fields within geriatrics, such as geriatric depression.

Other visionaries have seen trends or needs within their specific fields. For example, a prominent cognitive-behavioral psychologist and anxiety researcher, Dr. Edna B. Foa, saw a need for effective treatments for obsessive compulsive disorder (OCD). As a result, she developed exposure and response prevention therapy which has become the gold standard of treatment for OCD. Later, noticing a distinct need in the marketplace, Dr. Foa created an exposure-based treatment for post-traumatic stress disorder (PTSD): prolonged exposure (PE) therapy. She has helped clients and trained clinicians all across the world with this highly effective therapy. Among her myriad career achievements, Dr. Foa was the chair of the DSM-IV Subcommittee for OCD, was awarded the Lifetime Achievement Award presented by the International Society for Traumatic Stress Studies, and was given the Distinguished Scientist Award from the American Psychological Association. These are the results of a strong career vision combined with a solid understanding of market need.

WHAT ARE YOUR MARKETING GOALS?

It is important to have a clear idea of what your marketing plan is at any given point in time. It will change over time and will need to be updated. For instance, if you are applying for clinical internships, your goal may be to market yourself in a strong way relative to competitors so you get your ideal internship placement. As you move forward in your career, you may want to market yourself to certain agencies for jobs or to market your services to private practice clients. You may later create a series of workshops or products to market. Whatever stage you are in, it is important to be crystal clear about your goals at that point in time.

After you have completed your thorough situation analysis, it is time to set marketing goals. What are your marketing goals over the next year? the next two years? five years? What image do you want the public to have of your company or practice?

The best career and marketing goals are SMART goals. We discussed this idea in Chapter 2 when we talked about developing objectives in line with your mission statement. Here are a few good examples of SMART goals:

- Obtain training to develop a specialty in treating alcohol dependence within the next two years by working with a mentor who specializes in addictions. Receive two hours of supervision per week, complete three training cases, and independently see clients by the middle of the second year.
- Build my private practice (by marketing activities including speaking engagements and networking) to a full practice of 22 clients per week over the next 18 months.
- Complete professional licensure within the next year. Finish my postdoctoral training in six months; complete licensure application immediately upon completion of training; study for the national licensing exam (20 hours per week for four months); take the state and national exams; and get my license in the mail and frame it!

Write down your SMART marketing goals here:

_____

_____

_____

_____

STRATEGIES TO FOCUS YOUR MARKETING

Your goals will only be as good as you are able to implement them. As you know from working with clients in therapy, having a good set of goals is only half the battle—now you want to see those goals achieved. Once you have your SMART marketing goals, it is time to develop your marketing strategy.

THE SIX PS

Many marketing specialists talk of the "six Ps" of effective marketing: people, price, place, product, promotion, and positioning. These make up the biggest pieces of developing a marketing strategy, as follows:

- *The selection of the target market.* People: To whom are you marketing? Who do you want to have as your client? Who do you want to take notice of your work? Who do you want to attend your workshops or seminars? Price: Who can afford your services? What can they afford? How much are you able to spend on your marketing efforts?

- *What are you trying to sell?* Product: Are you trying to market yourself as a product, in your career? Why are you marketing yourself (new job, promotion, etc.)? What specific services can you provide at an excellent quality? What mix of products and services do you want to provide?
- *How will people know about you and your services?* Place: How are clients going to learn about your services? Will your business be local or national? Promotion: What will you do to tell people about your services? How will you promote yourself or your work to your ideal clients?
- *Your overall marketing message.* Positioning: How are you going to differentiate yourself relative to your competitors? What is your expertise or what gives you an advantage over the others who do what you do? Why would a client choose to work with you or why would someone want to hire you instead of another candidate?

IF YOU DO NOT SELECT A TARGET MARKET, YOU MAY NOT HAVE A MARKET

A target market is the best group for you to sell to. This is determined by the SWOT analysis and the research done on both potential clients and the competition during your situation analysis phase. Some people refer to this as your niche or specialization.

You have done this before, whether you know it or not. When you applied to graduate school, you most likely did a SWOT analysis and then decided which schools were in your target market. You weighed your own strengths and weaknesses (internal analysis) and then looked at the opportunities and threats in the market of graduate programs (external analysis). Let's say you had excellent clinical experience and skills but less experience with research. You would realize your professional strengths and then look into clinical programs. If you found an excellent clinical program with many opportunities, but it happened to be in the city that was most saturated with therapists (threats), it may have been less appealing. You also likely compared yourself to your competition — who gets into these schools, and which school would you be most competitive to get into? As you can see, marketing applies to many aspects of your career.

When choosing a target market, you want to consider which one is most attracted to your strengths and less concerned about your weaknesses. You can also target markets that other competitors are ignoring. If, for example, people were ignoring an incredible training program in Idaho, but you would love to go to Idaho, this could be an excellent opportunity for you to capitalize on lowered market demand.

Major problems arise for many individuals and companies that do *not* select a target market. Their idea is, "Why should I limit myself when I am capable of doing many different things?"

One way this "jack of all trades, master of none" syndrome may come up is by trying to see many different types of clients at once. If your practice consisted of some children with developmental disorders, women who were in domestically violent relationships, men who were depressed and suicidal, teenagers with adjustment issues, and adults with anxiety disorders, you would understandably feel pulled in many directions, and a number of negative consequences could result. You may feel unfocused and overwhelmed by all the complex cases to conceptualize and treat. If you were being supervised, you would struggle with how to best use the supervision hour when you had so many different issues on the table. Clinical care could suffer. If you were in private practice, you would have a hard time showing clients why they should see you if they perceived you as seeing any client who might walk through your door. You would have a hard time focusing your marketing efforts and could waste valuable time and money. For example, to obtain referrals, would you try to partner with school psychologists, psychiatrists who treat anxiety disorders, domestic violence hotline advocates, or whom? Don't fool yourself—no one has the time, energy, expertise, or training to do it *all*.

I learned firsthand the importance of targeting your marketing—actually, I have learned it firsthand many times. One example is when I was applying for my clinical internship, the year of full-time clinical work prior to receiving my PsyD. My strategy was simple: Apply to tons of different programs, and one will surely want me. Does this sound like a good strategy? One of the problems here was that I did not develop a vision for myself earlier in my training. (If you are still in graduate school while you are reading this and you worked through Chapter 2 and have a vision, you are ahead of the game!) I was actually prioritizing cities, so I had some aspects of a vision, but my overall strategy was not the best. I ended up applying to college counseling centers, community mental health centers, medical centers, private hospitals, and one veterans hospital. Surprise, surprise, I did not get interviews at all of these places. I actually got interviews at the places that would have best matched my SWOT analysis, had I done one—the places where my experience best met their criteria and where I would receive the best training for the direction my career was heading. These things happen for a reason. I could have saved all that time, energy, and money that I invested in the 12 programs that were not in line with my (undone) SWOT analysis and career vision, simply by conducting one.

Once you have decided to begin narrowing down your prospects to a target market, there are three more steps to take:

1. Conduct some market research to find out where there is a need for your services. Ask people who would refer clients to you what referral needs they have; search on the Internet to determine who else is doing what you want to do; read journals and newspapers to figure out where trends are heading and how you can get involved.

2. Begin narrowing down your market by demographics. For example, examine the demographics of your current and past clients, consider who your ideal clients are, and think of where you can fill a market need. Some general demographics to consider include age, gender, diagnosis, ethnicity, work position, salary, and geography. For services like therapy, geography is typically your local setting, since most of your clients will be local. For services such as public speaking, seminars, workshops, or executive coaching, your market may be broader geographically. You also want to consider the psychographics of your ideal demographic. What are their needs, challenges, and problems? What motivates them? What are their personality features? When do they seek services?

3. Decide how you are going to make yourself and your services different from your competitors. First figure out what your competition is doing, both successfully and unsuccessfully. You can learn from what they are doing both right and wrong.

POSITIONING AND COMPETITIVE ADVANTAGE

The last P is about finding your competitive advantage. Positioning is exactly what it sounds like: how you position yourself or your business relative to your competitors to create a distinct competitive advantage for your services or products.

A company's positioning should do a number of things. It should appeal to the selected market and communicate why its products or services are different from those of its competitors. It could also explain how a particular product solves a need of the target market. Whatever positioning is decided upon, it is imperative that a company delivers this positioning consistently in *everything* that they do.

There are many different ways to position a product or service. For example, one way to position a product is by price: "It's the cheapest one out there." For buyers who are highly price sensitive and whose primary buying criterion is cost, positioning based on price is an effective strategy. Customers who shop at stores like WalMart are typically price sensitive, and WalMart has done phenomenally well from price positioning. When positioning is done based on price, it is also typical to adopt a quantity approach. This is because products can generally be produced less expensively in high volume, and because you need to sell more to be profitable. For many mental health practitioners this is not the best strategy, because for services like therapy, teaching, or consulting, time constraints limit how much you can sell. Most therapists, for instance, do not want to provide more than 25 to 30 hours per week of psychotherapy.

Another positioning stance is that of quality. Quality can be perceived many ways, such as through brand recognition, cost, performance, testimonials, or experience. Brands like BMW have a high quality position in the market. Positioning based on quality can be a very important strategy for service businesses. Therapists can attract clients who are less price sensitive and more quality sensitive by marketing efforts aimed at showing effectiveness of the treatments. This would allow you to work less and earn more. Of course, your positioning strategy needs to be consistent with your career mission. If you are dedicated to working with low-socioeconomic-status clients, this may not be the best positioning for you.

Many customers are attracted to positioning based on value; they are drawn to the best perceived deal, which is a combination of high quality and lower prices. This is a hard balance to achieve, because higher quality often entails greater expenses and costs to produce. Taking courses from an excellent professor in a state school with state tuition is an example of a great value-based buying decision.

According to Aaker (1998), positioning can be used to create a sustainable competitive advantage, one that combines all the things we have talked about so far. This means using your product/services strategy, your positioning strategy, your core competencies, your target market selection, and your competitor analysis to create an advantage in your career that can be sustained over the long term. Your career is a marathon, not a sprint. You need to develop a long-term vision that allows for flexibility when your life circumstances, values, priorities, and constraints shift over time. The best sustainable competitive advantage is one that creates synergy or, as Jack Welch says, "integrated diversity" in your career. You do not want to put all your eggs in one basket, but you do want to be sure you are putting your eggs into the right baskets for your career.

Record some of your core competencies and ways you can position yourself, your business, or your products to create a sustainable competitive advantage now:

_____

_____

_____

_____

_____

YOUR UNIQUE SELLING PROPOSITION

You combine your positioning statement and competitive advantage to develop a unique selling proposition (USP). According to Landsbaum (2004), a USP is a way to answer the two fundamental questions that members of your target market ask when evaluating whether they want to work with you: (1) What's in it for me? and (2) Why should I buy from you? Your USP not only highlights the potential benefits to clients (question one), but specifies what is completely different, unique, high quality, and special about the services that you provide. It is influenced by your personality and what exactly you have to offer that makes you different from others. You can use your USP to position yourself as *the* solution to your target market's problems, and show why you would be their preferred provider. The best USPs are short—either a sentence or a brief paragraph.

Interview with Robert Middleton

Robert Middleton is the owner of Action Plan Marketing and can be reached at www.actionplan.com or (831) 338-7790.

You have worked with many service providers. In your experience, what are some of the common mistakes made by mental health service providers in marketing their businesses?

Not understanding marketing: what it is, how it works, and what they should do. Many professionals confuse an activity (such as placing an ad) with what it really is: communicating what you do so people are interested and respond to what you do. Many people don't know the rules and strategies, or they resist marketing. They then engage in marketing activities that don't produce results, so it doesn't work.

Marketing is like a game of baseball. The correct strategies provide you with the baseball diamond, the bat, the ball, the batting gloves, and the rules of the game. Without the full set of marketing strategies, you are just running around on a field with no direction.

What three fundamental steps do you recommend for someone who is beginning a marketing program from scratch?

1. Get your message together. Focus on the problem or solution. Create your verbal message, such as, "I work with women who are in abusive relationships but don't know how to change their situations."
2. Put together high-quality marketing materials, including a web site. Professionals need to have a web site these days.
3. Use networking and visibility-increasing activities one piece at a time, based on the strategies that work best for your product or service.

When a professional is marketing a new product, such as a book or audio program, what do you recommend they do first?

You still have to have your strong message and materials, but you also need to know what the purpose is. Typically, it's not to sell books. Think of a book as an advanced brochure to tell people about the services you offer and what makes you stand out from your competition. Ask yourself, is this product communicating my difference and uniqueness?

Know where you want to go with it. Do you want to become an info guru? There are therapists who have become famous info gurus, such as Dr. John Gray in the area of relationships. They maintain clients and fill workshops quickly. Ask yourself, to what degree do I want to have fame and notoriety? If that is what you are interested in, you will have to put in time and effort. Dr. Phil wrote a number of books before becoming famous. A book is often a stepping-stone or milestone. It has to have a unique angle or edge to it.

Can you share a crucial piece of advice you were told or important lesson you have learned during your career as a marketing expert?
Once you have everything in place on the three basic areas (clear message, visibility, credibility), you need a keep-in-touch marketing campaign. Many people might only hear or see you one time. I learned early in my career about the importance of a newsletter, either e-mail or print. This is the single most powerful tool. Nowadays my newsletter is the only marketing I do. I just send out my newsletter to 32,000 people each week.

Almost nobody has a keep-in-touch marketing system. Your database is the most important aspect of marketing. Your office, books, and computer are not as important. Without a database, you are constantly reworking old ideas and searching for new contacts. With a database, I can fill a workshop quickly. I started building my database by networking and speaking. Now people mostly sign up through my web site.

RESOURCES

BOOKS

Aaker, D. A. (1998). *Strategic market management* (5th Ed.). New York, NY: John Wiley & Sons, Inc.

Landsbaum, M. (2004). *Streetwise low-cost marketing*. Avon, MA: Adams Media Corporation.

Levinson, J. C. (1998). *Guerrilla marketing* (3rd Ed.). New York: Houghton Mifflin.

Richardson, L. (1998). *Stop telling start selling: How to use customer-focused dialogue to close sales*. New York: McGraw-Hill, Inc.

Rotler, P. (2003). *A framework for marketing management* (2nd Ed.). Upper Saddle River, New Jersey: Pearson Education, Inc.

Willingham, R. (2003). *Integrity selling for the 21st century: How to sell the way people want to buy*. New York: Doubleday.

WEB SITES

American Marketing Association:

www.marketingpower.com

Markus Allen's free low-cost marketing resource center:

www.markusallen.com

Leexan Hong's X-Marketing Consulting LLC:

www.x-marketingconsulting.com

Robert Middleton's Action Plan Marketing:

www.actionplan.com

Joe Vitale's hypnotic marketing site with a lot of free information:

www.mrfire.com

My small business marketing company, Performance and Success Coaching, LLC:

www.PAScoaching.com

TERMINOLOGY

brand   Creating a distinctive identity for a company or product using words and graphics. This is often accomplished by using logos, taglines, and color schemes.

brand recognition   One of the goals of branding is to create a sense of familiarity, recognition, and positive bias associated with a particular brand.

competitive advantage   The way in which you differentiate your business from your competitors by capitalizing on your core strengths and opportunities and utilizing your competitors' weaknesses to make your business stronger.

market   Potential buyers of a given product.

marketing   A process of identifying human wants and needs, and developing a plan to meet those wants and needs.

positioning   Creating a distinctive image for a product or company in the minds of customers.

prospect   A potential target customer or client who has not yet been converted to a current customer or client.

selling   A process of identifying and filling people's wants or needs that creates mutual value for customers, salespeople, and their organization (defined by Willingham, 2003).

target market   The portion of the market that a company selects toward which to focus their marketing efforts.

visibility   Having a presence in front of your ideal prospects so they know of you and your products and services.

CHAPTER 4

Your Marketing Plan

When the product is right, you don't have to be a great marketer.
Lee Iacocca, former CEO of Chrysler

The secret of business is to know something that nobody else knows.
Aristotle Onassis, shipping magnate

THE MARKETING PLAN IN ACTION

Now we get to the fun part. You have advanced past Marketing 101. You know something about what marketing is, what makes it effective, and how to position yourself or your services. You have learned the building blocks of marketing plans. As a reminder, the six pieces in a marketing plan are:

1. Situation analysis
2. Marketing goals
3. Marketing strategy
4. Specific marketing tactics to support the marketing strategy
5. Implementation plan (including budget)
6. Method or methods to track progress of marketing plan

We discussed the first three of these in Chapter 3, where we learned that the situation analysis involves conducting an analysis of your strengths, weaknesses, opportunities, and threats (SWOT); that creating goals entails developing SMART goals; and that marketing strategy has to do with creating your positioning, competitive advantage, and unique selling proposition. In this chapter, we will use all of those ideas to create some specific strategies to help you implement your marketing plan and track its effectiveness over time.

MARKETING YOUR SERVICES

Before getting into the specific tactics you will want to use, it is a good idea to have a conceptual framework regarding marketing your services. Generally speaking, marketing a service is quite different from marketing a product. When people think about marketing, many of them think of product advertisements. But advertising tends not to work as well with many services as it does with products. This makes sense when you think about therapy, since the effectiveness of therapy depends largely on a good rapport and level of trust between the patient and therapist. These are qualities that typically cannot be communicated well in an advertisement.

Harry Beckwith is a bestselling author on marketing service businesses. One of his books is entitled *Selling the Invisible*—rightly so, because we are selling something that is intangible. Beckwith offers some keys to successfully marketing a service:

- Don't over rely on word-of-mouth advertising (do not assume that everyone will be out talking about how wonderful you are).
- Writing and publishing are excellent for marketing a service.
- Teaching and educating others about what you offer are great methods.
- Being clear in your message is essential. He says, "Clarity is expertise."

The latter point is a crucial one for a mental health professional. If you cannot be clear and concise in your message or purpose, how are others supposed to get it?

One way to formulate a clear message is to create a brief verbal description of your services, sometimes called an "audio logo" which communicates what you do and why others should be interested. Saying, "I'm a therapist" is not a good audio logo, because it does not clearly communicate what you do, and more important, it does not communicate the potential benefits of what you do. A better audio logo would be, "I provide stress management workshops to nurses and medical professionals to help prevent burnout and improve work satisfaction."

Another key point Beckwith emphasizes is how you visually present yourself when sending your message. In his book *What Clients Love*, he states, "Clients understand with their eyes. . . . Dress like the company you want to become. . . . If you're dressed for golf, be sure you're golfing." If we want to present a professional, modern, and up-to-date image, we need to convey this message in our appearance. This does not mean that you have to spend your life's savings on designer suits, but that you need to be conscious of how the way you present yourself will impact your efforts to market yourself or your services. If we want to show a client or employer that we mean business, we should dress for business. The way you present yourself allows room for personal expression and creativity, so it can also be a way to position yourself or show how you are different from all the other professionals out there.

SPECIFIC MARKETING TACTICS

Now that your marketing strategy has been developed and you understand some of the essentials of marketing a service, it is time to create marketing tactics to support the strategy. Tactics are the actual programs that individuals or companies implement to market themselves. It is important to develop marketing tactics that are consistent with your marketing goals, strategy, and budget. Some examples of tactics to consider are:

- Advertising
- Press releases
- Web sites and Internet marketing
- Public speaking
- Sponsored events
- Referral programs
- Direct mailings

The marketing strategies or tactics that you select depend on what specifically you are marketing. For instance, the best way to market a workshop is different from the tactics for building a practice, which is different from selling a book. We will look at some specific marketing tactics in later chapters about creating and selling a book, consulting, and private practice. After reviewing the chapters of interest to you, when you feel you have developed effective marketing tactics, you should write out the steps you plan to take to implement the marketing programs. Putting your marketing plan in writing is invaluable. It helps you to monitor your progress toward meeting your goals and to track which strategies or more or less effective.

GET CLIENTS

Of course, the goal of your marketing plan is to get new clients. As discussed in Chapter 3, gaining new clients generally involves a combination of marketing and sales strategies. Of the many possible strategies for generating referrals and filling your practice, the best ones for services are referral partnerships, networking and speaking engagements, and publicity and media work

CREATING STRATEGIC REFERRAL PARTNERSHIPS

In professional services, referral partnerships are one of the most effective ways to generate clients. A strategic referral partnership (SRP) is a win-win referral partnership with the goal of satisfying the client. In an SRP, partners either refer clients to one another or one partner refers clients to the other partner. An example of the former is a business consultant who partners with an accountant. When one has a client that needs the services of the other, he or she will make the referral. In the best-case scenario, the numbers of referrals that each partner makes to the other are relatively equal so the partnership continues to feel mutually beneficial. An SRP can also involve one party referring to the other without necessarily receiving referrals in return. This partner may receive a different form of benefit in exchange for the referral. If you are looking for an SRP to refer clients to you, it is critical that you know what is in it for them, in order to give them an incentive to think of you and refer people to you. Some examples of benefits to the referring partner include:

- *Financial.* In some industries, the referring individual can receive a referral fee. This is *not* true in most health care or licensed professions. One psychologist cannot get a referral fee for sending a client to another therapist. Referral fees are also not permitted in professions such as law, medicine, and financial planning. In some industries, however, referral fees are relatively common. If you are thinking about using a referral fee as your SRP incentive, be sure to take the steps necessary to insure that it is legal and ethical. You may want to contact the state board of your profession and the referral partner's profession.

- *Psychological.* The psychological benefit comes from knowing that you have a high-quality referral for your client or patient. You are able to feel comfortable and confident that the person whom you referred will receive high-quality services. Think about a time when you found a good psychiatrist, physician, nutritionist, or chiropractor for a client. It feels great to know that you have this SRP to make your job easier (you do not have to hunt around for a professional every time you need to make a referral) and improve the quality of the care you give to your clients.

- *Professional.* Sometimes developing an SRP with someone is a great way to improve your professional development. It gives you an opportunity to network with excellent professionals and learn from them. You can offer to do an educational program at no cost for the office of the referral partner. One of my clients went to the offices of her SRP and delivered stress management and wellness workshops for the staff. The SRP appreciated this and the SRP's staff benefited from it. My client had the opportunity to meet many professionals and gain referrals.

There are many ways that you can propose a referral partnership to someone else. The first step is to identify who you would like to partner with or ask for referrals. Here are some options to consider:

- Physicians, chiropractors, nurses, and physician assistants
- Attorneys
- Accountants
- Clergy and spiritual advisors
- Community leaders
- Professors and staff at your current or past university
- Other therapists (for instance, therapists who do short-term treatment and then seek referral sources for long-term work, or therapists who do not treat the clinical issue that you specialize in)
- Holistic or alternative medicine practitioners
- Dietitians or nutritionists
- School psychologists, guidance counselors, or teachers
- Physical therapists and rehabilitation specialists

- Professional association or agency leaders or members
- Massage therapists

As you can see, there are many different professionals and individuals who can serve as potential referral partners. It is generally best to pick your top two categories and then approach several people within those categories. You can use your connections and networks to find potential SRPs, or you can cold-call (i.e., contact someone whom you do not know). If you choose to cold-call, you can first send a letter of introduction along with your brochure and business card. Do not expect people to call you back based on your letter. Instead, plan to follow up with them shortly, typically within three to five days of when they would receive the letter. When approaching a potential SRP, remember to highlight the potential benefits to them and/or their patients or clients.

SRP Worksheet

Record your top potential SRPs and why they may want to refer to you (the benefit to them of doing so).

Potential SRP   **Benefit**

1. _____   _____

   _____   _____

   _____   _____

2. _____   _____

   _____   _____

   _____   _____

3. _____   _____

   _____   _____

   _____   _____

NETWORKING AND PUBLIC SPEAKING

Speaking to groups of people is a great practice-building strategy because it helps people to know, like, and trust you. When they see who you are and how you present, they begin to feel they know you and like you. Talking about a topic in your area of expertise helps to develop your credibility and inspire trust.

You can combine networking and public speaking. A great way to do this is by becoming a member of a high-quality networking group. Begin attending their meetings and discovering what is of value to them. Once you are comfortable in the group, you can offer to present at the next meeting. Speaking in front of the group will raise your credibility to a level above being simply a member of the group. If you are not interested in public speaking, you can still significantly benefit by becoming a member of networking groups and looking for SRPs.

Networking groups typically cost money to join. There is usually an upfront fee and a recurring monthly fee. The fees are highly dependent on the type of networking group. Upper echelon business networking groups, for example, can be very expensive to join (in the thousands of dollars), with high monthly dues as well. You may be able to find informal meetings or lunches with networking groups that will be significantly less expensive.

Take some time to think about your purpose in the networking. Are you looking for SRPs? Do you want to find potential coaching or consultation clients? Are you trying to build connections to help you with your job search? Are you looking for a mentor or a coach to assist you? Your answers to these questions will help you determine which groups are the best investment of your time, money, and other resources. To find groups, ask around, conduct Internet keyword searches, and ask members of professional organizations about some good groups in your area.

Networking is not only useful if you are looking to build a practice. Fostering your professional networks can help you advance in your current position or find your dream job. A significant source of networking that is often overlooked is your own company or organization. People typically think of going to networking groups or making outside contacts as being the best way to network. But do not underestimate the contacts that can be made where you are. You do not need to tell people that you are looking for a new job or that you are networking per se. Instead, you can build up your professional relationships to help you on many levels. One of the greatest benefits of networking is finding mentors, role models, and people you can learn from.

69

Through networking you can formulate and refine a *value proposition* for your career. A value proposition is a description of the worth or positive characteristics that you bring with you. It is what gives you your competitive advantage and unique selling proposition. Realizing your own value can sometimes be difficult. Through networking and talking with other professionals, you can recognize what you really have to contribute. Either you will see positive qualities in others and realize that you, too, have those qualities, or you will see less positive qualities and appreciate that you do not have those issues.

During the process of networking, you will learn how to market yourself, and people will give you feedback about your unique characteristics and qualities. Networking and marketing yourself can be awkward and difficult at first. Once you become used to it, however, you will understand that it is a skill that can get you far in your career.

C. J. Hayden (1999) recommends that you engage in networking activities such as these:

- Volunteering your services at organizations where you can make good contacts.
- Trading services with potential SRPS or others from whom you can learn.
- Serving on committees in order to increase your community visibility and build important relationships.
- Collaborating with others on projects.
- Going to leads groups that exchange information and contacts for the specific purpose of building leads.
- Sharing resources and swapping contacts with others.
- Reading the trade press of your field or fields so you are always abreast of what is going on.

Networking Worksheet

Record upcoming networking events or people with whom you want to network. Next to each, write the specific goal or benefit you hope to achieve from networking.

Networking Event or Contact   **Goal or Benefit**

1. _____   _____

   _____   _____

   _____   _____

2. _____   _____

   _____   _____

   _____   _____

3. _____   _____

   _____   _____

   _____   _____

PUBLICITY

Getting quoted in the media is a great way to build your credibility and visibility. Being in the media gives you immediate expert status. I asked a top publicist, Annie Jennings, the founder of the national publicity firm Annie Jennings PR (www.anniejenningspr.com, (908) 281-6201) a few questions about therapists getting media attention. Here is what she said:

Have you helped any health care practitioners to gain publicity in the past?
Psychologists and therapists are a large part of our client base. These professionals are very much in demand by the media because they are qualified sources of information. Anytime there is a story that is concerned with human behavior, the media likes to get psychologists to comment. The advanced degree qualifies them. They need to develop their expert status, which can lead to more notoriety, a book deal, and a bigger book advance. The nice part is that there are a lot of experts without the credentials, so the credentials will put you ahead.

Therapists need to realize how to use publicity to build their business by creating a platform. Building a platform is important in getting a book deal so the publisher can see whether the authors can compel enough sales on their own. Publishers will ask questions like do they have media credentials? Have they been called upon by media? Do they have an audience for their message? A publisher, like anyone else, needs to feel that they made the right choice. Media appeal helps create a certainty in the mind of the publisher so they don't have buyer's remorse about signing you as an author.

What are some of the mistakes you have seen professionals make when they are in charge of their own PR?
Some of the mistakes they make have to do with not knowing the tools of the trade. They don't understand the pitching skills, e-mail and voice mail etiquette, how the industry works. We do want to empower people to get their own PR. For instance, a long voice mail isn't listened to. Anytime you leave a message, consider it an audition. If you sound boring on the voice mail, they won't want to take the risk with you.

Many people don't understand how serious a job it is to pitch the media. A few people have the natural ability to pitch themselves, but many need to learn how to be fabulous. Everyone can learn how to pitch themselves and be fabulous on camera. Everyone has the potential if they want to do it. Once they learn the skill set, they become excellent.

Which type of media do you find is the most effective for promoting professional services firms in a way that gets clients?
It depends on your objective. Radio is excellent for sharing your message or creating or developing a new thought. For instance, if you want to create a message about how to deal with holiday stress, radio would be great. It is easier to get booked on the radio because there are so many stations and there is a high need for experts. You can get on smaller shows to learn your craft and then build to the bigger shows. We like radio because you get a longer time and you get to follow your own agenda. If you deliver a sizzling hot interview and you can keep people from leaving their cars because they are listening to you, then you know you are doing a great job. People will be willing to be late in order to listen to what you have to say. The host will then be very supportive in promoting your book or practice.

In print, on the other hand, you end up with only a line or two, but then you are able to say "as seen in . . . ," which is important. Then you can develop a media kit and an expert web site or media web site. This is good because other media will see where you have been. Other media like that; no one likes to be the first to bill you as an expert because you have not been tested yet. TV shows can now choose to book people who can provide a tape of themselves on other TV programs. This is why local TV is great, because you don't need the tape.

(*Author's note:* Annie Jennings PR has a CD on what you need to know about publicity. Visit www.anniejenningspr.com for more information. For an electronic book on getting media attention and more of the Annie Jennings interview, visit www.TheSuccessfulTherapist.com).

IMPLEMENTATION PLAN

Once you create your marketing plan, you need to do it. Many people come up with great plans, but do not actually implement them, realize they cannot afford to do what they planned, or do not measure the effectiveness of various strategies. Do not make these mistakes.

EVALUATE THE TACTICS

Since you cannot perform all of these marketing strategies at once, you can evaluate them to see which ones work best for your current goals, your time and schedule, and your financial resources. A marketing plan is just a plan. It is not set in stone or written in blood. It can and should be revised and updated frequently. A marketing plan is essentially worthless if it is created once and then never looked at again.

If you begin with one strategy and realize that it is impossible for you or that it is not the right strategy to help you meet your goals, put it aside and switch to a different strategy. A caveat to this recommendation concerns avoidance. If you want to put aside a tactic because it is not comfortable or because it is not giving you immediate returns, then it is a good idea to keep doing that strategy for a while longer. As you probably know, these things do not happen overnight, and, like many worthwhile things, they will take some work.

HOW WILL YOU DELIVER?

It is also important to consider distribution channels in the implementation section of the marketing plan. If you are looking to sell a book, for example, you should make the product available to customers in locations where they are most likely to need it, read it, want it, or look for it. For example, more and more companies are offering their products and services on the Web. You may determine that your target audience will want their book online, and then choose to create and market an electronic book.

After this section of your marketing plan is completed, you should be able to answer the following questions: Will these tactics appeal to the target market? Do these tactics communicate what the positioning is consistently and effectively? Will people have access to my services and products? What are my expected sales over the first quarter?

CREATE YOUR BUDGET

If you were going to sell a product, you would need to create pricing plans that would appeal to the target audience. If you wanted to sell a magazine to help low-income families, you would want to consider making it a free magazine (and get financing through advertisements or lenders or by making your company a nonprofit). Along the same lines, you need to come up with a marketing budget that fits your current financial situation. The budgeting section of your marketing plan should include a timeline and budget for the implementation process. You may have high hopes of joining an exclusive networking group that costs $5,000 to join, but if there is no way you can afford to do that anytime soon, it should be recorded on your plan as a future activity.

To calculate your budget, first estimate the costs of marketing over the next four months, and quarterly after that. Add up your expected costs. When you make the purchase, fill in the actual cost column so you can better estimate your budget for the following quarter. The results may look something like this:

Expected Costs First Quarter	Actual Costs First Quarter
Business cards: $70	$ 65
Design of brochure: $200	$ 200
Logo design: $450	$ 375
250 brochures: $400	$ 420
Web site development: $1,850	$1,850
Web site hosting (at $15/month): $60	$ 60
Web site domain name registration ($15 once a year): $15	$ 15
Web site updates: $200	$ 250
Cost of one networking event per week: $180	$ 350
Computer software: $300	$ 280
Ink for printer: $120	$ 290
Professional membership (annual fee): $250	$ 250
Coaching and consulting $1,000	$1,000
Total Expected Costs: $4,825	**Total Actual Costs: $5,405**

As you can see, costs can add up very quickly, so you want to be aware of both what you planned and what you actually spent.

When you look at the actual costs, you can see how some items cost more or less than what you had budgeted. For the items that cost less, you can figure out what you did to save and then repeat that activity. For instance, if you learned that there is a monthly coupon for a certain item or if you found a great graphic designer, you can continue with those activities. In the preceding example, some items cost a good deal more than was predicted. Computer ink cost more than twice as much as anticipated. This may be because you were printing your own brochures, which uses more ink than you are accustomed to using. Using this information, you can compare your costs with the cost of professionally printing your brochures to make sure you are making the best financial decision. Networking events also cost more than was predicted. In this example, you had predicted a cost of $180 over the quarter to attend one networking event per week, but actual costs were $350. Perhaps you only accounted for the entrance fee and not for the cost of meals, or maybe you thought the average entry fees would be significantly less than they actually were. If you made many good leads and connections at these events, they may be excellent investments. If they were not worthwhile networking events, then you may consider looking for other networking opportunities. It is better to spend more money on high-quality events than to look for cheap networking events that may be a waste of your time and money.

If you are unable to keep track of your budget or the financial side of your career, you may want to hire an accountant or bookkeeper to assist you. Keeping track of your expenses in the way I've recommended is also beneficial for accounting purposes. Most of the expenses listed can be declared against your taxes. Hiring a business consultant/coach can typically be deducted, as can most operating and marketing expenses.

TRACK THE SUCCESS OF YOUR MARKETING PLAN

Your implementation process should include a way to track how effective the various tactics have been for you or your business. You do not want to spend your valuable time and money on strategies that are not benefiting you and your career. If something has a clear long-term payoff or benefit, then you may want to include it as a strategy even if it is not currently providing rewards or is creating a deficit.

As discussed already, examining your budget can alert you to some wise or poor investments. Understanding which marketing strategy is bringing you the most benefit (referrals, connections, job interviews, etc.) will help you monitor the effectiveness of your marketing plan. Keeping track of the outcome of your marketing plan could be as simple as having new clients complete information cards asking them, "How did you hear about us?" There are a number of tools for the Web, such as WebTrends or StatCounter that analyze how visitors to a company's web site were referred to the site.

Over time, you can look at how much business or value your various marketing tactics brought in versus the amount of money spent on these tactics. The overall marketing plan should be tweaked based on which tactics worked effectively and which did not. Like your career vision and mission, the marketing plan is a work in progress, one that you should revisit and update to incorporate lessons learned the hard way as well as your great marketing successes.

Interview with Leexan Hong

Leexan Hong is president of X-Marketing Consulting LLC. You can contact him at www.x-marketingconsulting.com or by telephone at (800) 641-4023 or (215) 832-0380.

How can professionals use marketing plans in their careers?
Professionals should look at themselves as a business. This is especially true if they are health care professionals with their own practices. These individuals should approach writing the marketing plan as would any other type of business. Even if they don't have their own practices, they can still use the same principles. For example, performing a very thorough SWOT analysis on themselves could provide valuable insight insofar as what items they should highlight in their resume or where they need to improve their qualifications.

What is customer relationship management (CRM) and how can professionals use it effectively?
Customer relationship management (CRM), which is also referred to as customer relationship marketing, is the focus on establishing and

retaining relationships with current customers. Understand that from a marketing perspective, it is significantly less expensive to retain current customers than it is to obtain new customers through marketing tactics. This means that companies should understand who their best (meaning most profitable) customers are and what their needs are. It means proactively changing a product to meet these customers' needs. The best way for businesses to understand their customers is to ask them questions. Businesses should take every opportunity to ask customers how satisfied they are with their products. More important, businesses should demonstrate to the customer that their opinions are being heard. Understanding what a customer wants and needs goes a long way in developing a long-term relationship and maintaining that individual as a customer.

What are some marketing resources that you recommend to your clients?
There are a number of resources that I recommend to my clients. Most are low-cost marketing solutions targeted to small businesses. The two that I recommend most often are Constant Contact and Zoomerang. Constant Contact (www.constantcontact.com) is a low-cost, Web-based, e-mail marketing software that is very easy to use and very functional. There are a number of attractive templates for invitations, newsletters, flyers, and coupons that can be customized very easily. If you are proficient in HTML, you can create your own templates. Clients can download a list of customers' names and e-mail addresses and track which e-mails were delivered, which were bounced, and what links clients are clicking on.

Zoomerang (www.zoomerang.com) is a great product with which clients can create Web-based surveys in minutes. Clients can select from a number of question formats and place links to these surveys in e-mails or on their web sites. It is a quick and easy way to get feedback from their customers. The tool also provides graphic reports online that clients can view.

For clients for whom I think direct mailings are appropriate, I use infoUSA (www.infousa.com) to purchase mailing lists. They have an extensive database of consumers and businesses. They have a great on-line user database where one can select a list of names based on a nearly endless list of factors — gender, age, geographic location, as well as others.

Finally, for those interested in learning more about marketing, the American Marketing Association's web site, www.Marketingpower.com, is an excellent source of information. They have a number of free webcasts and articles on marketing-related topics.

How can professionals effectively use a database? Who needs one and why?

I think the two most important uses of a database are (1) keeping all customers information so that communication with them is quick and relatively inexpensive (e.g., direct mailing to all customers for a holiday sale); and (2) understanding who customers are. Depending on what demographic information they ask for, companies could potentially look at their customers' gender, age, income, and so forth. They can potentially also track their buying behavior—what do they buy, and when do they buy it?

Anybody can and should keep a customer database. What grocery store doesn't have a scan card? It sounds great for the customers because they have the opportunity to save money, but in reality grocery chains use it to know exactly who is buying what and when. Analyzing the data in a database can provide extremely valuable information about individual customers and what their needs are. Other information that could potentially be tracked in a customer database would be answers to the following questions:

- How did you hear about us?
- Why did you select our product over other products?
- What other products or services did you consider?
- How could our product or service be improved?
- Where did you look for information on the product or service (i.e., Internet, newspapers, friends or family, TV)?

What are the top five things you think people need to know about marketing their services?

1. *Do a thorough situation analysis.* I believe marketing plans fail because they make incorrect assumptions about their customers. A thorough situation analysis reduces the number of incorrect assumptions and

78

leads to a stronger marketing strategy and tactical development that is more likely to succeed.

2. *Make sure all aspects of your marketing are consistent with your marketing strategy.* Your marketing tactics and your products should accomplish two things: Appeal to your target market, and communicate your positioning clearly and effectively.

3. *Ask your customers lots of questions and keep track of the answers.* The more opportunities you can take to ask your customers questions (without annoying them), the better. If it takes offering a free product or service to get your customer to answer your survey, do it! In the long run, it will be well worth the investment.

4. *Track return on investment.* Make sure you plan a way to track which tactics are working best. Periodically take the time to analyze where most of your leads are coming from. However, don't stop there — track how much you are spending on these particular tactics. Look at which tactics are most profitable, not just which ones are bringing in the most business.

5. *Focus on delivering a superior product.* Nothing beats delivering a superior product. Work hard to learn what your customers want, and deliver it. A satisfied customer means return business and referrals, which is *free* marketing for you.

What are the top mistakes small business owners make in marketing their services?
One of the biggest mistakes that I've seen among my clients is that they try to guess what their customers want. Sometimes, because of time and cost limitations, you will have to make some assumptions. The more background research you have done in the situational analysis portion of your marketing plan, the better your assumptions will be. With fewer assumptions, you will be making sounder marketing decisions. Whenever possible, ask your customers what they really want from your product or service.

Another major mistake that small business owners make is not having a system in place to track return on investment. Whenever potential new customers contact you, make sure you ask them one simple question: "How did you hear about us?" This is the type of information should be tracked in your CRM database.

RESOURCES

BOOKS

Beckwith, H. (2003). *What clients love: A field guide to growing your business*. New York: Warner Books.

Beckwith, H. (1997). *Selling the invisible: A field guide to modern marketing*. New York: Warner Books.

Brinckerhoff, P. C. (2002). *Mission-based marketing: Positioning your not-for-profit in an increasingly competitive world* (2nd Ed.). New York: John Wiley & Sons, Inc.

Hayden, C. J. (1999). *Get clients now! The 28-day marketing program for professionals and consultants*. New York: Amacom.

Levinson, J. C., & Godin, S. (1994). *The guerrilla marketing handbook (guerrilla marketing)*. Boston, MA: Houghton Mifflin.

Wood, M.B. (2003). *The marketing plan: A handbook*. Upper Saddle River, NJ: Pearson Education, Inc.

WEB SITES

InfoUsa for mailing lists:

www.infousa.com

Web site development:

www.sitesell.com

Web site effectiveness analysis:

www.webtrends.com

Web site visitor analysis:

www.statcounter.com

Database and newsletter management companies:

www.constantcontact.com

www.zoomerang.com

Press release electronic submission:

www.prweb.com

Database management — Accudata:

www.accudata-america.com

TERMINOLOGY

audio logo   (also called the "elevator introduction") A short (60 seconds or less) introduction to the benefits of your services.

customer relationship management (CRM)   (also known as customer relationship marketing) The focus on establishing and retaining relationships with current customers by providing exceptional customer service and exceeding expectations.

CMO   chief marketing officer; the primary executive in charge of all marketing planning, implementation, and evaluation in a company.

opt-in list   A mailing list in which subscribers need to add and confirm their subscription. An opt-in list always includes the ability to opt-out.

educational marketing   A marketing approach that rests on providing prospects with useful and valuable information and resources.

market share   The percentage of one company's total sales of services or products in comparison to the total sales in that company's market of competitors.

segmentation   The process of dividing the market into meaningful groups of potential buyers that behave distinctly from other groups. Examples of potential factors to use to segment the market are geography, age, sex, income, and personality type.

strategic referral partnership (SRP)   A win-win referral partnership in which partners refer clients to one another, or in which one partner refers clients to the other. In the latter scenario, the partner receiving the referrals benefits from getting the referrals and the other benefits in other ways.

sustainable competitive advantage   Creating a competitive advantage that relies on strategic thrusts, such as differentiation, cost, focus, positioning, and synergy, that are likely to last over an extended period of time.

value proposition   A description of potential value or worth that one entity can add to another. In marketing yourself, it would be the way in which you could add a unique contribution to an agency, an organization, or another aspect of your career.

CHAPTER 5

Your Financial Plan: Building and Managing Wealth

If you would be wealthy, think of saving as well as getting.
Benjamin Franklin

Money was never a big motivation for me, except as a way to keep score. The real excitement is playing the game.
Donald Trump

BE THE CFO OF YOUR CAREER

A CFO is a chief financial officer. As the CFO of your career, you will ensure that your career is creating value for yourself and for those with whom you work. By creating value, profit will result. It is the job of a CFO to concern himself or herself with the level of profitability of a company. Likewise, you will need to be the one in charge of not only creating wealth and profit from your career, but also managing the income you earn.

Therapists may need to begin thinking in a new way in order to be a CFO. In the mental health field, we are simply not taught much about the financial realities of a career during graduate school. We get out of school and have large student loans to pay off, and low salaries that at times can be too little to live on, much less support a family. If we do begin to make money, it feels so foreign that we do not know what to do. We wonder if we should put it into a savings account, invest it, or just keep it under a mattress at home and look at it to remind ourselves that it really is there.

For all of these reasons, it is important to create a financial plan for your professional career.

I am a therapist who started out in the scenario I just described. While I am business-minded and money savvy overall, I do not claim to be an expert in financial planning. I was fortunate to receive a great deal of insight and consultation for this chapter from a financial adviser. Because of the extensive contributions and participation of this man, to whom I will refer as Andre, I feel confident that this chapter has accurate financial information that can greatly benefit you in your career.

Andre is a financial adviser in the Philadelphia area with a leading global financial services firm. He builds and manages comprehensive wealth for individuals and companies through a consultative process. Andre has a diverse European and American educational background, which includes an MBA in international business. He has been a captain in the military, serving both in the United States and overseas, and has worked in the technology sector with corporate clients. For further information or to send comments to Andre, contact me at larina@pascoaching.com.

Andre states that the material in this chapter will serve as a general guide, offering broad brush strokes of some financial concepts, which are interwoven as topics of importance followed by case reflections and some reader questions. We have chosen to use a case study to provide clear examples and illustrations of how some of the principles described in this chapter can be implemented in practice. This chapter is not meant to be a complete text or financial advice. No tax or legal advice is given here. It is merely an introduction to gain your interest (pun intended). Nothing discussed here is a solicitation to buy or sell a security or funds. Andre's non-compensated opinion is not representative of any company or companies and may conflict with the opinion of other financial advisers. You should seek specific advice as your situation may differ.

RETURN ON INVESTMENT

One of the most important concepts in financial planning and, in my opinion, in career planning is the idea of return on investment. This is commonly referred to as ROI. Financially speaking, ROI is the return (appreciation and investment income—interest and dividends) that you receive from a particular fiscal investment. This concept can actually apply to any aspect of your career performance, not only the financial aspects. With any activity that you choose to engage in, you can ask yourself, what is the return? What am I getting out of doing this? Is it worth it? Is it paying off as I would like?

If, for example, you find that you are working 65 hours a week to build a practice, you can ask yourself whether the payoff is worth the hours you are putting in. You may be working 75 hours a week as a consultant and making $150,000. If financial rewards are extremely valuable for you, then the ROI is likely to be high. If, however, you are constantly upset that you never see your family, the ROI of the 75-hour work week may be lower.

Sometimes the payoff is not immediate yet it is still a smart idea to invest your time, energy, and resources in the short term for the long-term payoff. No one wants to work forever with little rewards or potential returns. This is why you should regularly ask yourself about the ROI of various career decisions. You want your career to create as much value and profit for you and the other people involved with your practice and career as possible.

WHAT IS A FINANCIAL PLAN?

As the name implies, a financial plan is a way to prepare and manage your finances. There are several variations of a general financial plan. An overview approach is to add up everything you own, especially if it generates revenue (i.e., savings and investments); those are your assets. Everything you owe—loans, bills, and household expenses—are your liabilities. Your assets minus liabilities are your net worth. If you seek to have a high net worth, you can achieve that either by defensively cutting back your liabilities (expenses and lifestyle) or by offensively increasing your assets through greater savings or a larger income. If, for example, you are a graduate student in psychology or social work and your assets are low, one way to increase your net worth is to cut back on your expenses. You can reduce your entertainment costs by eating out less and renting movies instead of going to a theater. You can reduce your school expenses by checking books out of the library or buying used books instead of buying all new books.

Remember that a good plan has reachable goals with time limits attached to them. In order to firm up your plan, add a time limit. Base your goals on age or the number of years to reach an obtainable goal. You can get a free Wealth Care Kit to help you estimate your goals from the National Endowment for Financial Education at www.nefe.org. Click on "Multimedia Access," then under "Resources for Consumers" select "The Wealth Care Kit."

What Are the Components of a Financial Plan?

Again, there are many variations in financial plans, based on where you are in your career, what your financial goals are, and so on. When you begin to make a more specific financial plan, you include a higher level of detail, such as time lines and event scenarios. An event could be a death, birth, or marriage that would trigger an action. The plan would include an if-then scenario to determine your fiscal response to the event. Generally, this is input into some type of financial planners' software, of which there numerous types, both proprietary and public. You gain access to financial planning software packages when you work with a financial planner or adviser. These programs deliver a book-like report which includes the likelihood (based on a percentage) of obtaining your various financial goals. The plan can also be stress-tested to account for down years, and you can add the concept of "be prepared to" (BPT), which is more quantifiable then a general emergency fund. For instance, be prepared to replace your car every eight years at a cost of $20K to $50K; or, in Florida, BPT repair or replace problems from hurricane damage to your residence.

The Issues Addressed in Your Plan

The Cannon Financial Institute (www.cannonfinancial.com) has identified 13 wealth management issues that should be addressed in a more specific plan:

1. Investments
2. Insurance
3. Liabilities
4. Qualified retirement plan/ IRA distribution plan
5. Stock options
6. Business succession plan
7. Durable power of attorney at incapacity
8. Gifting to children/descendents
9. Charitable gifting during life
10. Titling of assets
11. Selection of executor/trustee
12. Distribution plan at death to spouse/descendants
13. Charitable inclinations at death

As you can see, constructing a proper plan takes an in-depth thought process. Going into each of these in detail is beyond the scope of this text, but the takeaway point is that you want to create a living document that can be developed over time. Just like the marketing plan, a good financial plan is not one that is created once and then filed away. Instead, it is continually reviewed and revised.

WHY DO I NEED A PLAN ANYWAY?

Simply put, if you fail to plan, you are planning to fail. If you're not beating inflation, inflation is beating you.

We often tend to avoid or put off those things we do not want know how to deal with. While this may be a natural tendency, do not make the mistake of doing it when it comes to your finances. By not planning your finances, you can:

- Make poor decisions regarding taking out loans and loan repayment.
- Neglect to take advantage of opportunities to either increase your income or decrease your expenses.
- Invest your money in ways that will not help you to meet your goals.
- Be unable to save or cover unexpected expenses that arise.
- Feel frustrated and out of control about your money.

WHETHER TO HIRE A FINANCIAL PLANNER

Andre, the financial adviser, attended a seminar by a large international financial magazine promoting their stock-picking software for the consumer/individual investor. The lead speaker stated, "No one cares more about your money than you, so do it yourself." Andre's friend, also a financial adviser, was sitting next to him and commented, "Yes, and I also do my own brain surgery, do my own taxes, and represent myself in court."

According to Andre, the world revolves around two things: time and money. We cannot control time, so we should get all the help we can with our money.

In any aspect of your career, it is a good idea to do what you really know and outsource the rest. You will save time and energy by enlisting help from those who know what they are doing; you may also save a great deal of money and frustration. Unless you are highly skilled in the financial arena, it is a good idea to work with a financial professional.

CHOOSING A FINANCIAL ADVISER

When searching for a financial adviser, use some of the techniques you would for any other family professional staff member—a doctor, lawyer, dentist, or an accountant. Start by asking your friends and coworkers for referrals. Check the local papers and yes, the local telephone book. Interview each one. Ask about their investment theories, their background and experience, and how they run their financial practice. There should be a common thread of understanding regarding your wants, goals, and needs. They should offer commitment to you for reasonable options and balanced recommendations that are suitable to you. Last and most important, choose someone with whom you feel you can comfortably work.

When do you use an adviser? The answer is the same as for a family dentist or accountant: always. Their degree of involvement is what varies. For instance, you have a check-up and a cleaning with a dentist periodically, but sometimes you need more care. You may need to have cavities filled, which requires a couple of visits. You may need a long-term solution like braces. Similarly, your adviser will work according to your changing needs. An adviser should be able to operate on suitable levels at various points during your life.

FINANCIAL PLANNERS AND FINANCIAL ADVISERS

There is a difference between a financial adviser (FA) and a financial planner (FP). Broadly speaking, the difference is based on compensation, certifications, and knowledge orientation. The FA is generally keenly tuned in to the investment community, aware of financial information, the exchanges, stocks, bonds, mutual funds, IPO's, annuities, and any other type of investment vehicle he can find and use to implement a plan. An FA is typically paid either commissions on the client's investments (which is common for a stockbroker) or a management fee, and does not charge a flat fee or an hourly rate.

Financial advisers are more connected to brokerage houses and are constantly observing markets and tactical and strategic conditions. They typically have a couple of licenses (referred to as a series) and are monitored by the Securities and Exchange Commission (SEC) and the National Association of Securities Dealers (NASD). Look for an FA with a series 7, series 66, and insurance license. Andre points out that most FAs do not have additional certifications. Over the past few years, he says, some FAs are completing the Certified Investment Management Analyst

(CIMA) training, Chartered Financial Analyst (CFA) courses, and some get their Certified Financial Planner (CFP) certification. Do not be too alarmed about the certification issue because he knows several licensed FAs without certifications who have successfully managed well over a billion dollars for years, and certification has never come up. Andre, for instance, is a generalist with a diverse education that orients him toward comprehensive wealth management. When clients want to focus on a specific investment, he calls on the appropriate specialist.

The financial planner is also a professional and can be an accountant, banker, lawyer, stockbroker and/or real estate professional. The FP operates from a different perspective than the FA, in many cases more strategic and less tactical then the FA. The FPs typically have certifications like CFP. Some are also certified public accountants (CPA) and CFAs. Financial planners are very involved with the new laws, regulations, tax changes, and bigger-picture estate planning types of issues, whereas the adviser is oriented to both the why and how of implementing the plan. Each have advantages to be considered.

THE COSTS TO HIRE A FINANCIAL PLANNER OR ADVISER

In most cases, a flat fee or an hourly rate compensates your financial planner. The hourly rates vary and typically start at $200 with a certain minimum number of hours. The flat rate also varies and can start anywhere from $500 to $6,000. Both arrangements include a thorough interview and the delivery of an extensive report. There are some commission-based financial planners, but Andre does not believe that this arrangement is in the client's best interest.

You use an FP to establish a map for your financial journey. It is your map and you can show it to whomever you like. After you have chosen your FP and created the financial map (FP report), you can find an FA to help you implement the plan. In selecting your FA, choose three potential advisers and give each of them a copy of the financial map. Ask them for options and a recommendation. You should select the FA with whom you feel more comfortable and whom you most trust to implement the plan. That is an example of the complementary nature of the two positions (FA and FP). It is not wise to use the planner to implement his or her own report, because there can be a conflict of interest or, as we say in psychology, a dual relationship. The FA acts as the first string and the monitor. In three to five years—the length of a market cycle—you can go back to the planner for a reevaluation.

Is Working with FAs and FPs a Good Use of My Limited Funds?

Before you start out on any journey, you want to have a map or a vision of where you would like to go. Your financial plan is integral in helping you get there. If your funds are limited, you may want to find a diverse FA. Sometimes just what you can afford will get you moving in the right direction. You can then find an FP who is willing to take you as a client so you can grow together. You can also initially seek an FA with FP capabilities until you can afford a separate planner to complement the adviser.

When You Want to Start Investing

Deciding when and how to invest is one of the most challenging parts of your financial picture. Of course, there are many individual factors to consider. Here are some initial ideas to think about.

The Initial Steps

A good way to start is to pick a financial adviser and work together to complete a profile that includes your investment objectives and risk tolerance. After you have chosen your FA and discussed your goals, the first step in investing is to build an asset allocation strategy, which is a weighting between stocks, bonds, and cash. This will help you to stay diversified in order to reduce portfolio risk, reduce the emotional response to market fluctuations, and seek a more consistent long-term performance and investment horizon. All of this, of course, is weighed against what is reasonable, balanced, and suitable for you.

After the profiling and background, the second step is the options and recommendations, which your FA assists with. The third step is to implement your plan, and the last step is to review it to make sure it is doing what it is supposed to be doing. When you review the status of your investments, you can identify which stage of wealth management you are currently in—generally, you are in either an accumulation, a preservation, or a transfer period.

The Right Mix or Allocation of Investments

It is crucial to consider the mix or variety of investments that you need in order to stay diversified. We have talked about how diversification can benefit multiple areas of your career. Diversifying your career activities can significantly enhance the financial performance of your career. For example, you can maintain a clinical job conducting therapy and receive passive income from books or other products at the same time that you are billing client hours. One of the great aspects of diversifying your career is that it reduces your risk and dependence on any one area. This often minimizes stress and maximizes the rewards of your career. Diversification in investments serves similar purposes in terms of minimizing risk and maximizing returns.

We know that no single asset class performs best in all economic environments. By diversifying, you are able to have more consistent returns and less portfolio market value volatility. We are basically talking about balancing among three broad asset classes:

1. *Stocks.* Stocks mean that you own (have rights to) a piece of a company. They have more risk and greater downturn potential than any other asset class in the short term (approximately a year or less). However, over longer holding periods, they provide the highest returns on investment and have the greatest potential to beat inflation. Stocks are sometimes referred to as equities.

2. *Bonds.* Bonds are IOUs. They are debts issued by municipalities, governments, federal agencies, and corporations. They have less risk and less volatility than stocks. Their value can react widely based on interest rate changes. They offer current income and limited upside potential for increased returns. However, the returns or yields are higher than cash.

3. *Cash.* Cash is basically a money market account. This is really a fund consisting of a basket of short duration instruments like treasury bills, short term CDs, and maturing bonds. They are very stable and liquid. However, inflation will erode your purchasing power over time.

We can break this classification system down to another level consisting of U.S. stocks versus international (non–U.S.) stocks. The same is true for bonds, which are sometimes referred to as fixed income investments.

We can further diversify among asset classes and styles. An adviser helps sort through the U.S. stock large capitalized (blue chips), medium cap, and small cap, which can also be divide into two styles: value or growth. International stock is commonly broken down into developed countries (like those in Europe) and emerging (like those in Africa). Bonds or fixed income can be broken down into time of maturity—short (one to five years), intermediate, and long-term (20 to 30 years) —and either international and U.S. There are also different types of bonds and fixed income instruments, like U.S. government, corporate, and municipal.

PUTTING IT TOGETHER

The adviser works with your profile (objective and risk) and your goal (long-term) to construct an allocation based on the investments just described. His value-add is to manage the per unit increased return while reducing the per unit risk. For instance, with a goal of purchasing a vacation house in a 20-year time frame, capital appreciation and an aggressive approach to investing may produce an asset allocation portfolio analysis of 80 percent stocks and 20 percent bonds. A goal of purchasing a car in two years may be something like 40 percent stocks and 60 percent bonds. The best asset allocation is derived from discussions between you and your adviser. The portfolio analysis is done periodically to review your progress. It is an ongoing relationship and process.

CASE STUDY

Let's use a hypothetical example to see how this all comes together. Brian Ramirez, PsyD, is a licensed clinical psychologist. Here is how he describes his current situation and goals:

> I am a 31-year-old, newly licensed clinical psychologist. I have been licensed since August of 2004. I am presently working in a community mental health facility, augmented by part-time work with relocated refugee patients and teaching AP Psychology at a local college preparatory high school. I have also started a private practice and have a potential part-time contract lined up with the local university. My goal is to maintain a full-time private practice consisting of primarily private pay clients with no more than 30 to 40 percent of my patients coming from managed care or other insurance panels. I would also like to augment my future practice with part-time (no more than 10 hours per week) community work.
>
> I presently have $129,000 in student loan debt. This includes both undergraduate and graduate loans. All of these loans are federally

based. I have recently consolidated these loans and have an interest rate of 2.75 percent for the life of the loan. The rate drops to 1.5 percent after 36 consecutive on-time payments. The loan term is 30 years. I have chosen to graduate the payments at a starting rate of $322 per month. In addition, I currently have about $8,500 in credit card debt that I intend to pay off by August 2005.

My monthly take-home income is presently $3,300 per month. This includes my salaried position of $33,000 annually at the community mental health facility and approximately $1,000 per month for five hours of teaching per week. In addition, I also earn approximately $300 per month for my work with the refugee population (three to five hours per week.)

I have secured office space in a highly successful private practice at a rate of $12 per hour. I have also developed a mentor relationship with one of the psychologists in this practice who has indicated a willingness to refer overflow patients to me. I now have one private pay patient at a rate of $125 per hour. This began two weeks after agreeing upon the office rental. My mentoring psychologist sees approximately 37 patients per week at a rate of $140 per hour. She is on no insurance panels and accepts no managed care. Her patients pay her directly or arrange to have their insurance carrier reimburse her directly for her full fee. She has reported to me that her operating expenses run about $2,400 per month, including a full-time office manager shared with two other therapists. Her estimated after-expenses, pre-tax income is approximately $215,000 annually.

Being trained in child and adolescent psychology puts me in a good position to be busy relatively quickly. I am also earnestly working to develop relationships with other potential referral sources to expedite the building of my practice. I would like to be in full-time practice as soon as possible and have set a time table of two years to achieve this goal. I am wondering where I should direct my limited funds and whether I should take out a loan to build my practice. As I have become accustomed to living a very modest lifestyle, I am comfortable with investment risk at this point in time.

REFLECTIONS ON THE CASE

Andre reviewed Dr. Brian Ramirez's case in detail. He feels Brian is at a unique financial crossroads situation between the balance of income and expenses, debt and investments, along the avenue of wealth accumulation, preservation, and transfer. Ideally, Andre would meet with potential clients in order to discuss their background, risk tolerances, and establish suitability (client profiling) to derive what is reasonable and balanced for that individual. The issues and opinions discussed are not meant for everyone. You should seek individual financial advice as your specific situation may differ.

Overall, the case as it is stated falls into two broad areas: financial advisement and business development. There are two main financial advisement questions. Brian asks the first one at the end of his profile: "Where should I direct my limited funds?" The intuitive answer is to invest where it will pay him the most return. It is never too soon or too late to start investing. However, some other considerations are:

- When will his investments pay him back?
- What are the tax implications?
- What is the return and how much risk must he take?
- What type of access (liquidity) to his money will he need now and in the future?

The second main question is how and if he should invest for maximum growth while considering taking on a business loan. These are actually three questions in two separate areas—business developmental finance and individual financial advisement. However, they are linked personally, which raises some of the unique issues a professional person or business owner has that a typical employee does not.

CLIENT BACKGROUND AND PROFILING

In many cases, to increase business means to generate more income and greater individual wealth. For complete analysis, we would want to know more about his living arrangements (owns or rents), transportation (public, owns, or leases), and social situation (married, single, children, and relatives). He may simply want to have a full-time private practice because he thinks it is the fastest way to acquire more money, which is not always the case.

INVESTMENT OBJECTIVES

Your investment objective and risk tolerance will help you determine how to invest. Initially, Brian's investment is for maximum growth. There are three broad categories of investment objectives:

1. *Capital appreciation:* investments that generally seek the growth of principal rather than the generation of income.
2. *Current income:* investments that generate income.
3. *Current income and capital appreciation:* investments that seek the generation of income and the growth of principal.

Brian's case would fall under the first of these, the capital appreciation objective.

RISK TOLERANCES

Brian also mentions he is currently comfortable with investment risk. Risk also falls into three general themes:

1. *Conservative:* Seeking to preserve principal with low-risk securities.
2. *Moderate:* Combining the potential for returns and lower risk of principal loss.
3. *Aggressive/speculative:* Seeking significant appreciation potential and willing to accept a high degree of principal loss.

On the surface, the aggressive approach may be right for Brian. He has a long investment horizon in which to recover from losses in a down market. Once an objective and risk profile is established, it is not locked in—it changes as your life events change. (Read *Against the Gods: The Remarkable Story of Risk*, by Peter Bernstein.)

WORKING WITH A BUSINESS ADVISER

A business adviser/consultant/coach discusses with you ways to expand, maintain, or contract your enterprise and falls under a different category of advice. One way to expand is with a business loan, especially if you want to do so quickly. However, this will create a liability that has to be paid back. Client referrals are another way to grow gradually over time; this perhaps is more of a managed growth approach. It may take longer but there is no loan to pay back. For business advising, I have had good results with Practical Options Group (info@practicaloptions .com), an accredited associate of the Institute for Independent Business (www.iibusa.org), which gives small businesses direct access to top business people.

SHOULD HE TAKE OUT A LOAN?

If you take on a business loan, your practice has debts that must be paid. Your business is tied to you personally, so if the practice does not make a payment, the bank comes after you and your assets. Of course, some loans are bad for you and some are good, depending on the rates. Consider also the level of debt you would be taking on. Be careful it is not too high, or disproportionate to your income or net worth.

Brian may want the loan for business reasons but may choose not to take it because of the risk to his personal wealth, which he wants to build. He could accept the business loan if he changed his risk tolerance to conservative and sought to preserve principal with low-risk securities, thus allowing him to pay any missed bank payments with his investments.

The decision regarding taking out a loan is complex. You are starting to see where trade-offs are made and the relationship between risk and return. How you invest will be dependent on that decision. Why does Brian have these issues with a loan versus investment? What is his real need?

Keep in mind that needs often change. The purpose of the business loan is not to just make money—he is already doing that. It seems he wants to make even more money, maximize his efforts, or reach a goal. A good financial adviser can help him maximize his returns while reducing his investment risk under his existing profile (investment objective and risk tolerance). For more on these ideas, read *Rich Dad, Poor Dad*, by Robert Kiyosaki.

LIABILITIES

As a balance sheet (assets and liabilities) adviser, Andre believes it is important to look at Brian's personal expenses and debt. At a minimum, they are below $3,300 a month ($39,600 per year), which Brian mentioned as his take-home income. He also said he is accustomed to a modest lifestyle (for more about this, read *The Millionaire Next Door*, by Thomas Stanley

PhD and Danko PhD). We will assume that Brian has some discretionary income after expenses that is greater than breaking even between his assets and liabilities. His long-term (LT) debt is $137,500 ($129K in student loans plus $8.5K in credit card debt). Remember that assets minus liabilities equals net worth. Let's look at assets, the other side of the equation. He hasn't mentioned a retirement plan or an existing portfolio (investments and savings). So a quick overview of his net wealth situation can be phrased as "–$137,500 LT debt, breaking even, nothing saved, and high potential income."

Let us begin by setting up an initial defensive financial battle plan to minimize expenses, costs, and spending. Brian should continue to maintain a modest lifestyle, keeping expenses under control or even bringing them lower if possible. He must *not* miss a payment on the student loans for the first three years. I cannot emphasize this enough. The reduction in interest rate that follows three years of on-time payments will provide a huge boost to his financial situation.

A loan can be considered good debt if its interest rate is at or below the inflation rate and the person's portfolio returns. Currently, the inflation rate fluctuates at around 2.5 percent per year. By locking in 2.75 percent fixed for your $129,000 students loans, Brian will bring down his real cost of money (debt service) to 0.25 percent. Inflation will eat away the purchasing power of the lenders' funds, not his. If the interest charged qualifies as a tax deduction, he wins again. Further, after 36 consecutive on-time payments the rate is then reduced to 1.5 percent, and his real cost of borrowing against inflation is –1 percent. In other words, it would *not* be cost beneficial to pay his loan off early when he has a low interest rate. He just needs to pay it off on time.

This analysis does not apply to the $8,500 credit card debt, which is probably at a high rate of anywhere from 9 percent to 21 percent per year. It is important to pay off this debt as soon as possible, and that is most likely why Brian targeted next August for completion. Paying off expensive debt is a high priority no matter what the amount. High interest loans are expensive debt, whereas loans that have a low cost of borrowing, at or below the rate of inflation and/or below your portfolio return, are inexpensive debt. The lower interest loans can also help you build a good credit report.

Doubling up payments on Brian's student loan will bring him out of debt sooner, but it will not make him wealthier. By giving an extra payment, he would be losing control of assets that could be making him money. He would rob himself of return on that asset and of two fundamentals for investing: the time effect of compounding and dollar cost averaging (we'll consider these concepts shortly). Big wealth deflators are debt with high interest rates, inflation, and taxes.

SAVING FOR RETIREMENT

It is never too early or too late to start saving for retirement. We are focusing our efforts on wealth accumulation. How and when does Brian want to retire? One of Stephen Covey's seven habits, "Start with the end in mind," can be applied here (Covey, 1990). Retirement planning is an involved, long-term investment process and strategy. It also takes into consideration more immediate concerns, like a mortgage payment or saving for college. Brian could end up being in retirement for the same length of time that he was working. If he is 31 now and retires in 25 to 30 years at age 55 to 60, it is possible he will still be alive at age 80 or 90. In many cases, to maintain your standard of living after retirement, you will need most of your current (pre-retirement) income level—in some cases, 75 percent—each year.

Social Security benefits cannot be depended on for retirement, and they were never meant to be, anyway. When Social Security was set up in 1930, it was a safety net for people 65 years old and older. At that time, 65 was the average life expectancy of women; it was lower for men. According to an Employee Benefit Research Institute (EBRI) study, you will get about $7,000 or 14 percent of your income from Social Security if you are over 65 with a post-retirement income of at least $50K. Therefore, Social Security is minimal and pensions are no longer being offered as they once were.

The closest thing to a retirement plan that you can get from a company you work for is a 401(k), which gives you the responsibility to contribute (usually up to $14K) and select investments tax deferred. Ideally, a 401(k) with a company match (50 to 100 percent) of some of the contributions (sometimes the first 3 to 6 percent) would be a great start. Brian may be able to contribute to retirement vehicles through a 403(b) (for nonprofits, health care professionals, or teaching professionals) where he works.

There is also the Individual Retirement Account (IRA), which is not attached to an employer and which you can set up yourself. The traditional or Roth IRA is with a financial institution that you can keep regardless of where you work. It also qualifies as a tax-deductible contribution ($4,000 in 2005) up to certain income levels. The difference is that with the Roth IRA, contributions are made on an after-tax basis and continue to grow tax deferred. This means that you initially pay income tax, then place money into your Roth IRA, after which the money and its interest are not taxed.

For private practices and other business owners there are also simplified employee pension plans (SEP), profit sharing plans, and savings incentive match plans for employees (SIMPLE). Brian would probably be interested in hearing more about a SEP, sometimes call a SEP IRA. There is a limit to the amount of qualified funds you can put aside from your income in any given year. It is a tremendous benefit to the investors to have tax-deferred moneys growing over a long period of time.

The general trend in retirement planning is a shift of responsibility from the government and employers to the individual for his own retirement plans and funding. There are also other vehicles that can help you save for retirement; a financial adviser can discuss what fits best for your particular needs.

USING TIME TO MAKE YOU A MILLIONAIRE

Dollar cost averaging and compounding are two strategies whose benefits increase over time. *Dollar cost averaging* is a systematic way of saving and investing, usually the same amount (or percentage) and usually at the same time (typically monthly). For example, instead of putting in a lump sum of $4,000 for a given year into a retirement account (Roth or traditional), Brian would make monthly deposits of $333. The deposits would be invested into the IRA's stocks, bonds, or mutual funds. This way he reduces his overall cost per unit. When the market is low, he buys more shares of stock; when it is high he gets fewer shares. Generally, over time, he will reduce his overall average cost per share, thus improving his potential returns. This strategy cannot, however, guarantee a profit or prevent a loss. The strategy's effectiveness is based on the assumption that Brian will have the discipline to make monthly deposits and will not emotionally respond to higher price per share. (Read *Start Late, Finish Rich*, by David Bach.) This strategy is ideal for long-term investment goals like retirement, because it smoothes out short-term market fluctuations and increases the compounding effect.

Compounding is the ability of interest to earn interest, such that 10 + 10 = 21. If, for example, Brian invests $100 dollars in a mutual fund that has a return of 10 percent, at the end of the first year it will be worth $110. In the second year, Brian's $110 earns another 10 percent so that at the end of the year it is $121. Therefore 10 percent + 10 percent = $21. If you made this investment when you were born and if you never touched it—no withdrawals or additions, and the dividends were reinvested—by retirement at age 65 your $100 would be worth over $49,000. Imagine if the starting figure was $10,000. By age 65 it would be worth over $4.9 million! Can you see the compounding effect and the time value of money?

Interview with Andre

Andre is a financial adviser in Philadelphia, Pennsylvania. To consult with or contact Andre, send an e-mail to larina@pascoaching .com.

Andre, in your opinion, what are Brian's greatest strengths from the case?

The first and most important is that he is living below his means. He is not captured by keeping up with the Joneses or purchasing status symbols early on. I see folks going down that road all the time, and you would be amazed at how much debt they are in and how stressed out they are because of it. Brian's second strength is keeping his debt to a minimum. He only has student loans and a controllable amount of credit card debt that he knows is a priority to pay off.

Where do you see him most financially vulnerable?

Brian does not seem to have a lot of understanding of investment performance over time. Thus he may be less willing to fully embrace the concept and be disciplined over the long term. Another concern is what he spends money on now. I do encourage rewarding oneself. However, if he forgoes an immediate need for satisfaction, he will gain mountains of personal financial confidence through a much higher credit and financing rating. In addition, more extravagant purchases can be accumulated over time as his income becomes more predictable and increasing.

What are some general suggestions for Brian?

He has a great start! Higher education is one of the paths toward a higher income. I recommend that you pay yourself first—put away a certain percentage (10 to 25 percent, or even more) or an amount after expenses every time you are paid. Deposit the maximum amount, while you can, in your retirement vehicles. Your increasing earnings potential could hit phase-out limits of future contributions like IRAs.

Living below your means (substantially or otherwise) is one of the paramount concepts to accumulating and maintaining wealth. Consider the utility of each purchase, especially big-ticket items like houses, cars, boats, planes, and starting a family. Are you really going out on the boat or to the vacation house that much? Is it going to pay you back? Review and migrate to higher sources of income. Unless you are doing community work for experience, delay the altruistic efforts for a couple years. You will be in a better position later, professionally and financially, to help those you desire.

What are some of your observations from your own financial practice that you would like to share?
We have reviewed some of the concepts in the case. Many of the clichés are true: Prior planning prevents poor performance; don't put all your eggs in one basket.

Begin financial mapping when children are born, or before. When children are born, you know that in about 18 years there will be four to seven years of education to pay for. The College Board's Annual Survey of Colleges estimated that in 2025 the cost per year to attend a public college will be $38,327. The lack of general financial understanding that most individuals have is very sad, specifically surrounding investment performance and asset allocation and the relationship of time versus money. This goes back to the maxim that failing to plan is planning to fail.

Another area of concern is funding for retirement. Do your own due diligence and follow the advice given if it makes sense. I have yet to hear from any of my clients, "I have underspent and oversaved—what do I do?" Lastly, maintain my belief that *you can become a millionaire and it is achievable during your lifetime*.

RESOURCES

BOOKS

Bach, D. (2005). *Start late, finish rich: A no-fail plan for achieving financial freedom at any age*. New York: Broadway.
Bernstein, P. L. (1998). *Against the gods: The remarkable story of risk*. New York: John Wiley & Sons.

Brown, D. L., & Bently, K. (1997). *Wall Street city: Your guide to investing on the web*. New York: John Wiley & Sons.

Clements, J. (1998). *25 myths you've got to avoid if you want to manage your money right: The new rules for financial success*. New York: Simon & Schuster.

Covey, S. R. (1990). *The 7 habits of highly effective people* (1st ed). New York: Fireside

Gardner, R., & Welch, J (1999). *101 tax saving ideas*. Kansas City, MO: Wealth Builders Press.

Glink, I. (1999). *100 questions you should ask about your personal finances: And the answers you need to help you save, invest, and grow your money*. New York: Times Books.

Kelly, J. (1997). *The neatest little guide to mutual fund investing*. New York: Plume.

Kiyosaki, R. T., & Lechter, S. L. (2000). *Rich dad, poor dad: What the rich teach their kids about money—that the poor and middle class do not!* New York: Warner Business Books.

Morris, K. M., & Siegel, A. (2000). *The Wall Street Journal guide to understanding personal finance*. New York: Simon & Schuster.

Naylor, P. W. (1997). *10 steps to financial success: A beginner's guide to saving and investing*. New York: John Wiley & Sons.

Orman, S. (2000). *The 9 steps to financial freedom: Practical and spiritual steps so you can stop worrying*. New York: Random House.

Rye, D. E. (1999). *1,001 ways to save, grow, and invest your money*. Emmaus, PA: Rodale Press.

Savage, Terry (1999). *The savage truth on money*. New York: John Wiley & Sons.

Stanley, T. J., & Danko, W. D. (1998). *The millionaire next door* (Reprint ed.). New York: Pocket Books.

Updegrave, W. L. (1999). *Investing for the financially challenged*. New York: Warner Books.

Web Sites

Learn more about the 13 wealth management issues:

www.cannonfinancial.com

Free wealth care kit:

www.nefe.org

UBS Financial Services and Private Bank:

www.ubs.com

Independent Business Consultants:

www.iibusa.org

A Dun & Bradstreet research web site for the public:

www.hoovers.com

The U.S. Government's Department of Commerce and Bureau of Economic Analysis:

www.bea.doc.gov

Ohio State University's virtual library resource:

www.fisher.osu.edu/fin/overview.html

The *Wall Street Journal*:

www.wsj.com

A great information resource:

www.bloomberg.com

Rueters—financial news:

www.reuters.com

CNN money:

www.money.cnn.com

The Securities and Exchange Commission:

www.sec.gov/investor.shtml

The CNN site for money—a general finance and investment web site:

www.moneychimp.com

Free SEC filings for businesses:

www.freeedgar.com

Investment information with a focus on bonds:

www.bondsonline.com

Public Debt Treasuries, a governmental web site—the Bureau of Public Debt:

www.publicdebt.treas.gov/opd/opddload.htm

Investment Company Institute—gives information on mutual funds:

www.ici.org

Mutual Fund Educational Alliance—gives education on mutual funds:

www.mfea.com

Free stock quotes through Lycos search engine:

www.quote.com

Kiplinger's financial news for investors:

www.kiplinger.com

Yahoo's financial news:

www.finance.yahoo.com

Terminology

aggressive or speculative An investment approach that seeks significant appreciation potential and is willing to accept a high degree of principal loss.

asset The items on a balance sheet that add value or generate revenue, like savings and investments.

balance sheet A financial statement that includes assets and liabilities.

"be prepared to" (BPT) Funds to cover unexpected (quantifiable) costs so that one is financially prepared.

bonds Debts issued by municipalities, governments, federal agencies, and corporations. Bonds have less risk and less volatility than stocks.

Their value can react widely based on interest rate changes. They offer current income and limited upside potential for increased returns.

capital appreciation Investment that generally seeks the growth of principal rather than the generation of income.

cash accounts Basically a money market account. A cash account is re ally a fund consisting of a basket of short duration instruments like treasury bills, short-term CDs, and maturing bonds. They are very stable and liquid.

certified financial planner (CFP) A CFP analyzes personal and financial circumstances and prepares a program to meet financial needs and objectives. Some are also certified public accountants (CPA). They are accredited by the Denver–based Certified Financial Planner Board of Standards.

conservative An investment approach that seeks to preserve principal with low-risk securities.

current income Investments and earnings that generate income.

event scenarios Part of a financial plan that accounts for events such as a death, birth, or marriage that would trigger an action.

financial adviser A professional adviser who offers financial counsel.

IPO (initial public offering) A corporation's first offering of stocks to the public. When a privately held company goes public and tries to raise capital, in exchange for capital the owner gives the public investors shares of stock.

liabilities Everything that you owe, such as loans, accounts payable (bills you have not yet paid), and debt.

liquidity The degree to which your investments are available for cash. A high degree of liquidity means that you can have ready access to your funds. A low degree of liquidity means that your funds are unavailable without a penalty or that they are committed to long-term investments.

moderate An investment approach that seeks the potential for returns and lower risk of principal loss.

NASD (National Association of Securities Dealers) The primary private-sector regulator of America's securities industry, which oversees the activities of more than 5,100 brokerage firms, approximately 97,000 branch offices, and more than 659,000 registered securities representatives.

net worth   Assets minus liabilities.

NYSE (New York Stock Exchange)   Reported to be the world's leading and most technologically advanced equities market. The NYSE includes a broad spectrum of market participants, such as listed companies and individual investors. Buyers and sellers meet directly in a fair, open, and orderly market to access the best possible price through the interplay of supply and demand.

ROI (return on investment)   The yield or return resulting from a specific investment.

SEC (Securities and Exchange Commission)   A government agency that has the mission of protecting investors and maintaining the integrity of the securities markets.

stocks   Ownership of (rights to) a piece of a company. Stocks have more risk and greater downturn potential than any other asset class in the short term (approximately a year or less). However, over longer holding periods they provide the highest returns on investment and have the greatest potential to beat inflation.

value added   The additional value that an act, an individual, a service, or an investment adds to another individual or organization.

yield   The return from an expenditure or investment.

CHAPTER 6

Your Management and Operations Plan

Drive your business, let not your business drive you.
Benjamin Franklin

Management is doing things right; leadership is doing the right things.
Peter Drucker

BE THE COO OF YOUR CAREER

Your management and operations plan is basically the way that you run your business, practice, or career. If we think of your career as a company, you would have the CEO who creates the vision and strategy for the organization. You would then have your chief marketing officer (CMO), who oversees the branding and marketing efforts. There is a chief financial officer (CFO), who allocates the company's monies and creates fiscal policy. Now we have a chief operations officer (COO), who directs all the day-to-day business operations of the company. The COO works with the company's managers, who implement the operations plan. In typical businesses, COOs are in charge of departments such as production, distribution, management, or information technology. There is often a separate executive in charge of information technology; this person is known as the chief information officer (CIO). We will discuss the roles of the COO and CIO in this chapter.

As the CEO and COO of your career, you wear many hats. You are the overall leader (CEO) as well as a manager (COO) of your career. You need to continuously establish, reevaluate, and enhance your vision and strategy as a CEO, and you must create and meet regular business goals and activities as the COO. The COO takes on a great job and then gets the job done.

Many scholars believe that leadership and management are different but overlapping concepts. Leadership is traditionally what occurs when situations are dynamic and in times of change. When you are a graduate student, for example, you need to take on a leadership role in your career because your career is not yet fully established. At this point, you are creating the vision and laying the groundwork based on your core career values.

Leadership has been described as "doing the right thing," while management, which is often thought of as maintaining things during a period of relative stability, has been defined as "doing things right" (Whetton & Cameron, 1998). In today's continuously changing business environment, excellent leaders are also managers, and excellent managers are leaders, so the skills go hand in hand.

PRINCIPLES OF MANAGEMENT

Good management is vital to the success of a company or of your career. To illustrate this point, a study conducted by the U.S. Office of the Controller of the Currency found that two primary factors accounted for the failure of 162 national banks during the 1980s: a depressed economy and poor management. While many people in the 1980s assumed the failures were primarily due to the economy, the opposite was shown to be true. In fact, the distressed economy was rated as the sole cause in only 7 percent of the cases, and only 35 percent of the banks had depressed economic conditions. On the other hand, 89 percent of the banks were judged to fail due to poor management (Whetton & Cameron, 1998). High-quality management can lead to financial success; low-quality management can lead to financial failure. We want the former for your career, so let's look at some of the fundamentals of management to help you best manage your professional career.

Many of the fundamental principles of management are things that therapists are highly skilled in, such as verbal and nonverbal communication, stress and time management, self-awareness, problem-solving, creative thinking, and managing conflict. These principles are all extremely important in managing your career. For example, let's say that you are beginning a private practice and you are faced with a tactical challenge. You have found an excellent office space for a reasonable cost in a good part of town, but it has some problems. First, because there is only a very small window, it is kind of gloomy. Second, the room itself is very small. What is one thing that you could do to solve both problems? The creative manager in you takes over and you decide to paint one wall a light, sunny yellow. You effectively open up the space, making it appear larger and brighter.

INFLUENCING OTHERS

A good deal of effective management revolves around your ability to positively empower and influence others. You have seen how you do this with your therapy clients. Now think about how you can do it with other key players in your career.

Personal power is associated with four characteristics: expertise, personal attractiveness, effort, and legitimacy. Expertise is continuously developed through educational efforts, supervision, and so on. Personal attractiveness to others is created by impression management and positive behaviors. Effort is important because when others see you working hard, they want to help you out. Legitimacy arises when you continuously adhere to your own career vision and values. This means adhering to your professional and personal code of ethics and encouraging others to do so as well.

You can influence your supervisors, boss, or those in authority through what I call "issue selling" or "benefiting your boss." Issue selling is drawing your boss's attention to the specific issues or situations that you believe are most important. You must be able to convince your boss that the issue you raise is worthy of competing for her limited time. You can do this by first choosing an issue that is congruent with your beliefs and your role. It is important to select a topic that is solvable or changeable, credible, and compatible with the organizational culture. You can also form a coalition of other people who support your idea, or bundle that issue with similar issues. Benefiting your boss can be done by understanding and empathizing with her position, and asking yourself what you can do to help her out and to influence her decisions.

MOTIVATING OTHERS

Motivating employees, team members, and coworkers is another important management principle. In your career as a therapist, you can motivate people around you to help you succeed, such as your professors, bosses, and colleagues. You can also motivate others whom you are in charge of, such as assistants, supervisees, employees, office staff, and so on. Since the people who are supportive of your career are influential in your career success, you can also motivate them to continue their support and assistance.

As therapists, we know a good deal about what motivates human behavior and how to bring out the motivation of another person (through skills such as motivational interviewing). To summarize, here are some of the most effective ways of motivating others:

- Provide them with positive reinforcement for something that was well done or appreciated so they continue doing that behavior or increase the frequency of the behavior.
- Offer rewards that are valuable to that individual. If it is something they do not care much about, it will not be meaningful to them and can actually demotivate them.
- Provide training, assistance, and guidance as needed.
- Make sure the person has the necessary resources to complete assigned activities.
- Be available to offer feedback and input.
- Provide specific suggestions for making improvements.
- Set clear standards of performance or behavior.
- Provide forthcoming feedback on areas that need improvement.
- Develop effective and creative teams.
- Ask them for feedback on how they think you are doing and on your management style.

Kouzes and Posner (2003) put forth the idea that leaders and managers can motivate others by "encouraging the heart." They say that business and caring do not need to be mutually exclusive. They describe seven ways that you can encourage others:

1. Set clear, agreed-upon standards that consist of goals as well as values and principles.
2. Expect the best and believe in others' abilities.
3. Pay attention to what employees (or others in your career) are doing and why they are doing those things.
4. Get to know the people you reward so you can personalize your recognition of them.

5. Tell stories that connect people.
6. Celebrate wins with everyone in public ceremonies.
7. Set the example with your behaviors that are based on your own values and goals.

EMPOWERING AND DELEGATING

Empowering and delegating build on the motivational skills just listed. Delegating tasks to others, when done effectively, is a form of empowerment. An important area of psychological work is empowering people who are in disenfranchised or powerless groups. To empower means to help people develop self-confidence, necessary skills, and energy to accomplish something. The real source of empowerment is internal. You cannot really give power to someone; rather, they must accept it for themselves. There is not a limited supply of empowerment since it comes from within.

Delegating basically means assigning work to other people, but it is done with a specific strategy and goal. It becomes an art form when you delegate in a way that empowers people. This does not just mean assigning work to others when you are overloaded. Instead, it is used to create mastery experiences for others.

The first step in delegation is knowing *when* to delegate. Delegation should occur when people have the necessary skills and can learn from the experience, when people are committed to the project, and when there is enough time involved. Delegation works best when it is proactive rather than reactive.

The next step is to decide *to whom* to delegate. You want to consider individuals' talents, interests, expertise, strengths, and competencies when you delegate. When you can have people participate in the delegation process, you usually get higher buy-in. Describe the different tasks that need to be accomplished and ask them which activities they are most interested in and feel they could do best.

It is important that when you delegate, you really delegate. If you have worked in a place where someone micromanaged you, you know how belittling and frustrating this is. You must stay committed to delegating once you have decided to do so. This is part of the empowerment process. When you delegate and then micromanage, you do the opposite of empowering people. Allow people to do their best, make mistakes, and learn how to do even better. Check in regularly to see how things are going and determine whether the individual needs assistance. Even better, have them regularly check in with you as they need to. Offer feedback when difficult things arise, not in a punitive way, but in a manner that improves quality.

CONTINUOUS IMPROVEMENT

Continuous improvement is similar to the idea of total quality management (TQM). This concept refers to ongoing small changes in the direction of improvement. These ideas have been adopted from eastern cultures, such as the Japanese culture. Some people associate this principle with the idea of "zero defects," but it goes a step further. Instead, cultures that are dedicated to continuous improvement efforts are always actively looking for ways to improve. Many business theorists believe that this mind-set of the Japanese is largely responsible for their excellence in many product areas.

The principle of continuous improvement is one that can go a long way in the management of your career. If you accept your career development as static, you will be less innovative and creative. You may begin to feel stagnant or bored. You may never realize your career vision. When, on the other hand, you are constantly reevaluating things, you will feel more in control and satisfied with the progression of your professional life.

We have heard the idea that the important thing is not the destination but the journey. I agree with that sentiment and would add to it: "It's not the destination; it's a journey of continuous improvement." When you look at your livelihood as a process of which you are in charge and which is filled with opportunities every single day to develop a rewarding profession, you will add value for yourself and others on many levels.

This attitude can also take off a lot of pressure and help you to enjoy your career more. When you are micromanaging every aspect of your career, the result is often a sense of frenzy, frustration, stress, and anxiety. Instead, adopt the attitude that each decision is a small change toward your vision and notice the different way that you feel as you think about your career. This is the process of continuous improvement.

360-DEGREE FEEDBACK

The concept of 360-degree feedback has become popular in management consulting over the past decade. This is the idea that the best understanding of your own work performance comes from everyone who interacts with you on a daily basis. Previously, feedback was looked at as a top-down process in which your boss or supervisor evaluated you. With this newer approach, feedback is a continuous circle of information from various sources at every level.

This idea is similar to conducting a thorough mental health assessment. If you were assessing a child for ADHD, you would interview the child herself; interview the parent, parents, or guardian; interview the teachers and school officials; and give the child a battery of attention and continuous performance testing. If you relied solely on one source of information, your results would be less accurate (or even entirely inaccurate) and your recommendations would be less helpful.

In organizations, one critical component of 360-degree feedback is that you evaluate yourself in addition to having others evaluate you. From this information, you can receive self- versus other-perception of performance. This process tends to target job knowledge, performance, skills, and observable behaviors rather than personality style.

The idea of 360-degree feedback can be important in your career progression. You can conduct your own study and rate yourself on several areas and then ask others to rate you, knowing that although the results from others may not be completely accurate, you can still gather some good information. You can use this idea to keep a frame of reference when someone gives you feedback. If a supervisor criticizes you, you can keep in mind that that feedback is one source of information. Approach your career as your own management consultant, trying to gather continuous feedback for yourself to continually improve your career performance.

An extension of this idea is recognizing your ability to learn from everyone around you. One might think that learning is achieved through the process of direct supervision or teaching. This is of course true, but you can also learn from every individual you come into contact with during your career. I learned wonderful interpersonal skills from a receptionist I worked with at a community mental health center. I also learned the importance of keeping your goal in mind through chats with a custodian. I talked with this particular custodian several evenings while he cleaned, and he told me about his goal of saving money to return to visit his native Puerto Rico. With this purpose driving him to do his job well and stay focused, he was able to get to San Juan in a matter of months.

Your clients also tell you a great deal of information about your work performance, either directly or indirectly. You can use all of this information to learn how to improve your skills and create greater value for yourself and for those around you. With this goal, you can try to be around people who have knowledge that can help you learn more, assist you to overcome shortcomings, or inspire you.

Interview with Kathy Miller, MA, LCPC

Kathy Miller is the founding director and president of OASIS: The Center for Mental Health, in Annapolis, Maryland. The company's web site is www.oasismentalhealth.com, and Kathy can be reached at (410) 268-8590.

What have you learned about day-to-day business operations that has helped your business to be successful and profitable?
I surrounded myself with people who know more than I do about business and profit margins. I have personally learned that striving to be the best—and not just the first—is critical to success.

I listen carefully to any person who calls with a complaint. I take concerns to the staff to see if there is anything we can do to fix the problem. Someone from OASIS always calls the person back to explain what we have done to fix the problem—and typically, the call is from me.

I have learned to be more direct and I don't let a problem sit idle. I will try a solution, and if that does not work, I quickly adjust my approach. The resolutions may require that I deal with the head of a large insurance company, or the director of a practice—whatever it takes to ensure that OASIS receives what it needs to deliver service to our clients [and their families].

How do you lead, delegate, or motivate your employees?
I lead by delegating to staff and following up with meetings. I call staff and thank them for their help and recognize them when they go above and beyond. I try to be the one to field concerns or be the one to call back when we have missed the mark and frustrated a referring source or a patient (thank goodness this is not too frequent). I think the staff knows I am plugged in and monitoring what happens at OASIS but I really to try to treat them as professionals and not attempt to micromanage.

(Author's note: Read more about Kathy's company in Chapter 14.)

THE DAY TO DAY BUSINESS OF YOUR CAREER

The "daily grind" can become boring and uninspiring. In this section, we will explore how to create the most enjoyment, productivity, and fulfillment out of your daily work.

FOCUSING ON WHAT'S IMPORTANT

A career in the behavioral health care fields can be difficult because of the challenging and often stressful nature of the work. One of the best ways to deal with this is to make sure that every day consists of activities that are steps toward meeting your objectives and fulfilling your mission.

Many of my professors, supervisors, and friends have commented that I seem to have a strong ability to stay focused and accomplish a great deal. This is true—but I am not special or different from anyone else. I firmly believe that anyone has the potential to excel in whatever areas interest them when they clearly develop their vision *and* make sure that they are working to achieve that vision every single day. It is not enough just to know what you want. You must follow through. You must implement. And you must do it day after day after day.

This does not mean that you need to run yourself ragged trying to accomplish all of your objectives every day—quite the opposite, really. It means that you need to be strategic each day, recognizing how your actions fit within the larger picture of your career. It may be very tactical to take time off from working or to build into your schedule some relaxing activities to help you to stay focused and motivated.

Spend a few weeks explicitly reviewing how your daily activities are in line with your career values and vision. At the end of the day, ask yourself, "What did I do today that will help me achieve my career mission?" Write these activities down so you can see what you are doing and accomplishing. It is not enough to respond by saying, "I studied today because I'm trying to finish my degree," or "I saw six clients because that is what the agency requires." These types of thoughts put something else in control of your career, either your school or your agency. We want you to be the COO and be in control each day.

One way to implement your goals every day is by following up your answers to the question "What did I do?" with the question, "Why?" If you are not able to answer this question, or if you say, "Because otherwise I will fail out of school" or "Otherwise I will lose my job," then you have a little more work to do. These types of responses describe avoidance behaviors, moving away from something. Try to reframe them as moving toward something—toward your goal. You will start to see more clearly how you can make choices consistent with your vision and values.

Then "I saw six clients because that is what the agency requires" becomes "I saw six clients today—three of them were for relationship issues, since I want to develop a specialty in relationships and start creating a private practice." Doesn't that sound a lot more motivating and energizing? Turning your attention toward where you are heading and why can both help you to get there and improve your job satisfaction along the way.

Your responses do not need to be only in line with your career vision, but can also be very effective if they are in line with your life vision. You may say, "I saw six clients today, which is enabling me to work at this agency in my ideal city where I am close to all of my family."

LIVING A BALANCED LIFE

Mental health care is a field with a high degree of burnout. I believe one of the main causes of this burnout is incongruence between our goals and our current behaviors and responsibilities. We can tolerate a great deal more stress and frustration when we know exactly *why* we are in the position that we are in. There is no perfect job—every job will have its share of frustrations. Making your goals SMART (specific, measurable, action-oriented, realistic, and timed) can help to increase motivation and prevent burnout. Even when a work situation is difficult, if you can clearly see how it benefits your long-term vision, and you can make your goals SMART, you will know your time frame and stay motivated.

Beating burnout in mental health can also be done by diversifying your work. Diversification keeps things interesting and furthers a sense of self-efficacy, the feeling that you have control over your career. Despite the relatively low wages in many positions, the difficulties practicing within managed care, the flooded market in many parts of the country, and other external factors, you learn that you can take control and maintain a leadership position in your own career.

Another important strategy in your day-to-day career operations is one that we in the mental health field know about very well: self-care. We often ask our clients how they are eating, exercising, sleeping, engaging in enjoyable activities, spending time with significant people, and finding areas to fulfill themselves. Of course, knowing something is different from doing it. It's amazing what having a life outside of the office can do for your abilities in the office and your happiness everywhere. We can feel much more genuine in saying these things when we do them ourselves. When I began to do a lot of writing (i.e., sitting) last year, I noticed that my exercise dropped way off. I was talking with a client about the importance of regular exercise and I suddenly felt I was not being authentic because I was not exercising and practicing what I was preaching. I used this realization to prompt me to begin exercising three days per week, and I have noticed significant benefits.

These concepts of stress management and work-life balance are things that you surely already know, but it is a good idea to review them and take inventory of how well you are putting them into practice. If you are in graduate school or recently out of school, do not neglect the importance of planning your career operations. This is the time when you are laying the groundwork for the way you will manage your career. It is much more difficult to break unhealthy habits than to not create them in the first place.

Regardless of where you are in your career, consider:

- How many hours you want to be working versus how many hours you are working.
- Whether you are involved in meaningful recreational activities (exercise, creative outlets, socializing, etc.).
- How you decide when it is time to start or stop working on a new project.
- What your eating and sleeping habits are like.
- How your physical health is and what you could do to improve it.
- Your efficiency and ability to filter out distractions when you are working.
- How the important people in your life feel about your work behaviors.
- How well you are meeting some of your most important life goals.

Use of Technology

If you are able to become the chief information officer (CIO) in your career, you can greatly improve your operations and effectiveness. But if you are like me, you may be thinking, "I am hardly someone who could be a CIO—technology is not my thing!" Remember that we are talking about CIO in *your* career, not the CIO of a huge technology company. To be an effective CIO, you may need to develop some basic computer and Internet proficiencies. Learning programs like Microsoft Excel and Publisher, for example, can be a great asset.

Use of Technology in a Mental Health Career

One way to improve the operations of your career is through the most effective use of information technology. Since the Internet is one of the most important applications of technology today, ask yourself whether your use of the Internet is as efficient and effective as possible. For example, if you are sharing Internet access with other computers in your household or office, or if you can function better when you are mobile (in your home or office) with your laptop, strongly consider using a wireless wide area network (WAN) in combination with a wireless router.

E-mail management is another crucial aspect of most professional careers. You can not only waste time by poor e-mail management, but you can miss opportunities, communicate the wrong message, or offend people. With e-mail communication, if you do not already have a filing system in place, start one. I recommend that my business clients keep no more than 20 messages in their inbox, that they file messages into appropriate folders once they have been acted on, and that they clean out their inbox at least once per week. These things may sound trivial, but the level of organization and corresponding increase in operational efficiency can be significant.

We all know how difficult it is to communicate our messages over e-mail and how easily statements can be misinterpreted. Keep this in mind as you create your messages, and decide whether something is important enough that it requires a telephone call to avoid any potential misinterpretation. Also, keep in mind the needs of the person whom you are e-mailing. If you are sending a message to a someone who has very limited time, keep your e-mail communication brief and to the point as you would any other communication.

With the latest privacy acts, e-mail correspondence with material of a sensitive nature or with clinical or private health information is not recommended. Lawyers that I interviewed for this book consistently stated that significant caution should be used when e-mailing any clinical material, because this behavior may open up risk and can threaten the confidentiality of your clients. In sum, e-mail is risky in terms of piling up and overloading your daily processes, sending the wrong message, or violating security and privacy. Use e-mail carefully and judiciously in your professional career.

Improve your Technology Skills

As a CIO, you will also learn when you need to outsource technological services and hire someone. Since I am not a techie (although I often wish

118

I were, and I have learned more than I ever thought I would know by running a company), I have relied on many consultants to help me. For instance, I hired Web designers to create my web sites, and I have a list of technology consultants that I regularly call on and to whom I refer my small business marketing clients.

Many therapists are like me and are not experts in technology. This is not our area of core competency, and we know only what we need to get by. I have found that this can become a problem, depending on your career goals. When I began my MBA program, I realized that I was not nearly as literate with Microsoft's PowerPoint as the business cohorts who were on my teams. Rather than embarrass myself and waste time, I decided to spend $25 and have someone catch me up to speed in an hour. I just put an approved sign up on campus and got several responses. The $25 turned out to be a good investment and saved me a lot of time and energy down the line.

If you can see how technology can assist you in your career and you are somewhat technically challenged like me, I recommend that you take action. Hire an undergraduate student at $12/hour to teach you some important programs or applications. Educate yourself by reading books and articles on topics most relevant for you. Spend some time on IT-related web sites and doing research on the Internet. If you are still a student or work in a university, take advantage of the computer services departments: Go to the free workshops and seminars and ask the specialists questions. Take this on as your own continuing education project.

Interview with Helen R. Friedman, PhD

Helen Friedman is a clinical psychologist in full-time private practice in St. Louis, Missouri. She can be reached at (314) 781-4500 or by e-mail at hfriedman5@earthlink.net.

You have been successful in private practice for some time now, despite the difficulties in the marketplace (managed care, etc.). What are some of the factors that you think are related to your success?
First and foremost is providing top-notch professional services. I am broadly and extensively trained, with 10 years of additional postdoctoral training (four and a half years in gestalt training and supervision, followed by five and a half years of supervision in marriage and family

systems at the Menninger Clinic). I regularly attend scientific conferences to stay abreast of cutting-edge information. I have worked hard to develop an excellent reputation as a therapist.

Second, I have been very lucky. I have followed what is in front of my nose, which has led me to a number of niches—areas that I happened upon before they became more widely covered by other professionals. I have presented original ideas on these topics at national and international conferences and then have given these talks locally, allowing both professionals and consumers to know of my work and expertise. I am a good speaker and speak from the heart. I am also active in professional organizations in my specialty areas. All of these activities have resulted in referrals both locally and nationally.

A third factor related to a successful practice is my steadfast belief that there will always be people willing to pay for quality services. I have never joined managed care panels and I refuse to accept their low fees. I have been strictly fee-for-service, with no sliding scale. Most of my clients do have insurance coverage, on an out-of-network basis.

What are some of the strategies you have adopted in the day-to-day management and operations of your career that have helped you to become successful?

Some very simple day-to-day strategies promote success. One is the prompt and personal return of telephone calls. Potential clients are often given the names of several therapists, and they may call and leave messages with several. If another professional calls them back first, the client may be lost. I do most of my administrative work from home before and after seeing clients in my office. A pager service alerts me to incoming calls to my office voice mail, so that I can quickly respond. I record my office voice mail greeting myself. Some clients have said that they chose me because they found my voice soothing and friendly.

During the first phone conversation with new clients, I take the initiative in telling them about my practice: hours, location, fee, and payment policy. This lifts the burden of asking off of them. Subscribing to the Holiday Inn slogan that "the best surprise is no surprise," I inform them that they are to pay at the time of the session, that there is a 24-hour cancellation policy, where to park, and so on. At the first session, I give them a handout that repeats in writing the pay-as-you-go and 24-hour cancellation policies, as well as provides information about confidentiality, and so forth. I have always done this. Having it in writing prevents potential misunderstandings.

I get clients in quickly and never have a waiting list. This sometimes means coming to the office an hour earlier or staying an hour later. Clients are continually entering and leaving therapy, so that overall, there is always room to accommodate a new client. I am also quick to help colleagues and the media whenever I can, or to make referrals to someone else who can. I accept requests to speak (though not as often as when I first started my practice), to do media interviews, and to offer consultation (for a fee or as a quick favor over the phone). People appreciate kindness and it is usually returned.

How do you use technology or other means of organizing and planning in your practice?

I use my computer word processor to devise forms for my practice. This allows me to easily update and modify them. For example, the newest addition to my "Client Information" form is a line for the client's cell phone number. Having this information is a time-saver.

My primary means of organizing and planning is via a professional appointment book. I also write my to-do list and reminders in pencil on the appropriate day and erase items as they are completed or forwarded to a future time. I record personal activities in red, professional activities in green, and media interviews in blue ink. This calendar provides a snapshot of my life, helping me to assess whether I am overscheduled or underscheduled, to see patterns in my practice (e.g., changes in number of clients per week), and so on, so that I can make any needed adjustments.

(Author's note: This is a great process, and the same organizational process can be done on a computer or a pocket PC. You can also synchronize various schedules this way without rewriting.)

How are you a manager of your own career?

I prefer a hands-on approach to managing my practice. I do my own books each day and have an accountant who does my taxes after I give him the numbers to enter into his tax software. I rent office space. The building management company provides cleaning and maintenance, allowing me to concentrate on the practice itself. I personally provide all of the psychological services. I refer outside of the practice for issues outside of my areas of expertise. I manage my career by knowing myself and my interests, so that I can focus on what is important to me and what I do well.

Do you have any learning experiences in the management of your career or mistakes made along the way that you can share?

Yes, I do. Years ago, having an answering service was the local professional standard. I used such a service, but over time I realized that the operators were too quick to label a message an emergency, simply because the caller was tearful. Then they would call my home at all hours of the night. I decided to switch to voice mail.

I have learned that when I put myself out, I always get something back. It may not be what I was expecting, but it is always something of value. For example, early in my career, I gave a talk on stress management to employees of the telephone company. The following week, when I obtained a new business number, I was informed that I had missed the deadline for inclusion in the next edition of the *Yellow Pages* by one day—no exceptions. I called the contact person for my talk and asked for her help. She made some calls and got my listing in. I was hoping for new clients from the talk; what I received instead was unforeseen but priceless.

What career management and operations advice do you have for therapists who may want to grow a practice while working in another setting?

For therapists in other settings who wish to develop a private practice, I advise using another therapist's office on an as-needed or other low-fee basis. Many established private practitioners are happy to defray their own costs this way. (I currently have four renters who use the furnished rental office in my suite.) Then, with the security of the other position for your bread-and-butter income, you can slowly build your practice, with little overhead.

In terms of day-to-day operations, I recommend a streamlined approach, keeping things simple and cost-effective. My annual expenses total about 10 percent of my gross. My clients pay at the time of the session. I provide statements, which *they* submit to their insurance, and then they are reimbursed directly. This eliminates time spent following up with tardy insurance payments or otherwise chasing money, as well as the need for a billing service. I have practically a 100 percent collection rate.

Is it important to keep the daily operations in line with a career vision?

I learned this lesson in high school during a driver's education class. Behind the wheel of a car for the first time, I asked the instructor how to stay in the center of the lane. He replied that if you look at a spot 50 yards ahead in the center of the lane, it will keep you on track. Similarly, knowing your goals and intentions (looking ahead) informs day-to-day choices, what you do *now*.

For example, one of my goals was to be a media psychologist. When television stations would call on short notice seeking an expert for a late-breaking news feature, I always said yes, even though this was disruptive. It meant pulling files on the topic at hand in the 15 minutes between clients, preparing sound bites, and sometimes rushing home to change clothes. After each segment aired, I was always glad I did it. Not only did these television appearances help to fulfill my goal of being a media psychologist, they also increased my visibility, enhanced my reputation, occasionally resulted in a new client, and earned me the esteem of my colleagues as a spokesperson for psychology—all worthy goals.

One caveat: Having a career vision, goal, or plan is helpful to a point, but if you adhere too rigidly to a preconceived notion of your career, you may miss opportunities. Follow your nose and see what is in front of you. Incorporate new experiences and ideas into your career vision. This may take you into niches and venues you never imagined! It did for me.

RESOURCES

BOOKS

Buckingham, M. C. (2001). *Now, discover your strengths*. New York: Free Press.

Feldman, D. C. (2002). *Work careers: A developmental perspective*. San Francisco: Pfeiffer.

Forsyth, P (2002). *Career management*. New York: Capstone.

Kouzes, J. M. & Posner, B. Z (2003). *Encouraging the heart: a leader's guide to rewarding and recognizing others*. San Francisco: Jossey Bass.

Manz, C., & Neck, C. (2003). *Mastering self leadership* (3rd ed.). Indianapolis, IN: Prentice Hall.

Whetten, D. A., & Cameron, K. S. (1998). *Developing management skills* (4th ed). Reading, MA: Addison-Wesley.

WEB SITES

Listing of psychology jobs:

www.psyccareers.com

Resource with links to psychology guides and jobs:

www.psychology.org/links/Career

APA listing of psychology careers:

www.apa.org/students/brochure/

Jobs for people with psychology training at all levels (bachelor's, master's, doctorate):

www.psych-central.com/careers.htm

Company that specializes in 360-degree feedback and describes it very well:

www.360-degreefeedback.com

TERMINOLOGY

benefiting the boss   The process of influencing upwards by showing your supervisor the potential unexpected benefits of your idea.

brainstorming   Creatively coming up with ideas or solving problems in a group or on an individual basis without censoring oneself or rejecting ideas.

COO (chief operating officer)   A corporate officer who manages the day-to-day activities of the organization. A COO is involved in the strategic business plan of a company as part of the executive team.

CIO (chief information officer)   The executive responsible for the overall technological direction and functioning in an organization. Like the COO, the CIO is involved in the strategic business plan of a company as part of the executive team.

continuous improvement   Small steps or incremental changes, implemented over time, toward making something more excellent.

corporate president   Can be the same as the CEO or a separate position. When separate, the president is usually entrusted with the direction and administration of its policies while the CEO is more involved with setting the vision.

empowerment   Helping others to feel confident in completing a task or accomplishing an objective.

innovativeness   Encouraging the development of creativity and ingenuity within a work team.

IT (information technology)   Refers to the use of technology to transmit information within or between businesses.

process management   Assessing, analyzing, and improving the activities performed by the work team.

self-managing work team   A team that maintains all levels of functioning; the highest level of work teams.

total quality management (TQM)   A system that searches for ways to improve the quality of work and reduce defects or imperfections.

win-win strategy   A solution that is mutually beneficially for all parties in a situation.

360-degree feedback   The process of collecting survey data from multiple sources to show employees how they view themselves and how others view their work performance and behavior.

CHAPTER 7

Creating Deliverables

If the only tool you have is a hammer, you treat everything as a nail.
Abraham Maslow

The entrepreneur is a visualizer and an actualizer. . . . He can visualize something, and when he visualizes it he sees exactly how to make it happen.
Robert L. Schwartz

YOUR BUSINESS PLAN AS A LAUNCHING PAD

You now have all the primary components of a business plan and probably have some ideas about how you can use these principles to develop your career. You have a vision and a mission for the direction of your career. You have a good deal of knowledge about marketing and how you can use it to move ahead. You understand the components of a financial plan and have at least started to think about how to incorporate some of those ideas. And you have a management and operations plan in place. Now we need to help you use these tools to diversify your services so you are not "treating everything as a nail," as Maslow put it.

This chapter incorporates all of these ideas and will help you to create some tangible products to add value to your career. One of the most important aspects of your business plan is to have a sense for new markets and opportunities. You can use your knowledge of business planning to launch into new areas without necessarily changing your career path.

The idea of this chapter is to help you develop, market, and sell deliverables while staying in your current clinical, teaching, research, or other position. Another great way to diversify your career is via paid speaking engagements (for an electronic book on this topic, visit www.TheSuccessful Therapist.com). Beginning in the next chapter, we will examine some other career options if you want to branch out into new areas or further diversify your career.

As a mental health professional, your services can be limited by the amount of hours you are able to work each week. If you primarily see clients, either in an agency or privately, you can only see a given number of clients per week. That number is determined by how many hours you want to work or are required to work, how many clients need and know about your services, your current priorities, and your professional limitations. The latter category includes your personal limitations (for instance, many therapists feel they cannot do their best work when they see more than 20 clients per week), the types of clients with whom you work, and other obligations such as trainings, meetings, and so on.

Creating deliverables can help you to broaden the type of work that you do. A deliverable is something that is to be delivered to another, typically for a fee. This is a common term used in business and typically refers to some form of product that one creates and gives to another. The deliverable may be part of a job, such as delivering a report or analysis. The deliverable may also be something for sale that a business owner sells to a customer. In this chapter, we will use the latter definition and think about different products that you can create and sell to customers or clients.

There are two basic ways of delivering something: active and passive. An active strategy for creating and providing a deliverable involves going out and doing something on a regular basis. For example, speaking engagements, workshops, seminars, therapy, and coaching sessions are active deliverables. Your reimbursement is based on the services you provide. Passive deliverables include products that can sell themselves, often while you are busy doing an active deliverable. Passive deliverables and products capitalize on limited time and resources. Once you create a book, for example, you will receive royalties while you are going about your daily business. If you see five therapy clients one day and earn $350, and you also sell 25 e-books (electronic books) that day at $15 each, you will double your income without adding extra time.

Some common products that can readily be adopted by mental health professionals include e-books, assessments, books, videos, CDs, articles and brochures, and audiobooks. We will discuss service-oriented deliverables in later chapters. For now, let's start conceptualizing how you can create products based on your experience and expertise.

PASSIVE INCOME AND EFFECTIVE MARKETING

Passive deliverables are wonderful because once you have put the work into creating and developing them (which can be a lot of fun), you are able to stay focused on your other endeavors while bringing in a passive revenue stream. These products can also be helpful in marketing your services. For example, you may purchase my electronic book on becoming a media psychologist. After reading the book and becoming inspired, you may decide you want further coaching on this topic and contact my company.

Using deliverables as a form of passive marketing serves many purposes:

- It generates passive income streams.
- It builds credibility and expert status.
- It provides a preview of your work so your ideal clients (the ones you can best help and the ones you most want to work with) become interested in you.
- It increases visibility of your service offerings.
- It benefits those who may not be able to afford your other services.

Using products is great marketing because you are providing something valuable to prospects, which makes them curious about whether you have other products or services that could benefit them. In order for this to work, your products need to be of high quality, closely follow ethical guidelines (what you create and sell must, for example, be within your areas of expertise and bounds of competence), and offer something of value. We have all had occasions of experiencing something of value and then going back for more. Whether it is tasting a delicious chocolate and then buying all of your holiday candy from that chocolate maker, or finding the perfect pair of jeans and returning to that store or designer for years whenever you need new jeans, the idea is the same.

WHAT CAN I OFFER?

You may now be thinking that this all sounds great, but wonder what you could create and sell. The best products are the ones that capitalize on your own core competencies. As we discussed in Chapter 3, figuring out your internal strengths and weaknesses (by conducting a SWOT analysis on yourself and your career) is crucial in positioning your career to make you most successful and satisfied. In determining what products you want to create and offer, it is critical to begin with your vision and mission statement and then use your core competencies to create something that you not only want to make but are wonderfully qualified to make.

In deciding what to offer, ask yourself three fundamental questions:

1. What am I uniquely qualified to offer?
2. What are prospective customers or clients interested in buying?
3. Who exactly would buy the product and how much would they be willing to spend?

Complete the Product Offering Worksheet to help guide you in deciding what products to focus on.

Product Offering Worksheet

My core competencies from the SWOT include: _____

_____

_____

My top three unique areas of expertise include: _____

_____

_____

_____

Rank your skills below in order of greatest to least skills:

Skill or Characteristic	Rank
1. Great at creative or fiction writing.	_____
2. Abilities in factual or nonfiction writing.	_____

3. Strong voice quality or soothing or relaxing voice. _____

4. Professional visual presentation/appearance. _____

5. Comfortable with being interviewed on audiotape or videotape. _____

6. Greatly enjoy writing and can write quickly and in a focused manner. _____ _____

7. Enjoy public speaking. _____

8. Clear verbal communication. _____

9. Have many ideas for writing electronic or print books. _____

10. Strong connections with writers to collaborate with. _____

11. Photogenic or camera-friendly. _____

12. Area of expertise that would lend itself to a book. _____

13. Would enjoy leading an exercise (such as a relaxation strategy) on tape. _____

14. Area of expertise that would lend itself to an audio program. _____

15. Area of expertise that would lend itself to a short book or brochure. _____

16. Area of expertise that would lend itself to workbook. _____

17. Area of expertise that would lend itself to an instructional or training video. _____

What content area do you think customers or clients are looking to purchase and how do you know this? Do some preliminary market research to best answer this question, such as interviews, surveys, or questionnaires. Here is a list to get you started, but add specific content area to it based on your unique qualifications and experiences.

❑ Relaxation. Specifically: _____

❑ Stress management. Specifically: _____

❑ Anxiety reduction. Specifically: _____

❑ Relationship improvement. Specifically: _____

❑ Communication skills. Specifically: _____

❑ Dealing with depression. Specifically: _____

❑ Adjustment. Specifically: _____

❑ Parenting training. Specifically: _____

❑ Healthy eating. Specifically: _____

❑ Body image. Specifically: _____

❑ Attention problems. Specifically: _____

❑ Helping a relative with a serious mental illness. Specifically: _____

❑ Assertiveness. Specifically: _____

❑ Learning and memory. Specifically: _____

❑ Training or education in your specific area of expertise for other professionals. Specifically: _____

❑ Other specific content area: _____

What similar products on the market would compete with yours, and how is yours different?

1. Competing product: _____

_____

   How your proposed product is different: _____

   _____

   _____

2. Competing product: _____

_____

   How your proposed product is different: _____

   _____

   _____

3. Competing product: _____

_____

How your proposed product is different: _____

_____   _____

_____

How much would members of your target market be willing to pay? Again, conduct research to answer this question. For example, look into what similar products are selling for (not just what people are charging, but what they are selling for), or survey your prospects and ask them what they think the specific product would be worth.

_____

USING THE PRODUCT OFFERING WORKSHEET

Once you have completed this worksheet, you can use it to figure out what the best *first* product is for you to work on. From the skills ranking, you will begin to clearly see which of your skills are the strongest. Analyze your top 10 ranked items first. Notice whether speaking or writing comes up the most often and the highest. For speaking, do you prefer to be shown on video or heard on audio? For an audio product, do you want to be speaking directly to the listener or be interviewed by someone else? For a writing piece, are you interested in creative versus nonfiction writing? Does your personality and style lend itself better to short versus long pieces?

If you are working on creating your first product, focus on one of the specific products described in the following sections. You want to use your existing skills and strengths for your first product so that it is the easiest to develop and so you can learn from that process to create additional products in the future. Typically, buyers of products such as the ones described here are interested in very detailed and explicit information that they can implement right away.

CREATING VIDEO PRODUCTS

If you feel comfortable being on tape and having potential clients, referral partners, colleagues, or trainees watch you on video, this can be a fantas-

133

tic option for you and a relatively easy way to create a product. One of the best aspects of creating a video is that there is a great deal of flexibility in terms of time commitment, quality, and expense. Depending on how you create it, a video product can be relatively quick and inexpensive or highly time consuming and expensive.

There are many forms of technology available today that can provide high-quality videos (DVDs, VHS videotapes, digital videos, etc.). Digital video is considered by many to be more versatile because you can copy it onto many formats. For the sake of simplicity, I will refer to all of these as "videos," and you can research which technological applications best serve the needs of the product you wish to create. You can sell hard copies of your video or post it on your web site with a paid link.

A VIDEO OF YOUR SPEAKING ENGAGEMENT

If you are very interested in speaking, one fantastic way to create a video product is to record your speaking engagements. This strategy works best for speaking engagements that are trainings or workshops and that deliver a great deal of practical information. It does not work as well for lectures that are theoretical in nature or presentations of research data. You certainly can record those lectures and offer them as a free product or introduction to your work, but they do not work as well for products for sale. If you are going to sell a video from one of your speaking engagements, you should first consult with an attorney and ask all the audience members who may appear in your video to sign a consent form that explicitly describes the purpose and use of the video.

To create a video of one of your speaking engagements, you have three options: create your own video with a high-quality camcorder or digital recorder; hire a freelance videographer to record your talk; hire a professional videography company to record your talk.

The first of these, creating your own video, is obviously the least expensive. If you are creating a product to sell, you want to be sure that it is of highest quality, so practice using the equipment prior to your talk to insure that the quality is excellent. Recording the speaking engagement works best if you will be relatively static or stable during the talk. You do not want to have someone (an amateur) holding the recorder and trying to follow you around with it. You would get the "Uncle Rick's wedding video" effect, which is unsteady and at times nauseating to watch. It isn't just because Uncle Rick had too many glasses of champagne—it is very difficult to hold a nonprofessional-grade camera steady. Set up a tripod from which to record your talk.

A freelance videographer has professional equipment but is less expensive than working with a larger company. You can search on the Internet on web sites (such as www.elanceonline.com) where people bid on freelance work, to find professional freelancers who have the capabilities of videoing and/or editing your tapes. To use these sites, enter a search term such as "videography" and then bid on the services listed. I have used these services to find graphic designers for marketing materials and had very good experiences. A freelancer may not have access to equipment for reproducing the tapes at a very high quality, but you can outsource that as well.

The most expensive option is to hire a professional firm in your area that creates videos, DVDs, or CDs with your visual imagery. These are professional companies that create commercials and other business products. Typically the cost for a service such as this is around $2,000 for a half-day filming, but the fees range widely depending on your geographical location, the size of the firm, the specific services you want, and so on.

A TRAINING VIDEO

There are two types of training videos. The first is to train other professionals, and the second is to train individuals in need of services. Let's discuss the training videos for other professionals first. Many of us watched training videos as we were learning how to do therapy. There are series of interviews and training tapes from master therapists and researchers who developed some of the theory and interventions that many of us know and use. You do not have to be one of the world's most renowned master therapists to create one of these tapes, but you do have to have something valuable to offer that has been established through empirical research or other ethically stringent practices. When you are utilizing someone else's theory or application, cite them on the video so it is clear you are not implying that you are the originator of those ideas.

Think of something about which you know a lot and about which you have received positive feedback from other clinicians or therapists. For instance, if you presented a topic at the American Psychological Association's national conference and had great attendance, wonderful response, and follow-up inquiries, that may be a good topic for a training program.

If you heard about a project that another mental health professional created and you think it could lend itself well to a video training program, ask them if they would like to collaborate on the project. Before you begin creating a training video, I recommend that you do some marketing research on the videos currently available. A good resource for purchasing videos is www.psychotherapy.net.

Interview with Victor Yalom, PhD

Victor Yalom is the president of Psychotherapy.net, an excellent resource for therapists which sells videotapes of the masters including Irvin Yalom, MD; James Bugental, PhD; Donald Meichenbaum, PhD; Insoo Kim Berg; and Steve DeShazer. Find out more at www.psychotherapy.net.

Can you tell us a little about your company, Psychotherapy.net? What is the aim or vision?

The genesis of the company was when I produced a videotape with James Bugental in 1995 after studying with him for about five years. He's an amazing therapist and we wanted to capture his work on video, so we had the tape produced. He was speaking at the Evolution of Psychotherapy conference in 1995, so I ended up selling tapes there. I thought, "This can make an interesting business." My passion is creating and selling videotapes that show therapists doing their work. There is no substitute for actually seeing therapists do their work.

What differentiates our site is that we try to focus on what makes people passionate about psychotherapy—not dry, academic articles, but what is it that therapists do that excites them? What are the qualities of a master therapist? How can those who are feeling disillusioned or stuck think creatively about using their skills in ways other than the traditional therapy session? Our site is creative and playful to capture that excitement. Our strongest content is our interviews with the leading therapists of their time. For articles on our site, we try to find articles or work with writers who discuss their personal experiences of being a therapist. Articles with the therapists' subjective experiences of their work are what we include.

How do you go about creating and selling videos?

We produce tapes and distribute them. We produced a tape on couples therapy which is both a training tape for therapists and also a tape that therapists can lend out to couples to provide psychoeducation. Selling videotapes is a tough business because, unlike with textbooks, we primarily sell to universities and training centers, and typically they only purchase one tape. So it is important to expand your products. We'll be selectively expanding our product offerings, perhaps including a Health Insurance Portability and Accountability (HIPAA) compliance kit, and increasing our video inventory.

You have other things on your site, like your hilarious cartoons.
The development of those cartoons has been a continuous creative process. I found the first cartoon on the Internet, and then I started coming up with ideas on my own. I have been drawing them myself, and every now and then I'll be in a session with my patients and it will inspire a cartoon. A client who was a black-and-white thinker inspired the idea of the cartoon with the penguins.

I think your site is a great resource. How can therapists get involved?
Advertising is one way. We get entries in our guest book and video orders from all over the world. People can get good exposure. And we have a links section for people to get their work out there and increase the traffic to their individual sites.

We also take articles from anyone who wants to submit them. We will consider articles from all of our readers. Our web site creates a sense of community and the ability to network with each other. We have an open submission policy and if it is appropriate, we will work with the author to craft an article that tells a story.

The other type of training video is one that other therapists can use with clients. These are typically psychoeducational products. For instance, when I worked in a state hospital, we used assertiveness videos or relaxation videos with the patients. The patients loved learning from this medium, and the videos demonstrated and modeled for the patients how to use the skills they needed to develop. You can get started by using your own nonprofessionally created video with your own patients to see how it is useful and how you can improve it before moving on to a more costly production.

You may want to secure funding from your department or agency to create the video. You can structure the ownership agreement such that you share royalties, or sell it to them for their continued use. Typically, whoever is funding the project will expect a return on their investment, which may mean that you cannot sell it yourself. If this is the case, you will not be earning significant income from the product. This is fine if your goals are to get a quality product out there, use it to market your services, and gain some experience with the video medium.

CREATING AUDIO PRODUCTS

Creating an audio product can be even easier than creating a video product, and it can also be more comfortable for the majority of people who are camera-shy. Of course, you have to be comfortable with your voice, and you may want to consider hiring a voice coach to improve your speaking abilities.

Similar to creating a video product, you have many options for how you create the audio. You can do it yourself by purchasing a digital recorder, hooking it up to your computer, and recording. The sound quality can be quite good without professional recording and editing. An excellent do-it-yourself resource is http://audacity.sourceforge.net /windows.php. It has a free program that you can download in about two minutes, plug your microphone into your computer, hit the record button, and record away. You can save the recording as a .wav file or another type of file. Then you can either post it on your web site for download or burn it onto a CD; then dub the CDs and/or use the CD to record onto a cassette tape.

The other option for cheap recording is simply to buy a cassette recorder with a microphone (probably less than $50 these days, depending on quality). This will work for something like an e-book on tape or a relaxation exercise, but the quality is not typically as high as with digital recording. If you use this option, you will want to price the product low or offer it as a free introduction to your services.

It is important to minimize all the extraneous noises around you to improve sound quality. It is also important to practice before you create your recording. Just record a short clip, play it back to see how you sound, and then redo it as many times as necessary. You may want to ask colleagues for feedback on your clip or consult with a voice coach.

You can also outsource the production and hire someone who has the necessary equipment to create the audio for you. For the most professional and costly option, you can make a recording in a professional sound studio. To make copies of your audio, you can do it yourself or hire a company that reproduces CDs or other audio products.

AN EXPERT INTERVIEW

An excellent and easy-to-create audio product is an expert interview. It can be done in four simple steps:

1. Select a specific topic in your area of expertise. This should reflect your unique selling proposition. I recommend conducting a SWOT analysis on your idea to determine whether there is a good market for that product and what your competitive advantage would be.
2. Determine your target market and list of prospective buyers.
3. Ask a colleague or business partner if they would be willing to interview you on tape. Offer them a flat rate or a partnership in the royalties for their time and help.
4. Create a list of questions for the interviewer to ask you that would allow you to provide all of the information you want to provide. Be sure that the information you are giving is action-oriented, unambiguous, and detailed so your users can really benefit from it.

A GUIDED EXPERIENCE

Another type of audio product is one in which you speak directly to the listener. There are many ways to do this. It's best not to record a lecture, because people find those difficult to attend to and not engaging enough to be maximally effective. Also avoid doing something that sounds at all like a sales pitch. People become annoyed by sales-y audios even when they are given away for free, so you definitely do not want to do this if you are trying to sell your product.

A great way to avoid these pitfalls is by doing an experiential audio. This means that you are guiding your listeners through the process on the tape. Some examples of this guided experiential process include:

- A guided imagery for relaxation or a muscle relaxation exercise.
- What to do when your child is throwing a temper tantrum.
- How to deal with being caught in the middle of an argument.
- Picturing the future that you really want.

CREATING WRITTEN PRODUCTS

Many therapists are wonderfully effective one-on-one with their clients but do not feel comfortable with or have no interest in being in the public eye. If this describes you, and if you are a strong writer, then written products may be the best option. If you are interested in developing your media personality for audio or video products but do not yet feel strong in these areas, you can certainly work with a professional coach to gain increased skills and comfort, and focus on written products in the meantime.

Many therapists are very comfortable with writing. If you think of all the essays, term papers, case studies, clinical reports, assessments, progress notes, theses, or dissertations that we have written in the process of becoming therapists, one thing is clear: We are highly experienced writers—arguably some of the most experienced of many professionals out there, since so much of our training and practical experiences are based around writing. If you are ready to take your writing to the next level and work to earn a profit rather than earn an A, then creating written products can be perfect for you.

One of the keys to effective written products is to create something novel and focused. Another important key is to know your target market well. Keep these keys in mind as you start to consider what you might write about, because you want to write something that not only is excellent but that sells. If it is excellent and does not sell, people will not learn how helpful it could be for them.

BOOKS

Writing a book is one of the best methods for quickly establishing credibility and gaining widespread exposure. Writing a book is also a big undertaking. Here are some points to consider if you are thinking about writing a book:

Pros

- Quickly achieve expert status.
- Increase your market of prospects or potential clients, collaborators, and contacts.
- Generate income through your advance and royalties.
- Gain a sense of professional fulfillment by being an author.
- Use writing as a creative and enjoyable outlet.
- Reach a broader audience of people who can benefit from your ideas but do not have access to them or cannot afford your services.
- Collaborate with a co-author or co-authors, which can be intellectually stimulating and enjoyable.

Cons

- Writing a book requires a *lot* of time and the associated sacrifice and can be mentally and physically exhausting.
- Many books are not cost effective in terms of time versus monetary payoff.
- To write well, many people need blocks of time set aside, which may not be feasible given family or work schedules.
- Getting a reputable publisher to publish your book can be difficult.
- Self-publishing can be expensive and you may be stuck with a large inventory of books if you do not sell enough.
- If you work with co-authors, there may be challenges such as structuring an agreement, dividing the work appropriately, different writing styles, and so on.
- Many writers never see royalties because the book does not sell past its advance.

PROFESSIONALLY PUBLISHED BOOKS

As mentioned in the pros and cons just listed, it can be difficult to find a top-caliber publisher for your book. If you choose to go this route, and you do find an excellent publisher, there are many potential advantages. From the perspective of credibility, the publisher is extremely important. When I first told people I was writing this book, one of the first questions I was routinely asked was, "Who's your publisher?" When I responded by saying "Wiley," people smiled or nodded and said, "Wow" or "That's fabulous." The publisher's name recognition will also help you to sell books, and your book can be listed on their web site and in their catalogs.

A misconception is that publishers will invest a lot of money in promoting and advertising your book. Another reason (if I have not yet sold the idea enough) for improving your marketing skills is that you will most likely need to show a publisher that you will be able to market and promote your book. Most of the top publishers use the author's "platform," or ability to promote the book, as a differentiating factor to help them decide which authors to sign. Your book proposal will need to include a marketing plan that describes how you will let people know about your book via advertising, speaking engagements, articles, conferences, promotions, partnerships, web sites, and other marketing venues.

Many major publishers require that you submit your proposal through an agent. A literary agent has expertise and experience in assisting in the development and submission of winning proposals. It is a good idea to get a referral for a literary agent through colleagues and other contacts. You can also search online or through books such as the 2005 *Writer's Market* (Brogan, editor, 2005). Be sure to look for an agent who specializes in the category or genre in which you will be writing.

When approaching an agent, write a query letter describing your project and selling the agent on why they would want to work with you. Most agents expect query letters through the mail, along with a self-addressed, stamped envelope so they can respond to you. The agent may request a proposal along with your query letter or may ask for a proposal later if they are interested. Your book proposal will typically consist of:

1. Author information and bio.
2. Proposed title, description, and introduction.
3. Table of contents and detailed description of chapters.
4. Marketing plan.
   a. Positioning: What does your book add that is new and compelling? Who is in the market for your book?
   b. Competitor analysis: What specifically are the competing books and how would yours be different, stronger, or better?
   c. Marketing strategy: What will you do to market and sell the book?
5. Writing samples or one or two chapters from the current work.

The agent will take about five weeks to review your query or proposal before letting you know if they are interested. If the agent agrees to work with you, they will submit your proposal to a publisher. Most publishers typically take about 30 to 60 days to review a proposal. They can reject it, accept it, or ask for modifications and resubmission. If the publisher is interested, they will negotiate with your agent regarding specific details such as the advance (the dollar amount of royalties that you would receive up front and upon final manuscript submission), the time to write it, advertising budget, and other details. The advance is important because many books do not make more than their advance, so this is the only money that you are guaranteed to earn.

Interview with Dr. Joan Borysenko

Joan Borysenko's books have been on the *New York Times* best-seller list. Find out more at www.joanborysenko.com.

What advice would you have for a new writer?

A publisher wants to know that you have a platform. This is what you need to figure out right away: "What is my platform?" It could be that you are giving a lot of local talks; you could volunteer your time. You will need to develop some following. My platform was being well known in academia and having good credentials (a doctorate from Harvard Medical School).

There are people who are go-getters and can create their own platforms. For instance, radio programs are always looking for guests. Work up some things for radio shows or write articles for small publications. The health food store in Boulder [Colorado], for example, has five free magazines. The publisher will want to see how creative you can be about getting yourself known. Show the publisher that you are good at getting out there.

Basically you do need an agent, and there are a couple of ways to find one. Go to a bookstore and look at books in an area that you are interested in writing about. Look at the acknowledgment page and see who the agent was. Then go to the writers' section of the bookstore and look for books (like *Writer's Marketplace*) that list agents. It is likely that the agents mentioned in the books you examined will be listed there. You need an agent who specializes in your kind of book. If you know someone who is a writer, ask them who their agent is. You can ask other professionals to endorse your proposal, which can help you to appear like a good investment to the agent.

SELF-PUBLISHED BOOKS

If you have difficulty finding a publisher for your book or you are not interested in working with a corporate publishing house, you have the option of self-publishing. Many authors choose to self-publish because of financial and control considerations.

On the financial side, if you self-publish, rather than receiving the average 10 or 12 percent of royalties from a major publisher, you would receive a greater percentage of your book's royalties. Of course, you need to pay the initial publishing costs yourself, which can be expensive (the average is around $6,000), so unless you sell many, many books, it is not likely that you will make a good deal of money through self-publishing. But some people do, when they have outstanding books that sell very well.

On the control side, when you self-publish, you are the one who has the final say. You don't need to worry about conflicts or clashes with your editor's opinions. You can choose your book title yourself. You can select the cover design and the book's layout. If you have a very strong, clear vision for your project, self-publishing can afford you a greater sense of control. On the flip side, you will probably want to hire a professional editor to review the manuscript, so you may run into similar situations that way—plus you need to pay them, and the good ones can be expensive.

When you self-publish, it is often a good idea to contract for print-on-demand services, which means that books will be printed as they are ordered. This helps you to avoid having a large inventory piling up, and reduces the expense of printing books that you do not need. I know some authors who self-published and have a garage filled with books they have yet to sell. You can also make changes and additions to the book when you print on demand.

Many authors begin with self-publishing and move on to publishing the book or a new book with a major publisher. Since publishers like to see a track record of success, they may be more likely to contract with you if you can show them that you sold 5,000 copies of your last self-published book.

Interview with Mark Levy

Mark Levy has written for the *New York Times* and has written or co-created four books. He helps authors to find their big idea and develop best-selling works. Mark's web site is www.levy innovation.com.

How do you take an idea and make it a best-selling book?
If you're writing a technical guide on how to do something, you can be straightforward on how you say it. But if you are writing in a saturated

field, you need to turn around the conventional wisdom. If you are agreeing with what's already out there, you are not doing something different. Find a niche and see what is missing; look for a galvanizing principle.

Take your strongest information—see what you're all about, then try to extract the strongest piece from your material. Go through all of your materials and see what is remarkable. My approach is not so market-oriented, which focuses on the audience need. My approach is that if you are already doing something well, let's take that and go with it. Let your material lead the way.

When you were a director of specialist projects for the third largest book wholesaler, what were some of the things about books that would turn you off?
Books that sounded like other books were uninteresting to me. Unless the topic was very hot right at that time, if it sounded like something else, it would not register with me. The only time a generic book will work is if the category is very hot. It is hard to know what will be hot by the time you are finished writing. You have to project ahead to see what the categories will be. If there is a predictable event that you can release something to coincide with, that is great. Otherwise create something different.

If you are coming from a clinical or academic background, what do you do to write a book that has a large appeal and could potentially be a best-seller?
You have to make the book human. Readers respond best when you talk about topics as they relate to human beings, not theory. When you explain an idea, discuss the human story behind the person who invented the idea. The great writers will write about a town in New Jersey or a rock formation but also discuss the human side, such as the park ranger who brought you to the site of the rock formation. People know that everything is presented according to the position that you take, and you need to put your position out there, saying, "This is my take on the information." Put your real voice in it.

For example, "Who am I to tell you this information?" This has to be personal. Give your position: "This is how I am saying it." This approach is truthful.

A lot of people take the tack that they are writing the definitive tract on the subject — or they do not write, because they think that they cannot possibly write the definitive tract on a subject. What you are writing is not the end-all in your subject. If you think it is, you are deluding yourself.

A conversational and casual tone works great. You can be conversational and not be overly friendly; you can also be commanding, assertive, declarative, and show your personality.

ELECTRONIC BOOKS

An e-book is an electronic book that is typically created in a format such as portable document format (PDF) and distributed electronically. E-books are typically self-published by the author, although it is now common for publishers to sell e-books through venues like Amazon.com.

E-books are typically less dense in text and there is more white space on a given page. E-books have a lot of headings and subheadings, making the text very readable and clear. Many e-book authors feel that e-books sell best when they are on a highly specific topic, are action-oriented, and have a clear niche market. Readers tend to like e-books that can be readily implemented and used, rather than e-books on purely theoretical topics. At the time of this writing, novels and fiction are less popular as e-books, but the field is continually changing, so that may not be true for long.

Creating an e-book is relatively easy. As with any product, the key is an innovative, creative, and unique idea. You need to think outside the box to create something that has not been done before. For instance, think about how your research areas would apply to current events or issues in the media. Or think about your most fascinating therapy case and what helped the person to change, and then create a how-to manual for making a similar type of change. Spend some time brainstorming without censoring any of your ideas, so you can be as creative as possible. Then run your ideas by colleagues, professors, friends, and, ideally, members of your target audience.

At this point, you can begin conducting your market research to see what is out there, how it is done, and how your e-book can be different. You also want to determine whether there is a need or an interest in the particular area. If you are doing your research on Amazon.com, for example, you can look under "Product Details" to gather some good information. You can see who is the publisher of the e-book (or audio product or book) and the sales ranks of books to get a feel for how different books are selling. A lower number means a higher rank. When a book is published by a publisher and released as both a book and an e-book, you can compare the data to see how they are both selling.

Once you have done your research and have a compelling case for moving ahead, you can begin writing. Many people create their e-book as a Word document and then transfer it to a PDF file. You can use any technology to create an e-book. Of course, you can hire someone to do the technical side for you. Since it is a simple technology, you should not pay much for them to convert your file into an e-book.

At this point I will turn to one of the world's leading Internet marketing and e-book experts, Dr. Joe Vitale.

Interview with Joe Vitale

Dr. Joe Vitale is the author of too many books to list here, including the number one best-selling book *The Attractor Factor* (Wiley, 2005), the best-selling e-book *Hypnotic Writing*, and the best-selling Nightingale-Conant audio program *The Power of Outrageous Marketing*. His main web site is www.MrFire.com.

If someone writes an e-book in Microsoft Word and wants to hire someone to convert it to PDF, what do you recommend?
There's no need to hire anyone or spend a dime. You can use the free Adobe PDF maker on their site.

People often raise the concern that e-books can be copied and e-mailed around while hard-copy books cannot. What is your take on this point?
You can secure the book so people have to use a password to access it. You can set this when you make your PDF. But I think you should worry more about creating an e-book worth stealing. There's very little theft out there. Besides, what little there is is like viral marketing: It helps promote you and your book.

In your opinion, how does an e-book differ from a hard copy book?
I love e-books. I've been published in every way you can think of, from traditional publishing to self-publishing to print-on-demand and e-books.

E-books are faster and more fun. You can also make more money with them. There is far less credibility in writing them, but far more wealth.

Is it better to self-publish an e-book or look for a publisher?
Do both. Sell it as an e-book first. As you get feedback, improve your book. As you are selling it, look for a publisher or agent.

What are your top five tips for writing a successful e-book?

1. Your title better grab attention.
2. Your material better answer problems.
3. Your book better be written to a target audience.
4. Your writing should be easy to understand.
5. Your length can be anything, but the shorter the better.

What are your top five tips for marketing an e-book?

1. Go to the target audience you wrote the book for.
2. Go to list owners who serve your target market.
3. Run Google Ads for your target market.
4. Send out a news release for your market.
5. Be big, bold, and outrageous.

Harrison Monarth is someone who specializes in selling services and then successfully branched out to selling products.

Interview with Harrison Monarth

Harrison Monarth is the president of GuruMaker School of Professional Speaking (www.gurumaker.com) and partner with me in Extreme Communicator (www.ExtremeCommunicator.com). We have co-created several products.

Can you tell the readers a little about your company, GuruMaker?
GuruMaker is comprised of a team of highly accomplished and skilled communication coaches, each being an expert in a particular communication specialty. My vision for GuruMaker was to develop a dream

team of coaches who can help communicators in business, politics, and the industries get their message across powerfully and memorably. With GuruMaker, we help people get results through communication. Period.

What are some products that you or your company have created?
We are in the process of developing an audio program based on a live communication workshop in Florida and an e-book on communication skills. Larina and I have created several e-books on topics such as cold-calling, charisma, and speaking skills.

As a service provider, what made you decide to expand your business to the product arena?
Products are an effective way to get your message out to thousands via different marketing channels. We can reach more people by selling products than we ever could on a face-to-face basis. Products create interest in the services we provide. Products also are a great passive revenue stream for a service provider.

How would you recommend that others get their feet wet when creating a product for the first time?
See what's out there first. Who else in your field has created a product on a similar topic? Is it selling? The number one rule to keep in mind is that any product you create has to be of superior quality. Your product acts as a messenger for your services, and if the product says "mediocre," people will transfer this perceived lack of care and quality to your services. Attention to every detail is critical. Find proven experts to consult with about different parts of your product every step of the way.

Is it a good idea to partner with others in creating products?
Partnering can be a good idea, as long as both partners are committed to excellence and can contribute real value to a product. It's important to perform due diligence prior to getting into any kind of agreement that binds you together contractually. Look at the prospective partner's references, body of work, and reputation. Consider whether this is the person or firm you want to be associated with, because their credibility or lack thereof can hurt or help you in equal measure.

You can find partners just about anywhere, as the opportunities for joint ventures are endless. Whether you partner with a best-selling author or with a writer just starting out, make sure you know exactly what it is you will be getting in the end as far as a finished product is concerned. Also keep in mind that partnerships are like marriages. You commit to someone for a period of time or for the life of a project. Make sure it's the kind of person that complements you and that you want to be connected with for a considerable amount of time.

BROCHURES

Who would pay money for a brochure? That is an excellent question, because most brochures are given out as a way to market your business and service so they are passed out for free. Yet it is possible to sell brochures. Think about it: Who might buy brochures? If your answer is people who need them to hand out to patients or to give as educational materials, you are on the right track! These types of brochures are not the typical advertising brochures that many of us are used to. They are much more educational in nature.

In general, there are two types of brochures that can be sold. The first is brochures for patients or clients. Let's say that you worked in a hospital and realized that one of the medical units had a significant number of patients with domestic violence injuries or children with behavioral problems. You could develop an educational brochure that you could sell to the hospitals so they could give out psychoeducational materials to their patients. This would enhance their quality of care, reduce expenses, and provide a better work environment for employees since they would feel good about handing out high-quality information.

The other category of saleable brochures includes those that you can sell to other clinicians to give out as a way to describe their services. If you have expertise in a specific treatment modality, such as hypnotherapy, biofeedback, or stress inoculation, you can develop a brochure describing that treatment approach. Other therapists can buy this brochure from you so they do not need to spend their time and money reinventing the wheel. You can make a general brochure and send them hard copies, or you can send them an electronic version and they can modify it to add a line about their specific services and contact information.

Developing a brochure is relatively easy technically, using a program like Microsoft Publisher or an Adobe program. I recommend gathering about 20 different brochures or informational pamphlets and seeing what you like and do not like about them. Be sure to keep yours visually simple but interesting by alternating text with graphics, having a consistent color scheme, and leaving some white space. You may want to hire a marketing coach or consultant to look over your brochure and give you feedback before going to press. You can print the brochures yourself with a high-quality printer and heavy brochure or pamphlet paper, or you can have them professionally printed.

SUBSCRIPTION NEWSLETTERS

Newsletters are also typically free because their primary purposes are marketing and building your database. It is possible to create subscription newsletters to send to your subscribers and earn passive income. These can be electronic newsletters (also known as e-zines) that you e-mail to your database or hard-copy newsletters that you send out to your mailing list. For an example of my marketing e-zine, visit www.PAScoaching.com and sign up (it's free).

Even when a newsletter is free, people become annoyed if it is all about sales and not about great content. We have all experienced this—we open an e-mail that is supposed to provide valuable content and find that it is all advertisements. We only wasted about 30 seconds of our time, but it is annoying nonetheless. For any newsletter, you need the following elements:

- A very specific target audience. You can create more than one e-zine if you have multiple target audiences.
- A clear value proposition. What *exactly* will your newsletter offer its subscribers?
- A professionally designed layout and format. Imagine buying a subscription to a magazine and having an unprofessionally designed magazine show up at your house.
- Several articles of different formats. Include some storytelling articles, some how-to articles, some research studies, and some success stories.
- Two to three announcements and promotions. Free or discounted services, such as teleconferences or coaching calls.

ARTICLES AND COLUMNS

Writing articles is a great way to establish your credibility and expert status. You are typically not paid for writing articles unless you have a regular column in a magazine or newspaper. But even if you are not paid, writing articles can help you establish your platform and get a book deal, help build your visibility and credibility, and give you experience with writing. Look for media that your target market is most likely to read. If you are a family therapist or a parenting coach, write articles for major parenting web sites, lifestyle sections in newspapers, or parenting magazines.

Interview with Debbie Glasser, PhD

Debbie Glasser is a licensed clinical psychologist, a past chairperson of the National Parenting Education Network, and the author of "Positive Parenting," a weekly feature of the *Miami Herald*.

What is your background and what type of writing do you do?
I am a licensed clinical psychologist and past chair of the National Parenting Education Network. Currently, I am the author of a weekly parenting column in the *Miami Herald* (a Knight-Ridder newspaper) and a freelance writer for various magazines, web sites, and newsletters of interest to parents.

What are some tips for psychologists interested in a writing career?
Here are five tips:

1. *Specialize.* When you establish yourself as an expert in a particular branch of psychology (e.g., elderly issues, child development, adult relationships, etc.), you increase the likelihood that you will be published. Because books and magazines appeal to unique markets, editors look for specialists and experts who will appeal to their readers. Besides, it is easier to write about what you know.
2. *Build your credentials.* If you're going to present yourself as an expert author, you need to establish your credibility. Pursue appropriate licensure, stay current with continuing education courses, and join organizations in your field of interest. The more you know, the more likely editors and readers will want to hear what you have to say.
3. *Write.* One of the best ways to break into the writing field is simply to write! The more you write, the better you'll get. The better you

get, the more likely you will get published. Attend writers' workshops. Write sample columns or chapters and ask trusted friends and colleagues to critique them.

4. *Work for free*. It won't pay the bills, but offering to work without pay can get your foot in the door as a writer. In fact, many psychologists get their start as writers by offering a free column in a local newspaper or magazine. Editors are always on the lookout for quality content, but they don't always have the budget to fund new columnists. Write a few sample columns in your area of expertise and send them to a local community paper. Include a brief cover letter highlighting your professional credentials and ask whether there's an opportunity to submit weekly or monthly columns at no charge. It helps to find publications that appeal to unique markets or communities. For example, a small community newspaper distributed in a neighborhood with a large retirement population might welcome a monthly column from a psychologist specializing in elder issues. Also, there are many web sites looking for free content. In exchange, they offer the opportunity to get published and establish your writing career. As you gain exposure and experience, you will be in a better position to publish your work — and get paid for it, too!

5. *Learn more*. There are many resources available for writers. Now's the time to apply those advanced research skills that served you well during the grad school years. A quick search engine query can open the door to countless sites and articles that can help nurture your talent and your career. Here are a few Web resources to get you started: American Society of Journalists and Authors (www.asja.org), Booktalk (www.booktalk.com), For Writers (www.forwriters.com), and Writers Weekly (www.writersweekly.com).

RESOURCES

BOOKS

Brogan, K. S. (Ed.), and Brewer, R. L. (Asst. Ed.) (2005). *2005 Writer's market*. Cincinnati, Ohio: Writer's Digest Books.

Edwards, J., & Vitale, J. (2003). *How to write and publish your own ebook in as little as 7 days*. Available at http://www.7dayebook.com/?hop= mhsouthon

Vitale, J, & Mok J. H. (2005). *The E-Code: 33 Internet Superstars Reveal 43 Ways to Make Money Online Almost Instantly—Using Only Email.* New York: John Wiley & Sons.

Katz, M. J. (2003). *E-newsletters that work: the small business owner's guide to creating, writing and managing an effective electronic newsletter.* Philadelphia: Xlibris Corporation.

Poynter, D. (2003). *The self-publishing manual: How to write, print, and sell your own book* (14th Ed.). Santa Barbara, CA: Para Publishing.

Taylor, D. (2004). *The freelance success book.* Electronic book available at http://www.writersweekly.com/books/1107.html.

WEB SITES

Site to find freelance services:

www.elanceonline.com

E-book covers:

www.ecovergenerator.com

Create PDF files:

www.adobe.com

Turn an e-book into PDF format:

www.neevia.com/express

Buy and sell digital and electronic books:

www.ebooks.com

Create audios:

www.audacity.sourceforge.net/windows.php

Joe Vitale's web site:

www.mrfire.com

Free e-zine directory and resources:

www.freezineweb.com

Free articles, tips, and information on e-zines:

www.go-ezines.com

The American Society of Journalists and Authors :

www.asja.org

Booktalk—lists literary agents, lots of information about books:

www.booktalk.com

For Writers—a great resource for writers:

www.forwriters.com

Writers Weekly—a free e-zine about freelance writing:

www.writersweekly.com

Directory of magazines interested in articles by freelance writers:

www.writersdigest.com

Terminology

active strategy   A type of marketing or delivery of services that involves direct contact with prospects or clients and is usually delivered live or on-line in real time.

audio product   A CD or other audio media that can be sold or given away to promote your services.

deliverable   Something that is to be delivered according to agreement; by extension, a task that one is responsible for delivering; something that can be provided and sold as the product of development.

e-book   An electronic book, typically created in a PDF format and sent to people over the Internet.

e-zine   An electronic newsletter that is sent out to a company's database. E-zines are typically used as a means to collect names and e-mails of web site visitors and build a company's database.

freelancer   A writer who serves as a free agent and writes for numerous publications, rather than serving solely as a staff writer on one publication. Freelancers often contribute regularly to the same publications. Freelancing has increased in popularity as more companies are outsourcing their writers.

passive strategy   A type of marketing or delivery of services or products that involves selling directly to clients or buyers, often without direct contact by the supplier. The product can be distributed through channels such as the Internet, partners, publishers, or other delivery systems.

CHAPTER 8

Be Your Own Boss:
A Full-Time or
Part-Time Practice

In business for yourself, not by yourself.

Ray Kroc, founder of McDonald's

If we all did the things we are capable of doing, we would literally astound ourselves.

Thomas Edison

IS PRIVATE PRACTICE FOR ME?

Before you take the time to read the rest of this chapter, first consider whether you would be a good match for private practice. I believe there are some essential qualities, both innate and learned, that make certain individuals an ideal match for private practice. Answer this short quiz to see if you have the mentality and motivation of an independent practitioner.

Am I Meant to be in Private Practice?

Honestly answer the following questions on a scale of 1 to 5, with 1 meaning the statement is not at all true for you and 5 meaning it is strongly true.

1	2	3	4	5

Less True ←→ **More True**

1. I often think about how I love (or would love) being my own boss and being responsible for my own successes or failures. _____

2. I do *not* typically long for a stable and consistent job. _____

3. It is typical for me to think that I naturally have what it takes to be a successful entrepreneur. _____

4. I have a strong support system to help me along when my career is challenging. _____

5. People have told me that I am independent and am good at being the one in charge. _____

6. I would (or do) enjoy going out and networking, marketing, and meeting potential referral partners. _____

7. I am strong with time management. _____

8. I am good at planning and managing my finances and income. _____

9. The idea of an uncertain career future is interesting, challenging, and exciting to me. _____

10. I could be called a self-starter. _____

This is not an empirically validated assessment measure, but if you found yourself scoring many 1s, 2s, or 3s, you may want to reconsider whether your personality or goals are best suited to private practice. That is not to say that circumstances will not change in the future, but before getting into it, you want to think about when the right time will be.

Now You Get to Use Your Business Planning Skills

If you have determined that you are a good match for private practice and are thinking about beginning a practice, now is a good time to begin doing your business plan. Having read the first half of this book, covering the essentials of business planning, you should have a pretty good idea about how to create a business plan, either for your career in general or for a private practice.

Remember that the purpose of a solid business plan is not just to secure loans or funding, but to set your mission and goals, determine who your target clients are, assess the competition in your market and differentiate yourself, ensure profitability, and grow your business. Of course, the first step is to create the vision and mission for your private practice. You can use some of the assessments and questions from Chapter 2 to help you create your vision, then record it here:

Private Practice Vision or Statement of Purpose: _____

_____

_____

_____

Mission Statement: _____

_____

_____

The next step is setting up concrete objectives that will help you to accomplish your mission. Your objectives will be time sensitive. For instance, when you first get going in private practice, an objective could be to secure 10 fee-for-service clients on a sliding scale each week, with weekly revenue totaling $925 per week. Once you start building your business, this objective will change.

List your top five goals at this point in time:

Goal 1: _____

Goal 2: _____

Goal 3: _____

Goal 4: _____

Goal 5: _____

Now we'll explore the three basic steps in creating a marketing plan.

PHASE 1: ASSESSMENT AND PLAN

The first step entails figuring out your market and niche. This stage involves conducting the SWOT analysis, maximizing your core competencies and competitive advantage, and deciding what market is most interesting and inspiring to you. Review the section in Chapter 3 on conducting a SWOT analysis and creating your competitive advantage.

Some people think of this as the planning stage. It is critically important and often neglected by private practitioners. Therapists are, understandably, eager to get out there and start seeing clients independently, earning an income, and doing what they do best, which is usually *not* marketing. But wait! Don't jump into water where you don't know the depth. Don't drive a car with a windshield so dirty you can barely see. Remember this analogy to creating your vision? You want to have a crystal clear vision for your practice that guides you along the way. Just like jumping into unknown water and driving with a dirty windshield, marketing without a plan is dangerous to you and your career.

This initial stage of marketing your practice will lay the groundwork and foundation that will determine the future of your career. In therapy, we conduct a thorough evaluation and create a treatment plan for this very reason. If we had our clients come in and just start talking, without having a view of the bigger picture, we may not serve them well or, worse, we may be propagating a dangerous situation. Understanding the larger picture is critical to making wise decisions.

This stage of marketing is about creating an *identity* for your practice. Many people look at their businesses or practices as their baby. This makes sense—you created it, developed it, nurtured it, and can take responsibility for its successes and problems. Imagine if you did not give your baby an identity by giving it a name. The name of your practice should come from the same place of love and excitement from which you would name a baby (combined, of course, with a solid business analysis for good measure). Your business's name should be in line with your unique core competence. For example, a private practice marketing client of mine, Denise Humphrey, hired me to help create her practice identity and develop the corresponding marketing materials. Denise used her own unique attributes, including her extensive background in

160

music, to create the identity of her practice. Denise's philosophy and vision is as follows:

> Performing music involves both art and science, as does conducting therapy. The science of music involves the learning of theory and technique, mastered to the extent that the final artistic expression is not experienced *as such*. Therapy is the same. The science of psychological theory and technique must be mastered in order to allow the art of human interchange to emerge as "natural" in the therapeutic setting. Timing, tone, volume, and even silence are essential in both arenas as expressions of beauty, feeling, transcendence, and meaning. This internal understanding of the musical correlations to therapy has exponentially empowered my attributes as a therapist. For me, the two are intertwined and form the basis of my practice identity.

Can you see how her use of vision helps her to create an identity and sense of passion for what she does? From this identity, her practice name emerged: *Creating Harmony*.

One of the most important aspects of this stage in your marketing is identifying your target audience. Complete this target market form to be sure you have considered all aspects of your target market. If you have more than one target market (which is fine as long as you do not have too many), complete this form separately for each population.

Target Market Profile

Clinical or presenting issues: _____

Geographical location: _____

Age: _____

Gender: _____

Professions or occupations: _____

Family composition: _____

Income or economic status: _____

Motivation for treatment: _____

Important lifestyle variables: _____

Other demographic variables: _____

From a marketing perspective, having a target market, a niche, or a specific area of expertise will make your marketing process much more effective. I will rephrase that: Marketing something specific works much better than marketing something general. There are dozens of reasons for this, many of which are psychological in nature. For instance, when referral sources know that you specialize in treating girls with depression, they will bring you to mind first whenever they come into contact with that type of client. From the client's perspective, when people buy a service, they want to work with whoever specializes in that service—they want the best. In general, buyers in the services industry (as opposed to buyers in the product industry) are primarily motivated by perceived quality, more than by price or other variables. Having a specific niche or area of expertise increases the perceived quality of your services.

PHASE 2: MARKETING MATERIALS

Phases 2 and 3 will be based on your target client profile created in Phase 1. You need to know *to whom* you are marketing in order to market effectively. Once you have a solid understanding of what you will be offering and to whom, you can begin to create your marketing materials, including your business cards, brochures, voice mail or e-mail, websites, letterhead and envelopes, press kit or media kit.

The most important thing about all of these marketing materials is that they are consistent and that they communicate your core message. Remember that people do not care as much about *what* you do as about *how well* it works. A common mistake that therapists make when creating their materials is discussing their services at length. This is a problem for two reasons: first, the lengthiness, and second, believe it or not, clients do not care much what you do. They care about how it will help them, what benefits they will have from therapy, whether they will get better, and what problems will be solved.

Always keep in mind your code of ethics when creating your materials. You do not want to guarantee or promise results, since that would not be an ethical practice. It is okay, however, to say something like "Many clients experience a reduction in . . ." or "The literature shows a 78 percent effectiveness of our cognitive-behavioral treatments for panic disorder" (and cite the literature to which you are referring).

Another crucial component of your marketing materials is their visual attractiveness. They need to be visually consistent (same color schemes and graphics on web site, brochures, cards, etc.), professional, aesthetically pleasing, clear, and concise. Just as a company portrays its corporate image through its marketing, your materials will communicate a great deal to prospective clients or referral sources. You may wish to hire a graphic designer and/or a marketing specialist to review your materials before going live with them, since your reputation in the field is extremely important to your career success.

You can create business cards yourself. Creating a web site from scratch is not cost (or stress) effective for many people, but creating your cards and brochure can be relatively easy and enjoyable, and you will save a lot of money that way. If you create your materials yourself, you can then print them yourself with a high-quality printer and paper, take them to a professional printer such as Kinkos, or send them to an online printing service. I do not recommend printing and cutting your business cards yourself since they can turn out looking unprofessional. There are many online services that are very inexpensive and have quick turnaround time. Two that I recommend to my clients are 48 Hour Print (www.48hourprint.com) and Vista Print (www.vistaprint.com). You can hire a freelancer to create your brochures and business cards or you can go with a major design company, which is likely to be considerably more expensive but can be worth it.

PHASE 3: ACTIVE AND PASSIVE MARKETING STRATEGIES

Here is the fun part. If you have followed the preceding two steps, you should feel confident to get out there and market your professional services. There are a number of ways to do this. The most general classification for the different marketing strategies is passive versus active strategies. Some strategies accomplish both objectives.

ACTIVE MARKETING STRATEGIES

As the name implies, active strategies involve getting out there in front of people. When building a therapy practice, the people you will be seeking out are typically referral partners. It is generally considered better (from both a marketing and an ethics perspective) to market to referral partners rather than to individual clients. From a marketing perspective, this relates to the principle that if you "give a man a fish, he'll eat for a day; teach a man to fish and he'll eat for a lifetime." If you can show referral sources the benefits of referring to you, you may have enough people to fill your practice on an ongoing basis. From an ethics perspective, you need to be careful not to market to clients who are in a state of duress. For information about APA ethics regarding marketing, go to http://www2.apa.org/ethics/code2002.doc.

NETWORKING AS ACTIVE MARKETING

One of the best active marketing strategies is networking to create strategic referral partnerships. A strategic referral partner (SRP) is someone who will send you clients because the relationship is mutually beneficial. Let's say that a primary care physician (PCP) referred you a client with generalized anxiety disorder. The optimal way to nurture this referral partnership is first by sending a letter thanking the PCP for the referral. Second, provide the highest level of care possible (which you would do anyway). Third (assuming the client provides a consent to release information), send a progress report to the PCP and/or phone her for collaboration on the case. Fourth, send a termination summary complete with follow-up recommendations to the PCP. This physician will be motivated to refer to you again because she is well aware of the quality of services you provided since you are keeping her informed.

To build your professional networks, connect with former classmates or alumni of your undergraduate or graduate school programs. Talk with other professionals in your community and attend networking events or professional association meetings with allied professionals. Your state and local professional associations are excellent places to meet referral partners. You can also do cold-call networking by sending out letters and introducing yourself to strangers who could become good SRPs. Remember to clearly highlight the specific potential benefits to that individual. You can warm these contacts if you have an intermediate contact person. Then you can say, "Mary Ellen mentioned your work to me and I recognized that we may be able to send one another clients."

One of the best ways to gain strategic referral partners is actually counter-intuitive: Instead of looking for people who can refer to you, look for people to whom you can refer. Then start making as many high-quality referrals as possible. Pick your SRPs wisely and select people who you *want* to refer to. Your reason for making the referrals should not be solely to fill your practice. Instead it should be to help out or benefit the referral partner and client. For more on the principle of giving as a component of marketing success, see Joe Vitale's *The Greatest Money-Making Secret in History!*

SPEAKING AS ACTIVE MARKETING

In my experience as a marketing coach, networking to meet potential referral partners is tied for first place with public speaking, in terms of the most effective strategies to build a practice. For an e-book on professional speaking, visit www.TheSuccessfulTherapist.com. Public speaking is one of the most active of the active marketing strategies because you are literally out there in front of people. Being in front of people will not only put a face with a name but will put a personality with a name. Speaking in your local community helps you to gain both visibility and credibility with the people in your work area. Since speaking can be such an excellent marketing strategy, strongly consider doing it for free when you are trying to build your practice. Offer to provide free talks or seminars when it will put you in front of your target audience of potential referral partners. Do not provide free talks if you cannot see the people in your audience as excellent SRPs. Here are some questions to ask yourself in deciding whether speaking for a particular organization or group is an ideal opportunity for you:

- Do I respect this group and the work that they do?
- Do these people come into regular contact with my ideal clients?
- Is there some way I can help these people (e.g., by referring them clients)?
- What might motivate these individuals to refer clients or patients to me?
- Can I provide something of value to this group or the people they refer to me?
- Would the clients they refer to me be able to afford my services (or do they have insurance I take)?

There are some keys to be aware of when using speaking as a way to market your services. Many therapists do public speaking engagements and then wonder why they are not getting referrals from the talk. You need to think of the talk as a method for showing people how they or others can benefit from your services. Here are six top points to remember:

1. Give handouts!
2. Put your contact information on every page of your handouts.
3. Bring plenty of business cards and brochures.
4. Offer a resource for free, like an article or a stress management tape.
5. Find a way to initiate follow-up contact with your audience members.
6. Demonstrate the effectiveness of your services by making your workshop experiential or by telling great success stories.

PASSIVE MARKETING STRATEGIES

Passive marketing strategies involve activities that help you to build credibility among potential clients or referral partners without having to physically get in front of them. These strategies help you to get seen by many members of your community. People who tend to be more introverted or reserved generally feel more comfortable with passive strategies. The word *passive* has a somewhat negative connotation, but these marketing strategies are not negative. They do, however, tend not to be highly effective when used on their own. When used in combination with the more active strategies, you can find the optimal mix of marketing strategies for building your practice.

WRITING ARTICLES, BOOKS, AND NEWSLETTERS
If you enjoy writing and are skilled at it, then you may want to include writing strategies as part of your marketing mix. Typically, writing is a form of advertising that is free, other than the time you spend writing. You do not have to write books to successfully use writing as a way to build your practice. Since writing books takes months and years, if you want to build your practice quickly, you can write articles, newsletters, and letters to the editor of your local newspaper.

To generate new clients through your writing, be sure to make a connection between your written piece and your ideal client base. Consider your topic, the publication, the readers of the publication, and where in the publication your article or letter will be placed. Offer your articles to local magazines and free papers. Letters to editors in local newspapers are a nice free way to put your views out there. Since these letters are often opinionated, be aware of creating potential controversy and the impact it could have on your professional reputation. If you are submitting articles to local media outlets, create a couple of articles that tie your areas of expertise into local events. Local media likes to report on community events and topics.

Writing articles in newsletters can be very effective, especially if you write for a newsletter that has a large circulation. You can begin your own newsletter or you can offer articles to existing newsletters. Look into some businesses in your city or town that may serve your potential clients. Ask if they have a newsletter, and if so, let them know that you have an article you would like to contribute for free if they are interested. You can also submit your articles to large e-zines. Your article may receive national or international exposure, which can be good but not necessary if you are trying to build a local business in your community. Some e-zine submission sites that I like include http://ezinearticles.com and http://www.ideamarketers.com.

PRIVATE PRACTICE FINANCIAL PLAN

The financial plan for your private practice is comprised of funding the start-up of your business, setting your fees and costs, and managing your finances, cash flow, and taxes.

FUNDING YOUR NEW COMPANY

The first consideration in your financial plan is how you will fund your practice. Options include:

- Saving while you are still working in another position.
- Working part-time to cover your expenses and earn some start-up capital, and then beginning your private practice part-time.
- Borrowing from family or other personal support systems.
- Financing with debt equity through loans.
- Financing with debt by leasing office space and supplies.

The most common sources of debt financing used by private practitioners are commercial banks and lending companies. Commercial banks are the places from which people typically think of acquiring funding. Banks offer small business loans, and you can set up your business checking accounts and other services with the same institution. Bank loans may be secured, which typically means that you offer something as collateral in case you default on your loan (Stout & Grand, 2005).

Many therapists balk at the idea of using a loan to secure the initial funding for your practice. While debt equity is not ideal, many if not most small businesses rely on debt for funding. When you start to think of your practice as a business, you may recognize that this is a viable option for you. Of course, it is important to consider your personal feelings about loan-based funding. If it makes you very uncomfortable to take out a loan and it would lead to significant stress in your life, then it may be a better idea to look into the other sources of funding mentioned here.

To figure out how much you need for your start-up loan, first add up all of your start-up costs, including rental security deposit and first month's rent, office supplies, furniture, marketing materials, attorney and consultant fees, and so on.

Second, add up your first six months of operating expenses. If you do not have a solid marketing plan in place for obtaining clients, add up the first 12 or 18 months of operating expenses to give yourself more of a cushion. Operating expenses include costs such as rent, Internet, telephone, electricity heating, and so on. If you want to begin using more detailed accounting methods, divide your operating expenses into fixed versus variable costs. As the names imply, fixed costs do not change month by month (insurance, parking, loan repayment, rent) whereas variable costs fluctuate each month (utilities, marketing, office supplies).

Third, add up the totals from all of these categories. Then add up all of your current sources of funding from savings and subtract your expenses from this total. If you end up with a negative number, that is the amount you need for a loan. To minimize risk, multiple that number by 1.20 to add a 20 percent cushion.

FEES AND EXPENSES

Your business's income statement consists of income and expenses. Your major source of income in a traditional practice will be your client fees. Your expenses will consist of the fixed and variable costs just discussed. Since your hourly fees will make up most of your income, setting the optimum fee is extremely important. You will need to do some research and some math to determine what your hourly fee will be. Check with your state and national organizations and survey your local marketplace to get the necessary information to set your fee. Complete the Hourly Fee Analysis form to help figure it out.

Hourly Fee Analysis

1. The national average hourly fee in my profession is: _____

2. The average hourly fee in my state in my profession is: _____

3. The average hourly fee in my city or town in my profession is: _____

4. The local average hourly fee for someone in a similar area of specialty is: _____

5. My target client could afford to pay how much per hour: _____

Once you have set your hourly fee, you need to decide whether you will run a self-pay practice or get onto insurance panels to take insurance. In making this decision, consider these questions:

- How would your income be affected by taking some insurance fees versus others, and versus self-pay only?
- Would taking insurance allow you to work more with your target population?
- Given your marketing plan for potential referral partners, would you reduce your referrals if you did not take certain insurance plans?
- Do you have a philosophical, professional, or theoretical stance or opinion on the use of insurance in today's health care climate?
- How is your local market for self-pay clients? This is important, because some local markets are primarily self-pay whereas others are primarily insurance-pay.
- If you do not use insurance, could you create a sliding scale fee that enables you to see clients who cannot afford your hourly rate?

Whether or not to take insurance can be a difficult question. Many independent practitioners choose not to use insurance in their practices because of the paperwork, fee caps, and so on. If you think you would like to get onto panels, you need to contact each insurance company directly and request an application to be a provider for their specific panel. Create a list of which insurance providers are used the most in your area to see which would be the best to apply to. Talk to friends and colleagues to learn the pros and cons of various insurance companies. Some insurance companies may tell you that they are not currently accepting new providers, or they may require specific qualifications before they will accept you onto your panel. If they do approve your application, they will send you a contract with their requirements and coverage. If you become an approved provider for their network, you may still need pre-authorization for sessions, which the client can obtain.

If you decide to go with a straight fee-for-service setup, you can certainly initiate a sliding scale fee. However, according to lawyers I interviewed, you should be careful to adhere to the following five guidelines:

1. If someone is going to submit for insurance reimbursement, they cannot be given a sliding scale fee.
2. You must always follow the rules and regulations of insurance providers. If, for instance, a patient has insurance on which you are a provider but does not want to submit an insurance claim, the patient should not be given a reduced fee since you are a provider.
3. You should have a standard sliding scale fee chart that you can show to patients to illustrate how you objectively establish the fees based on income level.
4. You should request last year's tax information or a paycheck to show you the client's income when you are setting the fee.
5. You must rely on objective criteria when setting the fee, not factors such as the referral source, your interest in the case, your perception of risk or liability involved with the case, and so on.

If you are not taking insurance, your clients may want to submit insurance claims themselves. If they have out-of-network benefits, they can go to any licensed psychologist or counselor and use their insurance. They can check whether they have out-of-network benefits by calling the phone number on the back of their insurance cards. If they do have out-of-network benefits, they can pay you your set fee (not sliding scale) and then file a claim with their insurance company to get reimbursed for whatever percentage their insurance covers.

Another fee issue is whether or not to take credit cards. In answering this question, first decide how you feel about it. If you are concerned that you may be encouraging poor money management or that it will raise other issues in the therapy, then you may not be comfortable taking credit cards. If you do take credit cards, your clients could be appreciative for the convenience. Be forewarned, though, that there are financial implications to your decision to take credit cards. Most credit card services charge a monthly fee (anywhere between $5 and $100 or more) and take a percentage (the average is around 2.8 percent) out of your fee. If you will not be taking enough credit cards to justify the monthly fee, you can use a service such as PayPal (www.paypal.com), which will take a percentage (around 3 percent) out of the charge without a monthly fee.

MANAGING YOUR CASH FLOW AND ACCOUNTING

While some therapists elect to do their own accounting, if you are not either a CPA, very experienced with accounting, or someone who really enjoys accounting, I recommend that you hire a good accountant. When you interview accountants, ask them whether they work with other professional service firm owners. Before you sign a contract with an accountant, make sure that the agreement lists an annual fee cap to show that accounting services will not be higher than a certain amount (such as $850) per year. This will ease some of your worries about their hourly billing.

You will need to create a system to manage your own business's cash flow throughout the year. An accountant cannot do her job without the proper records and information. To maintain your accounting records, you can use a computer-based program such as QuickBooks to record expenditures (business expenses) and income. Check with your accountant to find out what type of program they use and what expenses are deductible so you can keep track of everything. There are other programs, such as Therapist Helper, that some therapists have found useful in accounting. You can also keep track of expenses in a well-organized Excel spreadsheet.

PRIVATE PRACTICE OPERATIONS PLAN

The daily operations in your business will dictate the efficiency and success of your practice. Strategic time and practice management can result in your ability to see more clients, treat clients more effectively, reduce your level of stress, control your finances, and accomplish your career objectives. How you run your business on a daily basis will determine whether or not you are able to turn your career vision into a reality.

CONTINUOUS IMPROVEMENT

On a daily basis, look for ways to improve your practice. Take, for example, the physical environment of your office. Make sure you have ordered all your supplies so you are not suddenly out of printer paper. Look around the interior of your office and ask yourself if the environment is creating the experience you want it to, or what you can do differently. Keep your office clean and presentable. Question whether the fees you pay for your fixed and variable expenses are reasonable compared to what others are paying. Assess the positive and negative qualities of your office location. Consider hiring a receptionist if you do not already have one. These types of variables can help you to add incremental daily improvements to your business.

MEASURING RESULTS

In treating your practice as a business, it is critical that you measure the results of your actions. Here are some of the numbers that I recommend you track:

- Number of intake sessions and the percentage of intake sessions converted to individual therapy clients.
- Number of cancellations and the reasons for them.
- Percentage of clients who are self-pay versus insurance-pay (and what types of insurances are used).
- Sources of new clients (who referred them).
- Which referral sources are providing the most new clients.
- Weekly, monthly, and quarterly income.

PAPERWORK AND RECORDS

Most likely you already know the general procedures for keeping records and notes. All of the rules that applied when you were working in an agency, counseling center, or other setting still apply when you are in private practice. Stout and Grand (2005) state that you use your paperwork and client records to help your practice run efficiently, to standardize documentation and routine procedures, and to comply with ethical and legal guidelines as well as third party payers, such as managed care organizations. They recommend using templates, such as those available from the Medical Arts Press (www.medicalarts.com). You can also ask mentors, supervisors, and colleagues for copies of the paperwork that they use. Be sure that whichever forms you choose to adopt are compliant with the Health Insurance Portability and Accountability Act (HIPAA). (For more information on HIPAA compliance visit www.hipaa.org.)

One part of your operations plan should be establishing a regular time to do your paperwork. If you do not already have a satisfactory system, do a little experimentation to see what type of schedule works for you. For instance, try completing intake assessment reports within the business day or within 48 hours, or completing each progress note immediately after the client session versus at the end of the day or end of the week.

Do not forget to create a receipt template that is professional in appearance so you can give your clients a receipt for their payments, spelling out what services they paid for. Include the appropriate clinical procedure terminology (CPT) code on your receipt. The most commonly used CPT codes are 90806 for a 45- to 50-minute individual therapy session in an outpatient setting, 90808 for a 75- to 80-minute individual therapy session in an outpatient setting, and 96100 for psychological testing (usually billed by the hour).

RISK MANAGEMENT

Clear, accurate, and timely documentation can assist in the operations of your business, improve your clinical services, and minimize risk. If someone brings suit against you, the client's records are going to be one of the most important pieces of evidence in the case. You should never include your value judgments or personal opinions that are not directly pertinent to the case.

To stay current on the legal and ethical guidelines of your profession and state, familiarize yourself with the regulations on a regular basis. You may want to initiate a practice that you will repeat during the course of your career, such as revisiting and printing out the ethical guidelines for your practice on a quarterly basis. Check the web site for your professional organization and your state board to get updated information.

Of course, malpractice insurance is necessary when you are operating a private practice. You can also check on the web site of your professional organization to get information on liability insurance providers. Select the insurance plan that is right for you based on your comfort with various degrees of risk, the degree of risk inherent in the client population with which you work, and financial considerations. There are generally two types of malpractice insurance. The first, occurrence coverage, is the more conservative of the two; it covers forever all the cases that you handled while you were subscribing to this insurance. The other type of policy is called claims-made and it covers only the cases you are seeing while you are still paying on that policy.

Interview with Leslie Hoy, MA, LPC

Leslie Hoy is a private practice therapist and personal coach, certified corporate trainer, and the president of Hi-Performance Coaching and Training in San Antonio, Texas. She can be reached at (210) 379-4403 or via e-mail at info@hiperformance.net. Her web site is www.hiperformance.net.

What are some of the lessons you've learned from developing a private practice? What marketing efforts have worked well and what has worked less well?

One of the best lessons I've learned is to diversify my business. I do not depend on only one source of income. There is just too much market instability, especially in mental health, these days to only depend upon one source. Another thing I have found helpful is to develop a good niche or two, and then market directly to those markets. I have several niches and I have developed good relationships with MDs and clinicians in these areas. One of my very best referral sources is a physician's assistant.

I would also encourage diversification among payers. In other words, if you are accepting insurance payment, try to spread out your patients among the insurance companies. I know of one clinician who received the majority of her referrals from one particular insurance company. For whatever reason, they stopped sending her as many referrals, and her practice suffered since she did not have other referral sources in place.

Certainly to be successful with a practice in today's environment, you really need to keep your expenses low. One group of clinicians that I know have independent practices but share a group of offices. This enables them to keep their overhead expenses very low. I also recommend maintaining your practice finances in something like QuickBooks. This allows you to keep close track of your income and expenses, and to know at any point just where you are financially. You can also set up a budget in QuickBooks, which I have done, and have found to be extremely helpful. Although this may sound like a lot, I know many of my therapist friends who do not keep track of their income and expenses and have no idea how much they are making until it is time to do their taxes for the year!

Interview with Gerry Bock, MA, CTS

Gerry Bock is a registered clinical counselor in Vancouver, British Columbia, Canada. He can be reached at gerry@bock.ca or by telephone at (604) 574-6555. His web site is www.lifestressrelief.com.

You have had an interesting career path in the field of mental health.
My career path began as a lay counselor to peers at the age of eight. I assisted in school peer-based counseling programs and other volunteer work throughout my school and university years. I have felt as if I have always been a counselor. I attended university a number of years after graduating high school, knowing that the career I desired was being a counselor in private practice. Having been employed and involved in family business from the age of 12, I was also very familiar with the way in which business operated and I had an entrepreneurial mind-set, along with the confidence that comes from early business successes in other areas.

My university training focused on marriage, family, and crisis counseling (now called critical incident stress management), as these were areas I had the most passion and interest for. I believe that passion and interest are crucial for genuine success and a feeling of fulfillment in a chosen career path. I began providing independent professional services for a fee as a soon as I completed the MA program in counseling psychology. I also continued my studies toward an MBA with a goal of completing this program. Because my practice became very busy, very quickly, I never finished the MBA. I completed my entire BA through MA program in five years, owing primarily to my passion to learn more and be highly effective in my work, a commitment that continues today. I became involved in the local counselling association early in my practice and currently serve on the board of directors in the role of chairman of member services.

What are some of the valuable lessons that you have learned?
Four lessons come to mind:

1. It is important to find a career to study and prepare for that you have a passion for. If you have a specific area of interest within a field of study, explore that as early as possible.
2. Once you have identified an area that you are passionate about, go out and volunteer as much as you can with this type of client base. Get the word out that you are interested in these areas.
3. *Learn to market yourself* early in order to maintain control of your career direction. Being known as a specialist in one to three areas is also very helpful in marketing.
4. Develop many contacts and referral sources in related areas; this will assist you in referring to others as well as having them refer to you.

Can you give an example or two of a time when having a vision for your professional career helped you to make a decision or advance your career?
More than anything, I love and enjoy my work in the session room. I have a passion to become familiar with what treatment modalities are available in my areas of interest and then find creative and effective ways to assist my clients. What may be unusual for my private practice is offering support and expertise in nutritional supplements and spiritual support related to crisis and stress. I became proficient in these areas in order to offer these additional benefits to clients. The underlying spiritual and physical causes that maintain a crisis or keep a client stuck should never be overlooked, in my opinion.

When you have defined areas of interest, it is much easier to promote yourself as you stand out from others in the field. For example, I have been the only one in my area offering treatment for dental anxiety. No one else does that here, and it fits within one of my areas of expertise, treatment of anxiety disorders. People seem to relate better when they feel you are speaking directly to them, not to a wider, more general audience. If you are a person who experiences dental anxiety, you are more likely to go to a professional who specializes in that than to a counselor who specializes in anxiety disorders. The population is easier to reach, as well, because it is more of a focused target market.

Have you made any mistakes or have there been things that you wish you had known as you grew your practice?
I wish I had had a business coach to assist me at the beginning. I was not aware that these people even existed when I started my practice more then 15 years ago. The only real business or career advice I had from a peer was, "Do not stay working for an agency too long as it is a low-paying dead end where others are in control of your future."

I had to be a pioneer in marketing myself, and I made a lot of mistakes. My biggest mistake was probably not researching the markets before writing my brochures for topics of focused interest. I wrote about all sorts of areas that interested me, without a good focus on areas that the market needed at the time. Market research is crucial to market success. It does not have to be formalized or complicated research. Asking some of your potential referral sources what they may be interested in is good face-to-face, referral source relationship–building research.

I also made the mistake of not spending the money up front for professional identity early on in my practice development. I had a home-based office that was located in an upstairs room in a townhouse. I also had inexpensive furniture in that office which was not entirely color coordinated. I have heard of others who conduct sessions in their living room. In my opinion, these may not have been direct ethical boundary violations; however, they still feel amateurish and unprofessional. I believe that clients overlooked some of these faux pas because they enjoyed the relationship with me, or because they got good results from the work.

Today, if I was starting a practice, I would do whatever is required to have a moderate professional identity. The home I live in now was purchased specifically because it had a separate area for my home office. The clients have a separate entrance, separate waiting room, and separate bathroom. The outside door has a "Welcome, Please Walk In" sign on it. Inside, I have a small bar fridge with cold drinks (juice, soda pop, water, diet drinks) and a TV/VCR on the wall with cable and a remote control. In my interview room, I have a candy dish with both good-quality snacks and candies. Some clients have to bring their kids because they cannot get a sitter at the last minute, and there is also a table for homework (this helps avoid some of those late-notice cancellations). The interview room is soundproofed so that clients in the waiting room cannot hear anything that is said in the interview room. To me, this sends a strong message to my clients that I am concerned about their feeling of being served and provided for, and addresses the need for privacy and professionalism.

I prescreen clients on the phone now by taking between 15 and 30 minutes to ask what they desire to see me about and to sketch out some possible approaches to the problem on the phone. I find this approach saves me a lot of time as it screens out the shopping crowd. If I know what the client is looking for, I can direct them to a colleague who could help them, perhaps more effectively then I could. This way I do not spend time with booking, waiting to see if they will show up, and possibly ending up referring them on anyway. On the other hand, the discounted session will bring you a lot more clients who may not otherwise attend at all. A good rule of thumb is this: If you have a lot of available time, it is not expensive for you to give it away at a discounted rate. If you are busy, limit the number of freebies per week to avoid a revenue drain.

Do you recommend that private practitioners get involved with delivering speaking engagements including lectures, workshops, and seminars?

This helps to get your name and reputation out to the public, especially in specific and focused areas of practice. However, if you are not comfortable speaking publicly, or if you are not really well versed in a subject that you are presenting on, avoid this one until you are.

An alternative twist to this is the free or low-cost monthly support group meeting. Having these type of meetings allows you to develop contacts and referral sources more easily, especially if you control the size of the group and require preregistration. Many of these contacts may also want your monthly e-zine or newsletter, which keeps you in touch with the prospects, many of whom will become clients. Also, you may consider inviting some of the group members who have good success with you privately, to come back and share their successes.

Do you have any tips for creating an effective brochure?
I believe that brochures must be written topically and have good exercises and added value to be really effective. A prospective client has no reason to read a brochure about you versus a brochure about others, unless they are motivated by something about the title or the topic. Write for your prospective reader's interest, not for your own.

(Author's note: Gerry welcomes continued discussion on these topics.)

Interview with Henry C. Fader, Esq.

Henry Fader is a corporate and health care partner at Pepper Hamilton LLP, Attorneys at Law, a Philadelphia-based firm with 10 offices nationally. Mr. Fader can be reached at faderh@pepperlaw.com, and the firm's web site is www.pepperlaw.com.

In what ways have you helped mental health practitioners in the past?
There have been several categories. In the practice formation stages, I have worked with groups of individuals who want to form large practices. With ongoing practices, I have worked with therapists when they have growing pains and issues come up in their practices with employees and tax planning. I have also been involved with disciplinary and litigation issues. This has been not so much with malpractice as with sexual improprieties or drug abuse. I have seen people trying to interpret the laws on their own.

When a licensed professional is opening a private practice, what are some of the key legal issues for which they should seek the guidance of a reputable attorney?
Typically we get brought in after the fact when there's a problem—for example, medical doctors form an LLC and then questions come up about whether that is permitted. There are accountants who can assist you with setting up a practice, but it is a good idea to consult with a health care attorney. Many states require that you get permission from the state board before incorporating your practice. Before beginning a practice, you can receive counsel on the various business entities.

There are benefits, for example, in setting up a professional corporation. If you have more than one of the same professional, the benefit of a professional corporation is that the partners do not have responsibilities for the other partners' behaviors. If your practice is within different professions and you are the owner, you can be held responsible. If there is litigation, the entity can be sued. As the owner or shareholder, it really is your liability, but not your personal assets.

Forming a partnership or limited liability corporation (LLC) can also keep your liability for the work of other professionals limited. As the owner of the practice, you can limit your exposure to what you yourself have actually done with your own clients. If you are a sole provider, there is minimal reason to set up a professional corporation for these reasons. Protect personal assets from creditor exposure (you can't really protect your professional assets).

Can therapists and psychologists work as independent contractors for organizations?

Many organizations and clinics hire psychologists on a contractor basis. The issue of whether it is a true independent contractor relationship comes down to whether the firm directs and controls the person's activities. If they tell you that you must work 9 to 5, they give you the employee manual, and so on, I have to wonder whether it is really an independent contractor position. By definition, a contractor can decline to take the engagement. Look at the IRS's standards about whether you are an employee.

What are some new and important considerations for independent mental health professionals since HIPAA?

One of the things we have come across is that people do not understand the difference between being a covered entity and being a business associate. For example, with your lawyer or accountant or billing company, you should have business associate agreements stating that they may see some of your client information.

The use of e-mail and how you can properly protect identity, especially with behavioral health, is a very important issue. This is becoming an issue because many malpractice insurance companies are focusing on the fact that there is exposure for claims if information gets out on the Internet. They recommend using a secure server that encrypts the information until the client or professional logs onto the web site with a password. This is one way that people do it, but a problem is most patients do not have encryption software in their house. Most people are not as strict as they could be with this.

A good example of a secure program is in telemedicine. Big psychiatry and psychology programs are using this method. In Arizona, for instance, there is a state-run telemedicine system where most psychiatrists do therapy. It is real time with secured lines. The equipment required for this level of security is expensive. In this case, the state is sponsoring setup.

Therapy over the telephone—there is a real issue here. You have to ask yourself, are you properly licensed to provide services in the state where the client is for the consultation or therapy session? Most regulators have not kept up with these issues, so the law is not yet set. Pennsylvania is trying to pass the law that any out-of-state provider has to be fully licensed with malpractice insurance in Pennsylvania. That has not passed yet, so there are not set limits at this point. If you are in Pennsylvania and the client is in Ohio, the situation is unclear. From a malpractice perspective, you are in two different jurisdictions, and this opens you up for potential liability. The plaintiff can decide in which state they want to bring their claim to sue you. This is called forum shopping—choosing where to bring claim.

What are some good resources for professionals trying to find an attorney with experience in all of these areas?

The best source to recommend is the American Health Lawyers Association. These are attorneys who devote most of their practice to health care advice. Since lawyers cannot advertise their specialties, you can still find a lawyer who specializes in heath care. By associating with this type of group, the lawyer is identified with the health care arena.

Interview with Dr. Marta Otero

Marta Otero holds a doctorate in psychology and is in private practice in Dallas/Fort Worth, Texas. She can be reached via www.drmarta.com.

How did you decide to go into private practice?

I had a positive experience when I was young. I had to be tested for ADHD (inattentive type) and I continued to see the psychologist off and on whenever I had a problem through college. I wanted to be like him and help others the way he helped me. I wanted to be in private practice and follow in his footsteps. To me, it was never an option to do anything else in psychology. I also wanted to be my own boss and be able to pursue what interests me instead of working for an organization. In other words, I have the freedom to teach adjunct, write articles or books, see clients, test . . . The opportunities are endless. Lastly, family is important to me so I wanted to be in private practice to give me the flexibility I need for that. So far, I am happy with my choice, despite having to learn all of the different aspects that are not taught in school (i.e., the business side of it).

I chose to do an interview with you because you have developed a booming fee-for-service practice in less than one year. How did you do it?

Marketing and referrals! I meet with primary care physicians, pediatricians, school counselors, university and private school admissions departments, oncologists, attorneys, and any other type of legal, academic, and health care professional that might be able to provide me with referrals. I always have my cards available and I remain very active in the community. When someone refers me a client, I write them a personal thank-you note. I also take them to lunches and try to remain in their life so that they don't forget me. I do this by sending birthday cards, holiday cards, and so on. My intention is to do something marketing-wise (a phone call, lunch, a letter) about once a week. I also have one advertisement in a free magazine that has resulted in several clients. That is the only ad I have but it has been a good investment.

I have often supplemented my practice by contracting with Social Security attorneys and Social Security providers that require testing to approve benefits. This can also be done by contracting with child protective services, mental health and mental retardation offices, and the like. The pay is relatively low but the practice is good and it helps your income—it gives you something rather than nothing while you are building a client base. The work they require can range from a mental status exam and write-up, which pays $50, to full batteries, which pay about $500.

I began with a sliding fee scale. As I got more successful, I omitted the scale, except for a few special cases. I have had to teach myself to be tough in terms of collecting. Unless someone has a valid reason and a prior agreement with me, I treat my business as a business—fee rendered upon service. It is not like going to a dentist or physician where insurance pays. It is like going to a restaurant or getting your hair cut—you pay immediately. With the type of job we do, this is often hard but it's necessary. My mentor always reminds me that we have only one thing to sell and that is our time. If we don't respect that ourselves, as clinicians, we will not fare as well in private practice.

What marketing efforts have worked well and what has worked less well?

The main lesson I have learned is that I only learned to be a therapist in school. I didn't learn how to do anything else. I often wonder if this can even be taught in school. I have been lucky to have the world's greatest mentor, who is patient and knowledgeable. My advice to people is to find a mentor or supervisor when starting out. Don't try to do this alone. Even if you have to pay a mentor or a business coach for counsel, it is 100 percent worth it!

Admit when you know nothing. Ethically speaking, as well as from a personal standpoint, your clients are depending on you to know what you're doing. Having a chip on your shoulder or too much confidence could hurt you. Be humble and open to learning from anyone who will give you advice. Be a sponge. You don't have to do everything that others suggest, but listen to those with more experience. I still contact one of my friends from graduate school to bounce ideas around. I am forever grateful to his peer suggestions. Also, I have my own therapist. Without her, I might be in big trouble. The stresses of wearing the many hats and starting private practice can affect my personal life. She has helped me achieve better organization, self-care, and stress-reducing techniques.

What are the best and worst things about working in private practice?

Flexibility, freedom, never-ending opportunities, making your own decisions and money—these are the best things.

The most difficult thing is the business side of it. It is hard to be consistent about the business side. We have to stand by the fact that the services we provide are worth the prices we charge. If we stand firm, we will distinguish ourselves from other mental health providers. For example, I have one woman who is on Social Security and without a lot of money. She takes the bus and is always on time. Coming for therapy is an expense she values. I am more likely to provide her with a sliding scale fee or let her run a balance. I have another woman who ran up a huge balance (one of my biggest mistakes). She has children in private school and doesn't let them want for a thing. When I asked how she might pay off her balance, she became irate. Because I am more of a therapist than a business-woman, I allowed her to run this balance. The lessons I learned are that (1) this can't be done; (2) we as clinicians *must* value the time we sell; (3) we *must* be business savvy; and (4) without our own confidence, perseverance, and tenacity to learn how all of these hats fit together in the puzzle of private practice, success is more difficult.

How do you differentiate yourself from other mental health providers?

I have discovered that I am really good with clients age 14 and up. The bulk of my clients are in high school and college. Once you find where your talents lie, follow it. If you try to spread yourself too thin you provide less effective services. I also respect all others and don't try to do their job. I am the first one to say I need to consult or refer out to whoever can provide them with the best services. I have had that pay me back with referrals later from those I suggested go elsewhere and from those to whom I made referrals. Integrity goes a long way. Another thing I have used a lot is the fact that I speak Spanish. Being bilingual and working with people in their dominant language is a huge skill to have. So find your niche and *do* it.

What are some of the characteristics of therapists who, in your opinion, are most successful in private practice?

Ethics, integrity, organization, consultation, self-care, perseverance, tough skin, creativity, ingenuity . . . You don't have to have had the highest GPA or even have had the best graduate training. You have to have a good mentor and/or peer, be a good therapist, have a natural ability, be ready to wear *many* hats, and have a lot of patience and a sense of humor when you make mistakes. Know your ethics and your state's rules/regulations, and follow them at all times. This job does not come with an easy paycheck, by any means, and there is no safety net.

RESOURCES

BOOKS

Berstein, B.E., & Hartsell, T. L. (2004). *The portable lawyer for mental health professionals: An A-Z guide to protecting your clients, your practice and yourself* (2nd ed.). New York: John Wiley & Sons, Inc.

Frager, S. (2000). Successful private practice: *Winning strategies for mental health professionals*. New York: John Wiley & Sons, Inc.

Grodzki, L. (2000). *Building your ideal private practice*. New York: W. W. Norton.

Kolt, L. (1999). *How to build a thriving fee-for-service practice: Integrating the healing side with the business side of psychotherapy*. San Diego, CA: Academic Press.

Hunt, H. (2004). *Essentials of private practice: streamlining costs, procedures, and policies for less stress*. New York: W. W. Norton.

Stout, C. E., & Grand, L. C. (2005). *Getting started in private practice: The complete guide to building your mental health practice*. Hoboken, NJ: John Wiley & Sons, Inc. (*Author's note: If you can buy just one book, I recommend this one.*)

Vitale, J. (2003). *The greatest money-making secret in history!* Bloomington, IN: First Books.

WEB SITES

Medical Arts Press for templates:

www.medicalarts.com

Sites to submit articles:

www.ezinearticles.com or www.ideamarketers.com

Credit card charges:

www.professionalcharges.com

APA ethical guidelines:

www.apa.org/ethics/

Small Business Association:

www.sba.gov

TERMINOLOGY

CPT code Clinical procedure terminology used to describe the type of services rendered.

debt equity A form of financing that is based on loan funding from banks or other financial institutions.

forum shopping   The plaintiff's choosing where to bring claim when a therapist has practiced in two or more states.

risk management   The policies and procedures that reinforce the ethical and legal practices of your company or organization and reduce the likelihood of adverse legal action or litigation

SBA   United States Small Business Administration

secured loan   A loan that is typically offered by commercial banks that requires some form of collateral as security.

strategic referral partner (SRP)   A referral source who directs potential clients to you based on the win-win nature of your relationship.

CHAPTER 9

Life and Executive Coaching

The test of a good coach is that when they leave, others will carry on successfully.

Author unknown

One can never feel content to creep when one has an impulse to soar.

Helen Keller

THE FIELD OF COACHING

Coaching is a field that has attracted many mental health professionals over the past decade. It has been a rapidly increasing field, both in terms of the number of coaches entering the field and the number of people utilizing coaches. According to an article on executive coaching in the November 2004 edition of the *Harvard Business Review*, an estimated $1 billion is spent annually on executive coaching (Sherman & Freas, 2004).

Many factors can account for the widespread interest of therapists in the field of coaching, including their desire to:

- Work without the confines of managed care.
- Pursue an equal partnership between coach and client rather than a therapeutic relationship, which typically has a power differential.
- Break the confines of geography and work with clients across the country since coaching is traditionally conducted over the telephone.
- Help people pursue their greatest life or professional goals rather than reduce psychopathology.

- Earn a higher hourly rate.
- Minimize burnout resulting from working with clients on problems (with therapy) by instead working with clients on opportunities and growth.

WHAT IS COACHING?

According to the web site of the International Coach Federation (ICF):

> Professional Coaching is a professional partnership between a qualified coach and an individual or team that supports the achievement of extraordinary results, based on goals set by the individual or team. Through the process of coaching, individuals focus on the skills and actions needed to successfully produce their personally relevant results. The individual or team chooses the focus of conversation, while the coach listens and contributes observations and questions as well as concepts and principles which can assist in generating possibilities and identifying actions. Through the coaching process the clarity that is needed to support the most effective actions is achieved. Coaching accelerates the individual's or team's progress by providing greater focus and awareness of possibilities leading to more effective choices. Coaching concentrates on where individuals are now and what they are willing to do to get where they want to be in the future. (www.coachfederation.org/aboutcoaching/about.asp).

The ICF web site goes on to differentiate the coaching from psychotherapy:

> Coaching can be distinguished from therapy in a number of ways. First, coaching is a profession that supports personal and professional growth and development based on individual-initiated change in pursuit of specific actionable outcomes. These outcomes are linked to personal or professional success. Coaching is forward moving and future focused. Therapy, on the other hand, deals with healing pain, dysfunction and conflict within an individual or a relationship between two or more individuals. The focus is often on resolving difficulties arising from the past which hamper an individual's emotional functioning in the present, improving overall psychological functioning, and dealing with present life and work circumstances in more emotionally healthy ways. Therapy outcomes often include improved emotional/feeling states. While positive feelings/emotions may be a natural outcome of

coaching, the primary focus is on creating actionable strategies for achieving specific goals in one's work or personal life. The emphasis in a coaching relationship is on action, accountability and follow-through.

The differentiation between past and present work applies to many forms of therapy, but some types of therapy (such as cognitive-behavioral therapy) focus primarily on the present. Coaching also sounds at times like humanistic psychotherapy since it is not about giving advice and is about genuine empathy and positive regard. In my view, one of the most important distinctions made by ICF is that the intended outcome in coaching is not improved emotional states or the reduction of problems with psychological functioning. Instead, coaching typically has the goal of achieving specific work or life goals.

THE PROCESS OF COACHING

Coaching tends to have a clear series of stages from the initial session to assessment to goal setting to the action phase.

INITIAL SESSION

Most coaches offer prospective clients a complimentary first session to learn about the individual's interest in coaching, answer any questions that the person may have, describe coaching, see whether the coach and prospective client are a good match, and make a referral if necessary. This first session lays the groundwork for coaching, and the coach may provide additional resources like questionnaires, relevant articles, book recommendations, assessments, or models.

Many coaches also recommend that the potential client take advantage of other coach's free initial sessions so the clients can be sure that they find the right match with a coach. One of the fundamental differences between coaching and therapy is the partner status with coaching. There is no power differential, and it would not be strange or unethical to meet your client for lunch. As such, coaches heavily emphasize the relationship equality from the beginning and encourage clients to be sure they are compatible with their coach.

THE ASSESSMENT PHASE

After the client and coach decide to work together, most coaches conduct an assessment process, which consists of a combination of interviewing and assessment tools to provide objective information to improve the individual's self-understanding and to create a benchmark for setting goals and evaluating the progress of coaching. For an example of coaching assessments visit www.CoachingAssessments.com. Create forms and self-assessments for your web site at www.AssessmentGenerator.com.

I believe that therapists make such excellent coaches because of their assessment abilities that can be utilized in the first few sessions. Not only are therapists well trained in effectively assessing a client's situation, but they are well qualified to make the decision about whether the client is better suited for coaching versus therapy. During conversations with some coaching colleagues who are not therapists, I have at times questioned the ethics of having a particular client receiving coaching and not therapy. When psychological or emotional issues the primary issue the differential between coaching and therapy becomes foggy. For example, if the client appears somewhat anxious or depressed, but that is not the reason they have approached you (the reason is more of a coaching topic), is therapy or coaching more appropriate? Some coaches do not know how to make this distinction. Most coaches recognize that if someone is looking for help with "feeling depressed" or "having panic attacks," then therapy is indicated. However, many coaches do not recognize how feeling "bored" or "unmotivated" can be warning signs of depression. I believe that therapists' understanding of the entire spectrum of emotional functioning helps them to be great coaches and to best assess the situation.

GOAL SETTING

Setting specific measurable goals is an important component of coaching—sometimes the *most* important component. Often when clients become crystal clear on their life or career goals, they can easily begin accomplishing them. Goals are reassessed during the process of coaching, and assessments are continually conducted to determine the client's progress toward the goals. Coaching is similar to cognitive-behavioral therapy in this respect.

An example of a goal within life coaching is, "Develop improved work-life balance by limiting work hours to 40 hours per week." An example of a goal within executive coaching is, "Improve leadership skills by strengthening my core strengths and delegating the other areas in an effective and assertive manner." Notice how the goals are measurable and specific. A goal of simply "improving leadership" would not be as effective as a specific coaching goal.

APPROACH, MODELS, TECHNIQUES, AND CONCEPTS

According to the ICF, coaching draws from a variety of disciplines, including the behavioral sciences, business and management, spiritual traditions, and the arts and humanities. Various models and concepts are employed to increase the individual's self-awareness and interpersonal awareness, shift perspectives, motivate action and change, and add new frameworks for addressing opportunities and challenges.

While therapy utilizes a variety of techniques and approaches based on the therapist's theoretical orientation, the client's presenting issue, and the therapist's own style, coaching typically incorporates an appreciative approach. This approach has similarities to solution-focused therapy in that it focuses on what is right and what's working. The coach then helps the client to build on what has been working and focus on what is needed to get where the client wants to go. There is some use of social-learning theory in the way the coach often models effective communication skills and methods for individuals or teams. The appreciative approach helps people to envision and therefore achieve success rather than focusing in on the problems. It is a proactive or forward-thinking technique. Similarly to cognitive therapy, it relies a great deal on Socratic questioning.

When I began coaching clients, I found the transition from the therapy relationship to a coaching relationship to be somewhat difficult because it does feel different. Once I became used to it, however, I really started to enjoy the absence of a power differential. For instance, one of my small business marketing clients who lived across the country was in town, so we met for coffee. You would typically not do this sort of thing (i.e., meeting at a restaurant) with a therapy client. The equality of the relationship is one way that coaching differs significantly from both therapy and consulting. Consultants come in as experts and provide advice and specific feedback. Coaches act as partners, mentors, and confidants who ask the right questions and help clients gain answers for themselves to help the clients achieve their own goals (not the coach's goal for them).

It is important to note that specific interpersonal and multicultural variables can create a power differential in coaching as they do with any relationship. The ethical coach always keeps in mind the impact of race, socioeconomic status, religion, work position, culture, language, and other variables of diversity that can impact on the relationship.

COACH TRAINING

Many therapists who are thinking about transitioning into coaching wonder whether they should get training and how to do so.

WHY TO GET TRAINING

There is not currently a requirement that coaches be certified in order to coach independently as there is in many behavioral healthcare professions. Calling yourself a coach is similar to calling yourself a consultant. The title *coach* is not a regulated or professional title. This, of course, does not mean that you do not need to know what you are doing, just that you are not *required* to have certification. Because you want to really know what you are doing, a good case can be built for receiving some form of coach training.

First, you want to be able to do the best work possible. Coach training can give you a great deal of experience with the process of coaching and what tends to work and does not work. Second, training helps you to establish your credentials. Third, coaching is a highly competitive field and you will want to have some guidance to not only help you coach, but to learn how to build a coaching practice.

If you do not want to or cannot currently afford to enroll in a formal training, another option is to find a practicing coach to mentor you. Some coaches will mentor for free, while most will offer a discount from their typical hourly rate to mentor you or provide consultation on your coaching cases. This is a practical option and a good alternative to more expensive training programs. You can learn more about the coaching world and get hands-on experience and support.

Another option is to enroll in some day, weekend, or week-long workshops to learn more about coaching before you commit yourself to a program. Attending a workshop may help you clarify your interests in coaching and select the appropriate training program. If, for instance, you have not decided whether you want to do executive coaching, you could do a workshop to learn more. If you like the workshop and become inspired to learn more about coaching businesspeople, you can look for a program that has an emphasis on executive coaching.

WHERE TO GET TRAINING

There are many coach training programs available, with varying strengths and degrees of effectiveness. If you are still in graduate school, check whether your school has a training program, as more and more universities and colleges are beginning to offer coaching training, particularly in executive coaching. For example, the Massachusetts School of Professional Psychology has recently launched a new Professional Executive Coaching Certificate Program. Many other graduate programs offer classes in coaching and consultation.

You can also elect to take courses in other departments at your university. During my MBA program, I designed a self-study in executive coaching and organizational development, and received supervision by an expert in management and organizational behavioral, Bud Baker. I was able to do academic research through which I learned a great deal. I also engaged in interesting conversations with a mentor and learned much from his knowledge about how businesses work. This was an excellent way to learn about coaching executives and impacting organizations. You may be able to create a similar independent study within your psychology, counseling, or social work program. You can find an executive coach or life coach in your community to supervise and mentor you. By doing this, you can get course credit and learn a great deal about coaching.

There are many schools and training programs dedicated to helping coaches. One consideration when looking for a school is whether you want to get certified as a coach. If you are interested in obtaining certification in coaching by the ICF, check their web site to see whether the program you are interested in is an ICF accredited program. They list all their certified training programs on http://www.coachfederation.org /training/programs.asp?prog=1. You can also look at their approved Continuing Coaching Education Programs at http://www.coachfederation.org /credentialing/programs/cce-programs.asp.

In choosing a program, you may want to focus on a curriculum that trains therapists and helping professionals who are transitioning over to coaching. If you go to a more general training program and you already have extensive education in counseling and psychotherapy, you may find that you have already learned many of the skills discussed. Several or most of the other students in your courses may be coming from completely different industries, like engineering, marketing, advertising, or law. They may not have any experience whatsoever in interviewing, asking thought-provoking questions, conceptualizing a client situation, or promoting change. Therefore, you may feel more comfortable in a program with other therapists. On the other hand, some therapists-turned-coaches say that they learned a lot about the business world and other disciplines from other students in their coaching classes. The decision will be a personal one that you can come to after researching several programs.

I highly recommend looking into the coaching programs created by Terri Levine, one of the top professional coaches in the industry. Terri is the founder and CEO of Comprehensive Coaching U (www .comprehensivecoachingu.com) and The Coaching Institute (www.coach institute.com), internationally recognized programs that provide training to individuals and organizations that want to learn coaching skills.

Some other examples of programs that have training specifically for therapists include the Institute for Life Coach Training (www.lifecoach training.com); the College of Executive Coaching (www.executivecoach college.com); and Mentor Coach (www.mentorcoach.com).

Interview with Ben Dean, PhD

Ben Dean is the founder of Mentor Coach (www.mentorcoach .com), an organization that trains therapists to become coaches; and co-founder with Martin Seligman, PhD, of Authentic Happiness Coaching (www.authentichappiness.org).

Why do you think therapists make good coaches?
Therapists already have many of the skills that make good coaches. Therapists think they should abandon their therapy skills for coaching, but this is not necessarily true. The number one skill for coaching is empathic listening. Therapists are used to working with people to achieve goals. They are attuned to building relationship.

What might make a therapist more suited to coaching than therapy?
People who enjoy working with the high-functioning side of clients can be well suited to coaching. Everyone has a high-functioning and lower-functioning side. Coaching focuses on the higher-functioning side.

In my workshops, I ask people to list the characteristics of a great mentor. I then say, "Ask yourself: Is this path of being a transformative mentor in the life of others the right path for you?" At midlife, there is a call to live the unlived parts of your life and be authentic. It is not enough to say that you want to be a coach because you want to work with higher-functioning clients. It needs to be the right path for you, what you are meant to do.

Another reason that therapists sometimes enjoy coaching is that coaching can feel better. When you are working with a client as a therapist, you empathize with the misery and discomfort that the client is going through, whereas with coaching you are empathizing with the excitement.

What might some therapists need to unlearn to become effective as coaches?

In coaching, you are not typically deepening affect. You do not focus on the past or mine the past. You focus on helping people gain a vision of where they want to go. A really good therapist understands the contribution of the past, and this can be true for coaches as well. Appropriately used, an understanding of the past can give an understanding of the coaching client, but the focus remains in the present.

A therapist may need to unlearn the therapist identity and learn the identity of a coach to start feeling comfortable. Certain ethical boundaries are the same but some are different. More self-disclosure exists with coaching. A coach and client may become friends, and you could meet with them socially and exchange gifts.

The key difference between therapy and coaching is in the goal of the relationship. Toward a coaching goal, it is useful to use everything you have learned. It can be from your therapy practice to school to watching Captain Kangaroo. Whatever you know, you bring to the coaching.

One of the areas that can be difficult for therapists is that therapists are used to having mastery with therapy. It can be uncomfortable trying on the new hat.

What are some things that a therapist should look for in selecting a good training program?

Look for a good track record in helping therapists make the transition to coaching. This is very important. Find out whether you would be in a program with other helping professionals or people from different professions.

Ask whether the training program teaches group coaching skills in addition to individual coaching. One of the most exciting ways to build a practice is through virtual groups. We have groups where coaches can gain experience.

Ask if they support you and show you how to get clients. Also ask whether you are taught ways to handle risk and ethical issues by an expert in the intersection of risk management, coaching, and therapy. What options are there for support from a community of clinician coaches? Do people who have been extremely successful come back to talk about what they have done to make the transition?

We suggest that people start off as generalist coaches and then they can develop a specialty or a niche. A training program should provide generalist training with some opportunity to specialize. For instance, with Mentor Coach, people can pick a combination of master classes in small business coaching and executive coaching.

In your opinion, what makes a highly successful coach?
The first thing is very good training and ongoing supervision and support. The best coaches are constantly learning. You should understand the research and evidence-based coaching interventions. You need to know how to get clients. You need to be willing to practice things that make you anxious. When you try new things, you will feel anxious at first. If you can practice with anxiety, as your mastery increases, your confidence will increase. If you're doing niche coaching, have expertise in that niche area. Many of the successful coaches also do group coaching, trainings, and have other sources of passive income. It frees you up to have more than one source of income.

LIFE COACHING VERSUS EXECUTIVE COACHING

You may have heard life coaching called "personal coaching," "success coaching," or a number of other names. In coaching, there is generally a distinction between personal or life coaching and the more business- and career-focused coaching, which is often called "executive coaching," "career coaching," "work performance coaching," "business coaching," or "management coaching."

My coaching practice, for example, is primarily a business coaching practice split between executive coaching with top corporate executives and small business coaching with professional and entrepreneurs who are building their businesses and careers. Therefore, my coaching title is "Business Coach" and not "Life Coach." I typically recommend to my clients that they choose to specialize in either life coaching or executive coaching since they are such different fields. It is much better to be seen as a specialist than a jack of all trades but master of none.

LIFE COACHING

Life coaching focuses on helping clients to clarify, prioritize, develop, and achieve their major life goals. Some goals that many life coaches help their clients to attain include:

- Create a balanced life.
- Become accountable for life choices.
- Work towards a significant life change or goal.
- Improve goal-setting abilities.
- Enhance relationships.
- Build parenting confidence or skills.
- Re-evaluate future direction in life.
- Enhance communication abilities.

Life coaching has its pros and cons as compared to executive coaching. The primary pro for therapists transitioning their careers toward coaching is that many therapeutic skills are readily transferable to life coaching. Another positive aspect of life coaching is that it can be deeply rewarding because you are working with clients who are achieving their own personal mission in their lives.

One potential negative aspect that I see with life coaching versus executive coaching is obtaining new clients. While the field is continually changing, there are not always obvious direct referral sources for life coaching clients as there are for executive coaching clients. For example, a human resources director at an organization can fill your executive coaching practice, while you may find one life coaching client here and one there. Of course, with either field, a fantastic referral partner can fill your practice.

Another difficulty with life coaching is keeping your therapy hat off and your coaching hat on. If a client you are coaching begins to experience a relationship or other problem, it is common for a therapist to switch toward therapy mode, which may not be in the best interest of a coaching client. It may also be unethical, if you are seeing the client for coaching and not for therapy. Since the topics in executive coaching are so different from therapy topics, the distinction between therapy and coaching may be more clear in your mind with executive coaching than with life coaching.

Interview with Leslie Hoy, MA, LPC

Leslie Hoy is a personal coach and certified corporate trainer. Her company, Hi-Performance Coaching and Training, can be reached at www.hiperformance.net.

You do both coaching and private practice therapy. Can you tell the readers how you manage and differentiate them?

The easiest way to define the difference between the two is that in my private therapy practice, I address issues related to a diagnosis; in my coaching practice, I do not. For example, in therapy, I address issues related to depression, anxiety, chemical dependency, and so on. In my coaching practice, if I determine that someone might be depressed or exhibiting disabling anxiety, I would refer them to a therapist and, in some cases, an MD. It has been my personal coaching experience that I wait until they have addressed the therapy issue before I resume coaching. It can be overwhelming to engage in both therapy and coaching at the same time.

Another difference between the two is that I see therapy clients at my office. For coaching clients, I usually conduct the coaching sessions over the phone or on-site at their workplace. Billing is another area in which there is a big difference. For therapy clients, I bill at the time of service (or bill their insurance after the visit), whereas with a coaching client, I typically bill at the beginning of the month for that month's services.

Do you have any other advice for therapists who are interested in getting into coaching?

If you are currently employed by a company or agency, I would encourage you to keep your job as you are building your other sources of income—whether that be starting a private practice or starting a coaching business. I would also start putting money aside for when you leave your regular job to go into private practice or coaching. Cash flow can be an issue and it is always good to have a cushion of money available.

I think it is also extremely helpful to build a good professional support network for yourself. For the past four years, I have met with a group of three to four colleagues on a monthly basis. It is a great time to share information, obtain advice, vent, and just have the camaraderie. I also have another coach friend whom I have talked with via phone, on a monthly basis over the past two and a half years. We exchange resources, brainstorm, and offer each other accountability.

Executive Coaching

Executive coaching is the process of helping executives to develop their key abilities such that their work performance exceeds expectations. Executive coaching may be a better option for you than life coaching if you are interested in working with the business world.

Areas that executive coaching tends to focus on include:

- Develop critical leadership abilities.
- Empower and motivate your employees and improve work team performance.
- Earn respect and recognition.
- Positively persuade and influence others.
- Increase assertiveness and rapid decision making skills.
- Create a competitive advantage in your career.
- Quickly reach and surpass your career goals.
- Increase your income or get promoted.

Executive coaching has vastly increased in popularity over the past decade, in part due to changing business environments. Business landscapes are rapidly developing and employees are expected to keep up with the new pace. Companies are merging and downsizing, and the restructuring creates many new challenges and opportunities for employees and organizations. In our new century, managers are expected to be leaders, and leaders are expected to be increasingly visionary and high-performing. Because the business world is so competitive, executives fear that they will be let go if they are not performing optimally—and this is often the case. Human resources managers and other directors in organizations have been turning to executive coaches for assistance with developing their employees.

One of the advantages to executive coaching over personal coaching is that the average fees are higher. While you typically charge higher fees for executive coaching, your business expenses are often higher as well. You need to develop impeccable marketing materials if you are marketing to corporations. Business networking groups are expensive to join. The upside is that you often have access to more individuals as well as work teams.

Interview with Stephen Fairley, MA, RCC

Stephen Fairley is a best-selling author and president of Today's Leadership Coaching, Inc. Their web site is www.TodaysLeader ship.com and they can be reached at (888) 588-5891.

You have an extensive background in mental health. What skills did you find to be transferable to executive coaching, and what are new skills that mental health practitioners must learn?
Let me start by saying that I firmly believe coaching is fundamentally different from counseling and psychotherapy. That being said, there is some overlap in terms of the skills you use. The skills I found to be most transferable from psychology to coaching are mostly basic ones: active listening and setting SMART goals, identifying the client's strengths and weaknesses, creating a game plan, keeping the client on track. Whether you're working with a client in psychotherapy or coaching, you still need to be a good listener and you still need to ask insightful questions. However, there are five major paradigm shifts therapists and psychologists need to make in order to successfully transition from counseling to coaching.

1. *Problems*. The easiest way to explain the different kinds of problems you will encounter is with the following model. Imagine a scale that extends from −10 to +10, where negative 10 is severe psychopathology, zero is "normal," and positive 10 is a "superstar." It is the realm of psychotherapy to help people who are at a negative 4, 5, or even 10 and move them back to zero or normalcy. Coaching, on the other hand, starts with people who are at a 3, 4, or 5 and helps move toward a positive 10. While some may find this to be an overly simplistic model, it is easy to explain to clients and others when differentiating between your psychotherapy practice and your coaching business.
2. *People*. The people you coach will often be in a leadership position with management responsibilities. In my experience, they are much higher functioning than your typical psychotherapy client and will expect you to be more directive with them and be very active in the session. They will not hire you if you only ask good questions; you must also provide solid answers, especially in the business world, where they hire you for your expertise.
3. *Process*. The process you use in a coaching session will be much more directive than you may be comfortable with in your counseling ses-

sion. Clients expect you to take charge of the session and actively work with them as a partner in the process to help them rapidly achieve their goals. They are not so much concerned with insight as they are with action and accountability. I tell my clients, "Insight without action leads to frustration and failure." In business it's all about execution and accountability, not insight and information.

4. *Price.* According to the research I conducted for my book *Getting Started in Personal and Executive Coaching*, the average personal coach charges $130 per hour with a range of $40 to $300 per hour. The average business or executive coach charges $200 per hour with a range of $100 to $700 per hour. Most professional coaches charge on a monthly or quarterly basis, rather than an hourly basis, and they receive their fee at the beginning of each month. In small companies the person being coached usually pays the coach; in larger companies it is often the company who does the billing, except when the individual is asking for career coaching to make a transition.

5. *Place.* More than 70 percent of coaching is conducted over the telephone, not face to face. Many therapists have found this to be a difficult adjustment, there are some benefits: You can conduct coaching sessions from anywhere there is a telephone; you can easily see clients back to back; you can remove or reduce your office space; and it is often easier on both the coach's and client's schedule. Some coaches, including me, combine face to face with telephone sessions.

You transitioned from mental health to executive coaching and have been fantastically successful in the coaching world. How did you transition?

The theoretical orientation I was most drawn toward in my psychotherapy practice was a combination of cognitive-behavioral and brief strategic therapy, so the transition from counseling to coaching was fairly easy for me from a psychological perspective. The financial transition was more difficult, so I decided to set up an apprenticeship with a local business coach who had a long track record of success. Over the course of a year I learned a great deal, and in 2000 I launched my company, Today's Leadership Coaching.

What do you recommend that graduate students do to begin gaining experience with executive coaching?

Read good business books and magazines. I know graduate students are already overloaded with homework, but to make it in executive or business coaching you must know the world of business, and no psychology graduate program that I've ever heard of teaches you that. In fact, many of your professors may have never worked outside of an academic setting. If possible, take a couple business courses on leadership, management, marketing, sales, or economics. It doesn't matter if they are for credit or not. What you're looking for are people and experiences that will expose you to how business leaders think, how a company works, and the language of business. Just like psychology, business has its own terminology—ROI, CEO, COO, CFO, and 360 assessment, just to name a few.

What do you recommend that practicing therapists or psychologists do to gain experience with executive coaching?

There are dozens of coach training programs and a few that specialize in helping therapists make the transition. Look for ones who teach you more than just basic skill building. Consider forming a partnership with someone who is currently doing coaching and learning from them. If you really want to make a transition, you must learn how the business of coaching works. Visit www.MYOBforCoaches.com for more information on how to learn the business of coaching.

What are some of the personality traits that indicate a mental health practitioner may be a great executive coach?

If you enjoy working with higher-functioning clients and like fast-paced, intensive, goal-oriented sessions, then you may want to consider coaching. I believe most of these are skills that can be learned or a mind-set that can be changed.

Why are some therapists highly effective and successful with executive coaching?

From my experience, the therapists that are most effective with executives are the ones trained and skilled in brief strategic counseling or cognitive-behavioral techniques. Most clients want to achieve their goals fairly rapidly and their goals are typically behaviorally based—increase their sales numbers, successfully find another job, learn how to better communicate with their employees, or launch a new product line in the next six months. Therapists who want to primarily focus on the process of the coaching or are satisfied with asking powerful questions are usually not successful as an executive coach. It takes someone who is relatively thick-skinned, is willing to give and take direct criticism, and can talk the language of business.

What are the pros and cons of starting your own coaching company versus working with a larger company as a coach or consultant?
I'll list them for you:

Starting Your Own Coaching Company

Pros: You are your own boss (you have control of everything); it can be a great and creative process; you can specialize in any area you want.

Cons: You are your own boss (everything depends on you); there is no accountability; lack of financial stability.

Working with a Larger Coaching Company

Pros: They will usually find the work for you; you can choose to accept it or not.

Cons: You receive a lower fee; the work is not guaranteed; they often want you to push their programs to everyone you talk to.

What are the pros and cons of attending one of the coaching schools and becoming certified as a coach?
Certification as a coach is not mandatory and probably will not be for another several years. In 1999 there were only 15 coach training programs worldwide. There are now more than 160. Many of them simply teach basic skills that you learned back in graduate school. Being a certified coach currently does not mean much of anything in the business world, except when targeting Fortune 500 companies. If you are seriously looking for coach training, I recommend visiting www.peer.ca; it has a comprehensive list of all the different programs around the world and is an objective resource.

Any other comments about executive coaching as a career path for mental health professionals?
I've often said there are three things therapists don't like to talk about: money, marketing, and managed care. I recommend that you:

- Deemphasize your educational credentials; instead, emphasize your experience.
- Make up separate business cards with your coaching title on it.
- Create separate marketing materials for your coaching and psychotherapy practices.

- Go to networking events where your prospects go.
- Set aside a specific amount of time every week to work on your transition.
- Find a marketing coach to help you clearly understand the process.
- Develop a timeline for making the change (it usually takes professionals one to two years).

BUILDING YOUR COACHING BUSINESS

You can be the best coach in the world, but if you are not marketing your business and getting clients, it won't help anyone

MARKETING

Marketing a coaching practice can be difficult because many potential clients or prospects do not feel they *need* coaching in the same way that they *need* to overcome depression, a debilitating anxiety, or a family crisis. In fact, many coaches are not marketing their practices well enough to gain clients. According to Stephen Fairley's research (Fairley & Stout, 2004), more than 50 percent of practicing coaches are making less than $20,000 per year and have less than 10 paying clients in their practices. In fact, he found that 73 percent of coaches make less than $10,000 in their first year of practice and less than 11 percent of coaches make more than $50,000 a year during their second year of practice. Marketing and sales are the keys to growing your coaching business. If you feel these are not your strong points, seriously consider hiring a marketing or sales coach or consultant to help you out. It may be the most important business investment that you make.

Marketing your coaching business will utilize all the marketing information discussed in Chapters 3 and 4. I'll summarize the marketing materials and activities here.

The marketing materials that you will need to best promote your practice include:

- *Business cards*. Use the back of the card as well to bullet the benefits of your coaching.
- A *high-quality web site*. It is a good idea to include audio and video to personalize it and show the client the interpersonal nature of the coaching and importance of the client-coach match.

- *A brochure*. Your brochure should be in full color and not too busy with words and images. If you are doing executive coaching, the quality of this brochure is even more important since it will need to be at the same level of professionalism and branding as the company to which you are pitching.
- *Information sheets*. Create one-page handouts about your different programs and services.
- *A white paper or articles*. It is great to have a white paper (a brief on your company, a Q&A sheet, a news item, or an article) to hand out to prospects for free.
- *A media kit*. This is not typically necessary, but when you get into more media work it will become essential.

Once you have your marketing materials in place, you can begin marketing. Strategic referral partners can help you build your business and will vary based on what type of coaching you do. For life coaching, referral partners may include therapists and counselors, chiropractors, clergy, community leaders, dietitians, physicians, and other coaches. For business coaching, referral partners might include financial planners and advisers, accountants, human resources directors, executive recruiters, venture capitalists, or attorneys. Find your local networking groups where your potential referral partners go. Recognize that many high-quality networking groups have significant membership fees; choose the ones that will be most helpful for you attend, and invest your time and money wisely.

Many of my business coaching clients have found that professional speaking engagements are the best way to gain visibility and clients. I have also found this to be true for my coaching practice. By speaking, you are in front of many people at once and they get a chance to know, like, and trust you. It can be a smart idea to speak for free whenever it can get you out in front of your target audience.

There are many ways to write to market your coaching practice, including writing your own e-zine, contributing articles to other e-zines, writing articles for local papers or magazines, writing free special reports or short e-books for prospects, or writing and publishing books. Writing is a great way to share your ideas and establish your credentials as an expert. Deborah Brown-Volkman (2003) suggests that you can also make money from your e-zine. Once the membership is large enough, you can recruit advertisers to pay to advertise within your newsletter.

Promotions are a great way to build visibility for your coaching business. Offering discounts, free products, free coaching sessions, and promotions through partnering with another company (buy one service and get half off the other) can attract clients.

An audio logo is the way that you introduce yourself every time you meet someone new and can interest people in your services. It describes the type of work that you do and can engender curiosity in prospects or potential referral partners. A good one is *not* "I am a life coach." It *is* "I help people to improve their communication skills and find the relationship they have always wanted."

SALES

There can be a difference between marketing, which involves increasing visibility, and sales, which involves actually gaining clients. Marketing brings prospects to you, but the sales process turns those prospects into clients. Strong and effective marketing can make the sales process easier because clients may already believe that you are credible and trustworthy by the time you have your initial conversation.

Deborah Brown-Volkman (2003) states that the fear of selling is quite common within the coaching profession. This may be because coaches came from other professions where they did not need to sell. It may also be because the coach does not have a clear program or target market, or because the coach ends the initial call by saying, "If you are interested, please get back to me and let me know." She also states that discomfort with selling may arise because the coach is too focused on money (trying to earn money or feeling uncomfortable with their fees), or because they have not hired an experienced coach to show them the way. If you are uncomfortable with the concept of selling, keep in mind that the best way to sell is not to tell people what you do. Instead it is engaging in a client-centered dialogue in which you learn about the client's needs and determine whether you can help them to address their needs (Richardson, 1998).

RESOURCES

BOOKS AND ARTICLES

Auerbach, J. E. (2001). *Personal and executive coaching: The complete guide for mental health professionals*. Pismo Beach, CA: Executive College Press.

Brown-Volkman, D. (2003). *Four steps to building a profitable coaching practice. A complete marketing research guide for coaches.* Lincoln, NE: iUniverse, Inc.

Fairley, S. G., & Stout, C. E. (2004). *Getting started in personal and executive coaching: How to create a thriving coaching practice.* New York: John Wiley & Sons, Inc.

Flaherty, J. (1999). *Coaching: Evoking excellence in others.* Boston: Butterworth Heinemann.

Fitzgerald, C., & Jennifer, G. B (2002.) *Executive coaching: Practices and perspectives* (1st ed.). Lanham, MD: National Book Network.

Fortang, L. B. (1998). *Take yourself to the top.* New York: Warner Books.

Jay, M. R. (1999). *Coach 2 the bottom line: An executive guide to coaching performance, change and transformation in organizations.* Victoria, BC, Canada: Trafford Publishing.

Peltier, B. (2001). *The psychology of executive coaching: Theory and application* (1st ed.). New York: Brunner-Routledge.

Richardson, L. (1998). *Stop telling, start selling: How to use customer-focused dialogue to close sales.* New York: McGraw-Hill.

Sherman, S., & Freas, A. (2004, November). The Wild West of Executive Coaching. *Harvard Business Review*, 82 (11) 82-90.

Whitworth, L., Kimsey-House, H., & Sandahl, P. (2003). *Co-active coaching.* Palo Alto, CA: Davies-Black Publishing.

Williams, P., & Davis, D. C. (2002.) *Therapist as life coach: Transforming your practice.* New York: W. W. Norton & Company.

WEB SITES

Listing of coaching trainings:

www.peer.ca

ICF:

www.coachfederation.org

Assessments:

www.AssessmentGenerator.com, www.CoachingAssessments.com

Coach University's coach referral service:

www.coachu.com

Worldwide Association of Business Coaches:

www.wabccoaches.com

Ben Dean's company, Mentor Coach:

www.mentorcoach.com

Coaching training programs:

Comprehensive Coaching U (www.comprehensivecoachingu.com)

The Coaching Institute (www.coachinstitute.com),

Stephen Fairley's companies:

www.TodaysLeadership.com, www.BusinessBuildingCenter.com

Overcoming marketing blocks and resistance for coaches (my company):

www.PAScoaching.com

TERMINOLOGY

appreciative inquiry   The approach to coaching that helps people to envision and achieve success. It is a solution-focused approach rather than a problem-focused approach. It is a proactive or forward-thinking technique.

audio logo   A way to introduce yourself and answer the question, "What do you do for a living?"

COIs (centers of influence)   Highly influential members of the community who have extensive networks and potential to refer many clients to you.

coaching   A process that entails a professional partnership between a qualified coach and an individual or team with the aim of supporting the achievement of extraordinary goals and accomplishments.

enrollment   The sales process during which a prospect turns into a client or customer and elects to buy your services.

executive coaching (also called business coaching)   Coaching geared toward business executives, small business owners, entrepreneurs, or professionals, to improve work performance, business profitability, leadership skills, or career satisfaction.

personal coaching (also called life coaching)   Coaching aimed at an individual's life, spiritual, or relationship goals.

start-up   A new company that is in its first few years of business. Start-ups present good opportunities for coaching because there are more and more businesses each year in need of assistance with leadership development. Entrepreneurs often lack focus and have difficulty channeling their energy, and there is great room for change and assistance.

white paper   A professionally prepared paper about your company. It may include pertinent data or news, a Q&A sheet, an article, or other relevant information that can be useful to your prospects.

CHAPTER 10

The Forensic Field

An entrepreneur assumes the risk and is dedicated and committed to the success of whatever he or she undertakes.

Victor Kiam

Chance favors the prepared mind.

Louis Pasteur

ABOUT FORENSIC PSYCHOLOGY

According to the American Board of Forensic Psychology, forensic psychology is the application of psychology to issues related to law and the legal system (www.abfp.com). This definition is broad, as is the field itself. I have chosen to include it in this book because it is expansive and full of opportunities for interesting and lucrative careers.

I will generally use the term *forensic psychology* in this chapter, but the field of behavioral social sciences as they relate to law involves psychology, social work, and psychiatry. Typically psychologists and psychiatrists complete the evaluations. Psychologists, master's-level mental health professionals, and psychiatrists are all involved in various aspects of forensic treatment programs.

The field of forensics is attractive to mental health professionals for many reasons. Among these are the intellectually stimulating nature of the work and the potential for significant compensation. The payment and compensation structure for forensic work is different from traditional therapy work, and the fees charged are typically higher. Mental health professionals tend to give time away. For instance, if a client calls you with a question, you will generally call them back to discuss it without billing them. These types of conversations with clients may go on for 20, 30, or 40 minutes and still not be billed. In therapy, if a session goes a little long (say 65 minutes instead of 50), you tend not to charge extra. This is part of the culture of behavioral health.

When you get into forensics, you enter the culture of the legal profession. Hourly rates are higher. Billing is typically conducted in 15-minute intervals and all contacts are counted toward billing, whether it is a telephone call, a half hour spent writing a report, or 20 minutes spent reviewing materials. Several of the psychologists I surveyed who do both clinical and forensic work charge around $125 per hour for their clinical work and $200 to $400 or more per hour for their forensic work. It is clearly a lucrative field.

Forensics is also a highly fascinating and intellectually rewarding field for many. The work is often very interesting and engaging. Collaborating with professionals in various disciplines is a particularly enjoyable aspect of forensic psychology work. You have the potential to collaborate with attorneys, psychiatrists, judges, probation officers, court advocates, community counselors, physicians, social workers, and numerous other professionals.

Forensic psychology is not currently a unique specialty of psychology in the way that clinical and school psychology are. It is considered to be a specialty in the way that neuropsychology or child psychology is. Typically, forensic psychology falls into a subspecialty under clinical psychology. One can call oneself a forensic psychologist when one has the proper qualifications, but these are not set in stone in the way that, in most states, to be called a psychologist you must have a doctorate and appropriate licensure. The qualifications for being called a forensic psychologist after receiving one's doctorate can be the diplomate (ABPP), having completed an internship and postdoc in forensic work or corrections, or the sufficient level of training and supervision by a forensics expert.

Other terms that are used to describe forensic psychologists include: legal psychologist, criminal psychologist, forensics expert, investigative psychologist, correctional psychologist, police psychologist.

According to Scott Kidd, PsyD, a psychologist in private practice who does forensic work, some of the key areas in which mental health professionals are working include forensic evaluations, treatment of offenders, consultation, education, and research. There is a range of forensic evaluations that psychologists commonly conduct for criminal courts, such as competency (e.g., to stand trial, to waive Miranda rights, to testify), criminal responsibility (insanity), amenability to treatment, and dangerousness or risk of recidivism. Psychologists often conduct evaluations for civil courts as well, including involuntary treatment, guardianship, disability determination, child custody, and personal injury cases.

Mental health treatment for various offender populations is another key area of forensic psychology. Clinicians provide general mental health treatment to inmate populations and forensic patients in psychiatric hospitals. In addition, more specific treatment may be provided to particular groups of offenders. For example, specialized assessment of sexual offenders is a growing area of forensic psychology. Some of the other common treatment programs include groups for domestic violence perpetrators, shoplifters, DUI offenders, and juvenile delinquents. Substance abuse treatment, anger management, social skills training, and psychoeducational programs are common psychological interventions in correctional settings, according to Stacie Vernick, PhD, a psychologist who specializes in forensics.

Other key areas of forensic psychology include case consultation, fitness-for-duty evaluations of law enforcement officers, workplace safety and violence consultation, jury selection consultation, divorce mediation, and critical incident debriefings. Of course, research, supervision, education, and expert witness testimony are other responsibilities of forensic psychologists, as well.

The field is vast and has many options for mental health professionals in treatment, evaluation, and consultation. In summary, some of the areas in which the behavioral sciences and legal issues tend to overlap include:

- Domestic violence
- Interpersonal violence, safety, and aggression
- Criminal responsibility
- Competence, both civil and criminal
- Child custody and visitation
- Emotional injury (e.g., post-traumatic stress disorder)
- Memory related to abuse and crimes
- Mental disability or psychiatric disability
- Eye witness testimony
- Medical or psychological malpractice
- Confidentiality
- Duty to warn

- Involuntary treatment
- Correctional psychiatry
- Juvenile justice
- Professional ethics issues

There is a good deal of room to specialize and create a niche for one-self. Dr. Kidd believes that the more specialized one's expertise is, the more financially rewarding the work will be. For instance, jury selection consultation, expert witness testimony, and providing certain physiological assessments are often financially rewarding opportunities. If you have an area of expertise, then marketing your knowledge can also be lucrative by conducting seminars, trainings, or workshops for other professionals.

Dr. Kidd notes that, contrary to the way forensic psychology is portrayed by the entertainment industry (e.g., *Silence of the Lambs*, *Along Came a Spider*, *Profiler*), criminal profiling makes up a *very* small portion of forensic psychological work. Most forensic psychologists never obtain training in, or are asked to conduct, criminal profiling for law enforcement agencies. There are very few employment opportunities in profiling, and this work is often done by law enforcement agents with training in profiling.

AREAS OF PRACTICE

In general, the field of forensics can be thought of as being divided into criminal and civil competencies. The work of the forensic expert typically involves either testing and evaluation, treatment and rehabilitation, or consultation and education.

CRIMINAL COMPETENCY

Criminal law is intended to prohibit and punish specific acts against humanity, such as murder, rape, or other assaults. These types of crimes are seen as acts against society and the government, rather than solely against an individual. One of the primary factors distinguishing criminal from civil law is that with criminal cases, the government is always the party bringing charges against a defendant.

Criminal cases can result in various forms of sanctions, ranging from fines to community service to incarceration to (in some states) capital punishment. An interesting issue for mental health treatment providers is whether the public and professionals believe that criminal offenders can be rehabilitated. There is controversy surrounding whether the focus in criminal law should be punishment, deterrence, or rehabilitation. It is important that a treatment provider recognize his own belief system and how that may play a role in the treatment services.

Some issues in which behavioral health professionals are involved concerning criminal competency include: competence to stand trial, waiving Miranda rights, not guilty by reason of insanity, and death penalty cases. In the case of the latter, there is a high level of controversy in the legal system because you cannot put to death a person with mental retardation. People argue about this idea of "too dumb to die." Psychologists are involved with doing extensive testing, including but not limited to intelligence (IQ) testing. There are numerous issues in the IQ testing of offenders who may have had multiple IQ tests. For instance, there are reliability and validity concerns termed *IQ creep*. This means that with ongoing testing, IQ scores can increase over time and become less accurate.

CIVIL COMPETENCIES

Civil law, as opposed to criminal law, involves cases that are brought by individuals or companies rather than by the government. In general, civil law is separated into two divisions: contracts and torts. Contract law involves disputes about breach of written or verbal agreements and contracts. Tort law involves wrongdoing or harm that has been inflicted on someone or on a group of persons by another individual or group. The damages or injuries may occur either intentionally or through negligence. The determination of criminal versus civil law can vary by state. Since legal precedents are created by state, most aspects of legal psychology also vary by state.

Some of the many opportunities for behavioral health care providers on the civil side of the law include:

- Guardianships and child custody
- Testamentary capacity
- Evaluation of juveniles before the courts (either as delinquents or as abused children)
- Treatment of offender populations and domestic violence (note that some states treat domestic violence as a criminal offense)

- Risk assessments (attorneys may request an evaluation to help their client get back out into community; legal precedent is the Atkins case)
- Assessment of parental rights
- Educational due process (disagreements between schools and parents about the child's services)
- Personal injury cases (for example, with medical malpractice cases, psychologists may be called upon to look for emotional damages)
- Disability evaluations

EVALUATION

Forensic evaluations are typically conducted by psychologists with extensive training and experience in testing and measurement. Several courses in assessment (particularly with child assessment if that is your area of expertise) are necessary. Forensic evaluators need to have supervised experience with conducting assessment batteries in forensic or other settings and with writing high-quality reports.

Forensic assessments and evaluations are generally requested by third parties, such as judges, attorneys, and probation officers. As an evaluating clinician, it can be difficult to remain impartial and not be biased by your own values and opinions. We all like to think that we are objective in our evaluations, but in reality this is a difficult task. When you have a child in front of you whose future hangs in the balance, it can be tough not to have emotions subtly sway your evaluation. It can be helpful to keep in mind that the person you are evaluating is not technically your client. Your job is to help the courts form a judgment. Dr. Stacie Vernick emphasizes the importance of maintaining objectivity in court-ordered evaluations. According to Dr. Vernick, it is essential to remember that the court is your client and your role does not involve direct therapeutic intervention with the individuals you are evaluating. Instead, your task is to conduct an objective evaluation and to report your findings and, in some cases, recommendations to the court.

Evaluations typically consist of semistructured or structured interviews and formal testing. Interviewing skills for these evaluations are very important since that is one of the primary means of gathering information. Course work and education in testing and measurement is very important, but you need to get the real-world experience of administering and scoring tests and writing reports yourself. A good way to gain this experience is by actively seeking out practicum and training opportunities that provide opportunities to administer personality tests like The Minnesota Multiphasic Personality Inventory-2, Million Clinical Multiaxial Inventory-III, and Personality Assessment Inventory, and cognitive assessments like Mini Mental Status Exam, Wechsler Adult Intelligence Scale-III, Wechsler Memory Scale-3, and The Woodcock-Johnston Cognitive and Achievement tests.

If you are a practicing psychologist, a good way to gain experience is to find a forensic psychologist or neuropsychologist who administers many test batteries and offer to help out at low or no charge in return for supervision and feedback. It is important to build your experience with conducting these tests before you begin testifying in court.

When thinking about what type of evaluations you would be best at providing, consider expanding on your current area of expertise. If you have done a good deal of work with assessing children and adolescents, then you can begin to get into juvenile delinquency evaluations, child abuse assessments, or other evaluations pertaining to youth. If your expertise is in the evaluation and treatment of post-traumatic stress disorder (PTSD), many attorneys would be interested in hiring you for evaluations.

FORENSIC TREATMENT

Treatment programs in forensics are an option for any behavioral health professionals who are interested in getting into the field. You can explore existing opportunities or you can work on creating your own program. If you are interested in program development, offender treatment programs are very much in demand. Before beginning your own program, you need to make yourself aware of the relevant state laws, agencies (e.g., court systems, probation and parole departments, advocacy organizations), and policies in your area and, of course, have training in the specific area of practice. For instance, if you are thinking about beginning a program related to domestic violence, learn whether your county has mandatory arrest laws and gain experience by working or volunteering in a domestic violence agency. In addition, become familiar with agencies from whom you may seek referrals, such as county or municipal court systems, probation departments, or child protective agencies. Before starting your own treatment program, you should also consider possible funding sources, such as state or federal grants, other government sources, community agencies, or private insurances.

Case Study of an Offender Treatment Program

Wright State University's School of Professional Psychology (SOPP) developed a program called Preventing Abuse in the Home (PATH). PATH, which is directed by Kathleen Malloy, PhD, associate professor of professional psychology, is dedicated to serving victims of domestic violence through treatment to batterers in order to prevent abuse in relationships. PATH is the only local batterer intervention program in its area that is in complete compliance with the Montgomery County domestic violence protocol requirements. PATH therapists run a group treatment program based on social learning theory and help members to change their behavior through monitoring feelings, thoughts, and responses. It is a combination of psychoeducation and process-oriented groups.

This program receives many direct referrals through magistrates of the court or court administrators. Most referrals are through the perpetrator's probation officer (PO) after the court-mandated treatment. When treatment is court-ordered for the primary batterer or aggressors and the PO recommends the PATH program, the clients call directly to schedule an intake and, if they are accepted, begin treatment. When working in this type of program, it is extremely important to uphold ethical standards, particularly as they relate to confidentiality, since attorneys and POs can frequently request information.

Violence or Abuse Victim Treatment Programs

Group and individual treatment programs for victims of violence are opportunities to become involved with the forensic world. You can become involved in a treatment program for children or adults. Before going out on your own, gain some experience in an agency, such as a domestic violence agency. By working at such agencies, you can gain experience with treatment and also with the courts and legal system. For example, you can work as an advocate and go to court with a client who suffered domestic violence and is trying to obtain a protection order.

Consultation, Training, and Expert Witness

If you have experience with forensic work and are interested in providing consultation, there are many areas to become involved. You can provide consultation to attorneys regarding their cases. Sometimes attorneys consult with psychologists before accepting cases to determine whether their potential client is likely to have a legitimate or a strong case. The attorney may hire you for discussion and consultation without having you actually meet with their client.

One of the best ways to get hired as a consultant is to become known for a specific forensic niche area. When you develop an expertise within forensics, you will create a place in the minds of attorneys and other referral partners. Consultation essentially means applying your expertise to a specific situation, so the more finely honed your area of expertise, the more highly you will be regarded as a consultant.

A good way to further your area of expertise is to work with someone who is already highly successful in that area. Ask them whether you can become an apprentice to them. Generally, you get paid for your work (a percentage of the total billed) and gain experience. This is win-win situation. Many forensic psychologists will want to work in this capacity only with people who are already licensed or certified. Forensic psychologists can build their practices and professional development by providing training and consultation to other professionals who are interested in becoming more involved with legal work.

If you are interested in potentially appearing in court as an expert witness, the key is to link with attorneys who will call on you and recommend you to their colleagues. When you do a good job and build a relationship with the right attorneys, you can quickly become experienced as an expert witness. There are many online opportunities to network with attorneys. For instance, on www.expertpages.com, you can pay an annual fee, and when attorneys are looking online for an expert witness, your information will appear. Before paying for a service like this, try it out by conducting a search for the term you would be searched by. Say you enter the search term that an attorney may use: "expert witness trauma." Be sure that the directory you are paying to be listed in appears within the first couple pages (preferably the first page). There are also free listing services, such as www.expertlaw.com, which match up attorneys with expert witnesses.

FURTHER EDUCATE YOURSELF

If you are interested in learning more about forensic work, one of the best ways to get started is to enroll in a professional organization to become affiliated with like-minded therapists and learn about career opportunities. There are many great associations. If you are a member of the American

Psychological Association (APA), Division 41, American Psychology Law Society, is a great association. The American Association for Correctional and Forensic Psychology (www.eaacp.org) is an organization of behavioral science practitioners interested in the delivery of high-quality mental health services to criminal offenders. They also work to promote and disseminate research on the development, evaluation, and treatment of criminal behavior. The American College of Forensic Psychology (www.forensicpsychology.org) is another resource.

Take continuing education workshops and courses. For example, the American Academy of Forensic Psychology offers workshops approved by the APA for continuing education credits. These workshops are also accepted as professional training by the American Board of Forensic Psychology. This is important if you are considering pursuing a diplomate (ABPP), because they count as double credit toward its supervisory/continuing education requirements.

Another important consideration, as described above, is hiring a supervisor or consultant to serve as a mentor and educator for you. Find someone who is a diplomate in forensic psychology. Search on www.abfp.com /diplomate_search.asp to find an expert, or begin asking around or researching in your city.

There are many other training programs available that offer courses and certificates in various aspects of forensic work. Forensic Solutions LLC, for example, has a program of courses designed to help students and professionals develop criminal profiling skills.

They offer courses like Criminal Profiling, Advanced Criminal Profiling, and Applied Criminal Profiling. Completion of a certain number of courses will result in a Certificate in Criminal Profiling, which is not meant to certify criminal profilers or expertise, but rather to show that a course of study approved by Forensic Solutions has been successfully completed. (See www.forensic-science.com/courses.html.)

Interview with Scott T. Kidd, PsyD

Scott Kidd has a private practice in Dayton, Ohio, and can be reached at (937) 438-4622 or by e-mail at scottkidd28@yahoo.com.

Why did you decide to get into forensics?
I earned Bachelor of Arts degrees in psychology and criminal justice and a doctoral degree in psychology. I completed clinical training at a state prison

and at a domestic violence center, which allowed me to gain experience working with both perpetrators and victims of violent crimes. I received clinical training at a maximum-security unit of a state psychiatric hospital, as a co-facilitator of an outpatient adult sexual offender treatment group, and as a co-facilitator of a support group for children whose mothers were murdered in domestic violence incidents. In addition, I completed my doctoral dissertation on school shootings that occurred in rural communities. During my predoctoral clinical internship at Atascadero State Hospital, a maximum-security state psychiatric hospital in California, I provided treatment and assessment of mentally ill offenders and sexually violent predators. I was then employed at Atascadero State Hospital as a staff psychologist, where I worked on a unit for mentally ill inmates from the state prison system. Currently, I am running an outpatient juvenile sexual offender treatment program and conducting a range of forensic evaluations, such as competency to stand trial, sanity, and sexual predator evaluations.

One reason I enjoy working in forensic psychology is the challenge of getting the two systems to work collaboratively. Combining the two fields is a somewhat unnatural fit, like putting together pieces from two different puzzles. The legal system is based on an adversarial process while mental health care focuses on building a trusting therapeutic relationship and creating positive change. It's a welcome (and worthwhile) endeavor to demonstrate the benefits of applying psychology within the legal system. Forensics is an exciting subspecialty of psychology with a wide range of career opportunities. The cases are very interesting and the work is certainly never boring.

Is forensic psychology an excellent niche market in which psychologists can add great value and be highly successful?
Absolutely. There are even excellent niche markets *within* forensic psychology. The more highly specialized or expert one becomes in a particular area, the more lucrative opportunities will become available. There are many employment opportunities, such as private practice; employment with federal, state; or local governments; probation departments; correctional facilities; law enforcement agencies; and colleges and universities. In addition, as laws change, new opportunities are often created.

What are some of the important attributes, qualities, or interests that a therapist would need to have to be successful in forensic work?
I would say the same qualities that are important for any psychologist. Being patient, nonjudgmental, accepting of individual differences, and

open-minded are important qualities. Being aware of your own issues that may impact your ability to work in an objective manner with certain populations or problem areas is also important.

Given the frequent exposure to violent offenders and their offenses, and the no-win situations faced in certain legal cases (e.g. protective custody cases), a strong social support system is critical for forensic psychologists to avoid burnout or vicarious traumatization. You must be accepting of the potential for violence when working in a correctional or forensic psychiatric setting and be prepared to cope with the impact this may have on you personally or on your clinical work. In addition, you have to be somewhat thick-skinned because it is likely that, at some point in your career, you will work with clients and read case files where horrendous offenses have been committed. This is also why having a good social support system is important.

Another skill that will serve clinicians well is adaptability. Environmental circumstances often impact the services offered by forensic psychologists. For instance, working with an offender who is strapped to a metal bed in an isolation cell certainly impacts the approach one takes when trying to conduct crisis intervention.

What are your top five recommendations for how students or professionals should go about getting experience in forensic work?

1. Obtain a graduate education from an accredited program, preferably (but not necessarily) with faculty who conduct forensic-related research or clinical work. Some programs offer degrees in forensic psychology. Other programs offer an emphasis or specialty in forensics within their general clinical psychology program. There are also law and psychology programs, where students are able to earn both a law degree (JD) and a doctoral degree in psychology (PhD). However, it is not necessary to attend one of these specialized programs. Broader training and education in clinical or counseling psychology would also prepare you for a career in forensic psychology.
2. Look for opportunities to get clinical or other field experience working in a correctional or forensic setting or with offender populations. In my opinion, settings that offer training and experience in both the treatment and assessment of offenders would be ideal.
3. As with many areas of psychology, forensics is a very specialized field. I strongly suggest that clinicians obtain the necessary education, training, and supervised clinical experience to become competent in

the practice of forensic psychology before conducting this type of work. For professionals who are looking to expand their current practice, I recommend attendance and active participation in continuing education and other seminars/training. I also highly recommend that peer supervision or case consultation opportunities be established, in addition to becoming familiar with relevant literature.

4. Take psychology courses, including course in abnormal, clinical, social, personality, and developmental psychology; psychopharmacology; and neuropsychology. Also take criminal justice courses, such as introduction to criminal justice, theories of crime and deviance, juvenile delinquency, and criminal investigations.

5. Read case files. This is an excellent way to become familiar with criminal behavior, offender characteristics, and the systems that interact with offender populations.

How have you built your forensic assessment practice?
First and foremost, I wanted to have a strong background in general clinical psychology through education and clinical training. Developing certain areas of expertise has provided opportunities to work in niche markets, such as sexual offender treatment and assessment.

Another way I continue to build my forensic practice is by networking with other professionals. I do this by providing workshops for Probation and Children's Services Department employees. I meet with judges, magistrates, attorneys, probation and parole officers, caseworkers, and other professionals who may be able to utilize the services I offer.

Membership in professional organizations and participation on listservs with other forensic mental health professionals and attorneys has helped expand my referral base. Finally, continuing education, training, peer evaluation, and case consultation help me continue to strengthen my competence in practicing forensic psychology.

Interview with Eric Mart, PhD, ABPP

Eric Mart is a licensed psychologist in private practice in Manchester, New Hampshire. He specializes in forensic psychology. He is an internationally known expert on Munchausen's syndrome by proxy, is the author of *Munchausen's Syndrome by Proxy Reconsidered*. Dr. Mart's web site is www.psychology-law.com, and he can be reached by telephone at (603) 626-0966.

What are your main areas of practice?

They fall into two categories:

1. Assessment, Consultation, and Expert Testimony
   - Munchausen's syndrome by proxy
   - Criminal and civil competency
   - Testamentary competence and undue influence
   - Mental state at time of offense
   - Juvenile delinquency
   - Risk assessment
   - Child custody
   - Sexual abuse
   - Personal injury
   - False/recovered memory
   - Education due process
2. Clinical Assessment and Treatment
   - Assessment of adult and child attention deficit disorder/ hyperactivity
   - Psychoeducational assessment
   - Treatment and consultation with developmentally disabled and dually diagnosed (MR/EH) individuals
   - Short-term cognitive-behavioral treatment of children, adolescents, and adults

The testing piece is done by psychologists, but is there a way that master's-level therapists or social workers can become involved in forensic work?

You have to be licensed generally. It is not a specialty like school, counseling, or clinical at this point. There are licensed social workers who do forensic work, such as custody work and offender treatment. If you are a master's-level clinician, you can collaborate with a psychologist who can do the testing part. If you are in the treatment end, you do not need to testify much. If you are asked to provide treatment, the degree does not matter as much (if the court did not have confidence in you, you wouldn't be there in the first place). A doctorate can help you have an edge.

Why is forensic psychology a growing field?

Frankly, there are two reasons: First. There is a big misperception that it involves a lot of crime profiling. People think you will be on TV shows like *CSI*. People love court-related drama. Second, there *is* a certain amount of theater, drama, and excitement.

What would make someone a successful forensic psychologist?
You can't be afraid of public speaking and you must be willing to be questioned. I have seen many academic experts who wilt under cross-examination. You must be competitive and driven. You need to be on top of the literature. Energy and a bit of narcissism are helpful. Generally speaking, you will not get someone asking you about the all the latest information, because you are likely to be more sophisticated than they are. The best forensic psychologists like the challenge of being cross-examined.

Forensic work has a different vibe than therapy. In forensic evaluation, you are not there to be supportive, you are there to do an impartial evaluation. Forensics is not a place for being too touchy-feely. If you are there exclusively for the relationship with your client, you may be disappointed. You are not supposed to use a lot of yourself because you are not there to help them feel better, you are there for the court. Your job is to assist the court as an expert.

You need the best assessment skills you can get. I don't think you have to be an expert on every test, but you must be an informed consumer in testing and measurement. Good interviewing and assessment skills are important. Another important skill is your ability to take very good histories and use collateral sources of information. The number one factor that leads to people making good predictions is getting all the information up front. It is like being a detective. Suspend your own judgment in your forensic work so you do not have confirmatory bias.

How do you recommend that psychologists resolve the dilemma of needing a good deal of experience (with tests, etc.) to achieve expert status and finding this experience if you did not have formal forensic training?
I actually came in the back door myself without doing a forensic internship and postdoc. I am a school psychologist by training, which gave me a lot of background with testing. I entered the clinical world and ran into a mentor, Wilfrid Derby, PhD, ABPP (forensic and clinical), and he said, "You know, there is a lot of work out there in forensics." The cases are out there, but you need the training and supervision. He helped me start out by doing evaluations on juvenile offenses, which was a natural extension

of what I had been doing in schools. He supervised me closely. As I gained experience and comfort level, I moved off on my own—it was an apprenticeship model.

Look at what your strengths are and how they will flow naturally into forensic work. If you do a lot of work with children and families, custody work is a natural extension. If you work in substance abuse, you can work for the state doing substance abuse evaluations. If you are a school psychologist, it is not hard to get into due process cases.

Of course workshops, training, and more classes help you gain exposure and experience. You can publish to create greater credibility. Publishing swings a lot of weight with the court. You can present a paper at a conference and afterwards jazz it up and develop it for a peer-reviewed journal. These presentations and articles establish your credentials. With credentials behind you, you can go on to publish in law journals.

Referral partnerships seem to be very important in forensic work.

Definitely. If you work in juvenile court, develop relationships with probation officers. Cultivate those relationships. I used to bring a box of donuts, which was appreciated. Many therapists don't think of themselves as a product and do not think to sell themselves and relationships.

I think of referral partnerships like a restaurant: You need to constantly keep it filled—one busy night in the restaurant is not enough. You need a large network of people to refer to you. You need to have lots of probation officers and lawyers referring to you. Parent advocacy groups are good. Specific judges will refer to you too. It is generally word of mouth. Advertising is not effective.

How can people find a supervisor or consultant to learn from?

If you don't know someone in your area, look for a diplomate (ABPP) since that does show that they are qualified. You should look to see whether these people are reputable. They have their expertise and credibility to sell. If they have published in an area that interests you, that is good. Be honest about it, let them know: "I am shopping for a supervisor." The fees for supervision really depend on the forensic psychologist. I give people a break with my fees because it is personally rewarding to supervise. You can work with someone regularly or do a supervision hour when an issue comes up.

Many professionals choose not to go into forensic work because of a fear of testifying in court. Do you have any advice or recommendations for someone who is beginning to testify in court?
There are some good books on this topic. I remind myself that it is not a win-lose situation. Lawyers will say, "You're being paid, aren't you, doctor?" to try to intimidate you. Your best response is, "I am paid for my time, not my opinion." If you don't know, say so.

It is important to dress appropriately. A classic dark suit is always a good choice. Don't forget to take care of yourself. Eat and hydrate first. There's no way around the fact that it will take time to gain comfort, but you can do things to make yourself more comfortable in the meantime.

Remember that sometimes the attorneys are scared of you, too, because they don't know much about psychology. Other things you can do are to be aware of your anxiety, go to the restroom first, concentrate on the issue at hand, and keep in mind that you are not going to know everything. It happens to everyone—accept yourself as someone who makes mistakes. In my first competency assessment, I got up and they said, "How many have you done?" I answered honestly, "This is my first one." Everyone laughed. I joked, "Judge, everyone needs a first one." With many juvenile cases you don't testify, you just turn in your evaluation, so that is easier to start out with. Build these types of experiences—juvenile or district court cases tend to be more informal.

What are some of the liabilities and risks? How do people get themselves into trouble and what are your top risk-management recommendations?
The top risk area is custody. For psychologists in general, boundary violations and sexual improprieties are what get them in trouble. With forensic work, custody has the highest level of complaints. You can hurt your reputation by not doing well in court.

One of the biggest areas of trouble is moving between forensic and therapist roles. For instance, "I saw Mr. Smith for counseling and I think . . ." This is not good. Beware of the stealth evaluation: The lawyer will tell the client to go to the therapist and ask the clinician to treat the client for 10 sessions. This clinician cannot be an expert witness in court. If you were the therapist, you can talk about diagnosis, but you need to make it clear that you are there as a fact witness, *not* an expert witness.

Another area of risk is people who do not really have the knowledge to do what they are doing—people who have not read a book in 15 years and go into court with the thematic apperception test (TAT) and Rorschach.

You need to know your stuff. Make sure you have read all the new pertinent literature on the subject.

Be sure that you have the highest level of liability insurance. Board complaint insurance is necessary if you are going to do custody work. You will have complaints and need to be ready for it.

Know what the standard of practice is in those areas. For instance, I do work on risk management with a group of developmentally challenged individuals. If I had met the standard of practice, used due diligence, and done a good job, if someone sued me, I would have done what I needed to. Another common problem is not doing a formal mental status exam (MSE). Do not open yourself up for this liability—do the MSE.

RESOURCES

BOOKS

Arrigo, B. A. (2004). *Psychological jurisprudence: Critical explorations in law, crime, and society*. Albany, NY: SUNY Press.

Brodsky, S. L. (1991). *Testifying in court: Guidelines and maxims for the expert witness*. Washington, DC: American Psychological Association.

Ceci, S. J., & Bruck, M. (1996). *Jeopardy in the classroom: Scientific analysis of children's testimony*. Washington, DC: American Psychological Association.

Grisso, T. (2002). *Evaluating competencies: Forensic assessments and instruments (Perspectives in law and psychology)* (2nd ed.). Norwell, MA: Kluwer Academic Publishers.

Homant, R. J., & Kennedy, D. B. (1998). Psychological aspects of crime scene profiling—validity research. *Criminal Justice and Behavior*, 25 (3), 319–343.

Impara, J. C., & Murphy, L. L. (Eds.) (1996). *Buros desk reference: Assessment of substance abuse*. Lincoln, NE: University of Nebraska Press.

Impara, J. C., & Murphy, L. L. (Eds.) (1994). *Buros desk reference: Psychological assessment in the schools*. Lincoln, NE: University of Nebraska Press.

Mart, E. G. (2002). *Munchausen's syndrome by proxy reconsidered*. Manchester, NH: Bally Vaughan Publishers.

Melton, G. B., Petrila, J., Poythress, N. G., Slobogin, C. (1997). *Psychological evaluations for the courts: A handbook for mental health professionals and lawyers* (2nd ed.). New York: Guildford Publications.

Murphy, L. L., Plake, B. S., Impara, J. C., and Spies, R. A. (2002). *Tests in print VI edited*. Lincoln, NE: University of Nebraska Press.

Plake, B. S., Impara, J. C., Spies, R. A. (2003). *The fifteenth mental measurements yearbook*. Lincoln, NE: University of Nebraska Press.

Pope, K. S., Butcher, J. N., & Seelen, J. (2002). *MMPI, MMPI-2, & MMPI-A in court: A practical guide for expert witnesses and attorneys* (2nd ed.). Washington, DC: American Psychological Association.

Rogers, R. (1997). *Clinical assessment of malingering and deception* (2nd ed.). New York: Guilford Publications.

Specialty guidelines for forensic psychologists: Committee on ethical guidelines for forensic psychologists. *Law and Human Behavior*, 15 (6), 1991.

Walker, L. E. A., & Shapiro, D. L. (2003). *Introduction to forensic psychology: Clinical and social psychological perspectives*. New York: Plenum Publishing Corporation.

WEB SITES

American Board of Forensic Psychology and American Academy of Forensic Psychology:

www.abfp.com

American Association for Correctional and Forensic Psychology:

www.eaacp.org

Buros Institute of Mental Measurement—publishers of the *Mental Measurements Yearbook and Tests in Print*:

www.unl.edu/buros

APA code of ethics:

www.apa.org/ethics/code.html#6.06

American Psychological Association, Division 41—American Psychology-Law Society:

www.ap-ls.org

State-by-state domestic violence law:

www.womenslaw.org

Forensic science resources:

www.tncrimlaw.com/forensic

The American College of Forensic Psychology:

www.forensicpsychology.org

Forensic Solutions LLC:

www.forensic-science.com/courses.html

TERMINOLOGY

adjudication The judgment handed down in a legal case.

alimony Money or other financial support awarded to a spouse in a divorce, typically awarded when one spouse has been dependent on the other or has less earning power than the other.

annulment A court declaration that a marriage is invalid or nonexistent to indicate that the marriage never occurred legally. Church annulments are different from legal annulments.

appeal The process of going to a higher court to review the decision of a lower court.

arraignment The court hearing where a defendant in a criminal case is required to enter a plea.

asylum The granting of legal protection against return to a refugee, which can lead to lawful permanent resident status and eventually to citizenship.

attorney general The head of the state agency responsible for prosecuting violations of state laws by either defending the State or bringing lawsuits on behalf of the State.

base rate The frequency that a particular event occurs within a specific time frame.

competency The ability of an individual to perform a certain function, such as adequately participate in his own defense, give testimony, waive certain rights, or carry out particular responsibilities.

consent To give free and willing agreement.

criminal responsibility A defendant's accountability for his or her actions as defined by the relevant law.

damages The award of money to the winner of a lawsuit. *Actual damages* are awards of out-of-pocket expenses such as lost wages or hospital bills. *Punitive damages* are awards that are intended to punish the wrongful party for willful harmful action.

emancipation   The process by which a minor child is declared to be an adult by a court of law after petitioning the court for this right. The age at which a person can file for emancipation is set by law in each state.

expert witness   A witness who, by reason of education, training, or experience, has knowledge concerning the topic about which he or she is testifying.

ex parte   On one side only.

fact witness   A witness who is present to confirm objective quantifiable facts, but who is not there to provide opinions or judgments.

felony   A serious criminal offense, such as murder, for which the sentence can include imprisonment for more than a year.

guardian ad litem   The person assigned by the court to represent the interests of a minor child or incompetent person in legal proceedings.

indictment   A document issued by a grand jury which identifies the formal charge against a defendant.

injunction   A court order that prohibits someone from doing some specified act or orders someone to undo a wrong or injury.

liability   An enforceable accountability and responsibility which can be subject to civil remedies or criminal sanctions.

malingering   Deliberate feigning or exaggeration of a mental illness or physical disability to obtain some personal gain.

malpractice   Any professional misconduct or unreasonable lack of skill during a professional duty or relationship.

misdemeanor   A less serious type of crime that can lead to imprisonment for no longer than one year.

negligence   Demonstrating carelessness, lack of care, or failure to act reasonably or take reasonable precautions.

parole   The early release of an offender from prison, where the offender must either follow certain conditions of parole or serve the remainder of his or her sentence.

probation   The suspension of a sentence, where the offender must either follow certain conditions of probation or serve the original sentence.

protection order, order of protection, or restraining order   A court demand for someone to stop violations of laws or court orders, usually issued to keep someone away from another person in order to protect that person.

statutes   Laws passed by state or federal legislators. The constitution is supreme over all statutes, and statutes have more authority than regulations.

tribal justice system   The terms *tribal court*, *tribal court system*, and *tribal justice system* mean the entire judicial branch of an Indian tribe, including trial courts, appellate courts, and traditional methods for dispute resolution

violation   An act that is against the law, for which the state can imprison an individual for no longer than 15 days.

voir dire   The process during which the prosecution and defense attorneys question and select jurors for a trial.

CHAPTER 11

Opportunities in Consulting

To teach is to learn twice over.

Joseph Joubert

There is nothing so useless as doing efficiently that which should not be done at all.

Peter F. Drucker

WHAT IS CONSULTING?

Consulting is a very broad field, and consultants can work in virtually any industry. Consultants use their expertise to help solve a problem, direct a process, improve an outcome, or add a different perspective. In business, consultants often go into organizations to help them develop their business strategies, their human resources, or their financial performance. In the field of technology, consultants help companies improve their use of information technology. Any system that you think of can benefit from consultation.

A BRIEF HISTORY OF MENTAL HEALTH CONSULTING

Educational consulting can be traced to the 1920s when psychologist Lightmer Witmer helped school personnel to improve the education of children with disabilities.

Organizational development has its roots in Kurt Lewin's field theory (1951) which stimulated a human relations approach in the workplace.

In 1970, Gerald Caplan introduced his work, *The Theory and Practice of Mental Health Consultation*, which has greatly impacted mental health care consultation to various disciplines. Caplan's model described three aspects of consultation. He stated that:

1. Consultation is an egalitarian relationship.
2. Theme interference (a gentle confrontation of the consultee's ideas) is present.
3. Consultation has its own taxonomy (e.g., client-centered, consultee-centered, consultee-centered administrative, and program-centered administrative).

Today, some of his initial ideas about consulting are debated. For instance, as behaviorism and behavioral consulting have increased, the notion of an egalitarian relationship has been challenged. In this type of consultation, the consultant is clearly the expert or teacher who models new behaviors or describes various contingencies. The idea that consultation only occurs between two professionals has also been questioned. For instance, Heller (1985) shares the view of social workers that mental health problems are often at the community level and that work with community groups can be an excellent use of consultation (Brown, Pryzwanksy, & Schulte, 2001).

Consultation versus Other Services

Consultation is often confused with other helping professions and professional services. This is true in part because people use the term *consulting* in a colloquial manner and apply it to many different things. I'd like to clarify how consulting is different from some of the other topics discussed in this book, namely coaching, supervision, teaching, and therapy. *Consulting* can actually be an umbrella term and can include some coaching, supervision, or teaching, but they are distinct fields.

Consulting versus Coaching

Consulting is different from coaching (discussed in Chapter 11) in several ways. First, the consultant utilizes an expert status, whereas the coach works from an equal status. While coaches work as partners with their clients, aligned toward the client's goal, consultants are generally hired for their specific expertise in an area that the client needs to improve.

Second, consultants advise while coaches ask. Coaches engage in the process of appreciative inquiry, asking a series of poignant questions to get clients to consider things differently. Consultants, on the other hand, tend to give clients specific recommendations and advice about action steps to take. Of course there is a good degree of crossover—consultants may also ask meaningful questions, and coaches often assign homework and action steps.

The third difference between coaching and consulting is the timing. While people often hire a coach when they have a specific situation or have a major change coming up, they also hire coaches for general self-improvement. Consultants, on the other hand, are generally called in to help with a specific situation. Consultants generally work with their clients on definite projects with clear timelines, whereas coaches often work with their clients over months and years.

CONSULTING VERSUS SUPERVISION

Clinical supervision is different from consulting because a supervisor is directly overseeing the supervisee's case. In most supervisory relationships, the supervisor is legally responsible for the case and for any risks or problems that may arise. The consultant, however, provides the consultee with ideas, assistance, and information without retaining clinical or legal responsibility over the case.

A supervisor is also often in an evaluative role and assigns grades or recommendations to the supervisee, while the consultant is rarely in an evaluative role. Supervisors are also generally seen as authority figures. Consultants, while they are experts in a subject matter, do not typically have the same authority role. If you are thinking about providing consultation (rather than supervision) to a clinician and want to have a clear understanding of your legal involvement in the case, you may want to discuss the situation with your attorney and create an agreement that clearly defines your role.

CONSULTING VERSUS TEACHING

Traditionally, teaching is thought of as a didactic process between a teacher and a student that occurs in the classroom. Teaching is typically imparted through lectures and homework (Brown, Pryzwanksy, & Schulte, 2001). While the roles and conceptions of teaching are certainly expanding, generally speaking, consulting is less formal and more applied than most teaching. The process of teaching often entails instructing students on theory and the background behind constructs and principles, whereas consulting does not typically get into theory so much as the hands-on application of knowledge. Teaching a consultee a new method or process can certainly be part of consultation. The consultant may model a desired behavior or may teach the idea in an applied manner based on the specific circumstance at hand.

CONSULTING VERSUS THERAPY

The focus of therapy is typically on reducing psychopathology, psychological dysfunction, or emotional difficulties within an individual, group, or family. Consulting, on the other hand, is not focused on psychopathology. It may be aimed at improving a problem, but it normally deals with systemic or organizational difficulties. The intense nature of the therapeutic relationship is not seen in consultation relationships. In addition, emotional processing and affect change are not typically goals of a consultation relationship.

CONSULTING THEORY

Consulting typically has group, business, or organizational goals rather than individual goals. A good portion of the theory underlying consulting work is systems theory (Katz & Kane, 1978). As applied to organizations, this theory states that organizations are generally open systems. An open system is a system that receives information from outside of the system, is affected by information outside of the system, sends information outside of the system, and has an impact on factors outside of the system. Boundaries are permeable; the environment greatly affects the system, and the system affects the environment. An analogy is the human cell.

Organizational systems have both formal and informal leadership structures. The people involved with leadership are those who make decisions and influence the organization. Systems are also composed of implicit or explicit goals and values, as well as structures or hierarchies. An organizational system will have financial and technological systems within the larger organizational system.

Perhaps the most important aspect of most organizational systems is the human component. The psychosocial system within an organization has a major impact on whether the organization's objectives are met (Beer, 1980). This is why mental health and behavioral consultants can have such a significant impact on the performance of organizations and the satisfaction of those within the system.

CONSULTING PROCESS

The process of consulting is quite similar to the process of therapy. Much of the terminology and concepts will sound familiar to you. The first step is to diagnose the situation. Since you are using a systems approach, you will not be diagnosing individuals; instead, you will be identifying the organizational problems. Beer (1980) recommends diagnosing the organization's efficiency, effectiveness, and health. Health can be thought of as how well the organization responds to changing conditions and external demands. The diagnosis should start at the macro level (the system as a whole) and move down to the micro level (how, for example, a team leader and team members are interacting and performing).

The next step is to develop an understanding of the goals of the organizational initiatives and who would be involved with meeting these goals. It is also important at this stage to recognize the internal and external supports and constraints for these goals and the organizational feedback mechanisms (Brown, Pryzwanksy, & Schulte, 2001).

Goals are then set based on the results of the analyses of current systems, objectives, constraints, and supports. It is critical that goals are set in operational terms so the client (the organization or department) can see how the consulting is helping them to reach their goals. If a goal is not measurable, it will not be clear how you, the consultant, are helping the system. An example of an operational goal would be to reduce employee turnover by 10 percent over the next six months and 20 percent over the next year.

Following the goal-setting phase is the intervention phase. As with therapy, this is the point where assessment and analysis are complete, goals are set, and changes will begin to occur. In contrast to therapy, the goals are not typically related to emotional status and relationship functioning. Instead, they may be designed to reduce costs, increase efficiency and changes, minimize organizational strains, or increase organizational goal attainment (Beer, 1980). As with therapy, the types of interventions selected will vary based on consultant, client, and situational variables.

Interventions may occur at the individual, group, department, or organizational level. An intervention may be *acceptant*, which is similar to the client-centered therapy of Rogers in which the consultant uses empathic listening skills and expects growth to result. The interventions may be *catalytic*, in which the consultant actively encourages people to make decisions for themselves. Another type of intervention is a *theory-based* intervention, which can draw from any validated model in the social sciences. A fourth form of intervention is *prescriptive*, where the consultant serves as the expert and prescribes solutions. Consultants can also use *confrontational* interventions by asking probing and challenging questions in a supportive manner (Brown, Pryzwanksy, & Schulte, 2001).

CONSULTING AS AN EXCELLENT CAREER OPPORTUNITY

The great thing about the behavioral sciences is that consultants do not need to only work within their industry, mental health. As I mentioned previously, a consultant can address just about any industry, system, problem, or process. Be creative in thinking about how your skills can apply to various settings and situations and how you can get out there and provide help through consulting.

The world of consulting presents excellent opportunities for mental health professionals because knowledge of the behavioral sciences can apply to many industries. In this chapter I discuss the three areas of consulting that are in demand right now and that I believe therapists are wonderfully equipped to provide. These areas are business consultation, family business consultation, and consultation to schools or educational consulting. I believe consulting merits a full chapter in this book because, in my opinion, it is one of the best career opportunities for therapists, for six reasons:

1. Consultation is intellectually challenging and rewarding. Applying your expertise to new markets requires constant innovation and creative thinking.
2. You can reach a broad audience by consulting to groups and organizations. One therapist I know has been doing educational consulting and has helped a dozen schools change their processes and provide better educational systems for hundreds of students.

3. Consulting as a rule is a lucrative field. You can typically bill at higher hourly rates than you would for individual therapy.

4. You are needed. If you have a great deal of knowledge in specific areas of behavioral health, there are many organizations and businesses who need you and can significantly benefit from your services.

5. Consultation is active. One of the things I most enjoy about providing consultations is that it gets me out of the office. If you are someone who likes to be physically active and who enjoys meeting new people and merging into new cultures and settings, you might enjoy consulting.

6. Consulting sells products. If you have created books or other products (or plan to), consulting helps you accomplish two tasks at once: consulting and selling your products.

CONSULTING TO CORPORATIONS

Many therapists and other mental health professionals make wonderful transitions into the corporate world as consultants. No licensure or certification is required in order to be a consultant. You can designate yourself as a consultant and the burden is then on you to prove your expertise in that area. A therapist can leverage her training in the behavioral sciences to create a strategic marketing position for herself in the business world.

While it is important to use your extensive experience working with different people, you want to use your therapist title with caution. It may not be the best idea to identify yourself as a psychologist or psychotherapist when you present to a business setting, because many businesspeople have negative preconceived notions and stereotypes about "shrinks." Also, using your clinical title is not an accurate way to describe the role that you will have as a consultant. Some other titles that mental health consultants to businesses have used include: psychological consultant, corporate psychologist, business psychologist, behavioral consultant, performance consultant, behavioral specialist, corporate trainer, communications specialist, team building consultant, change consultant, organization development specialist, corporate therapist, and human resources consultant. The titles utilize varying degrees of reference to one's background as a therapist. You can strategically decide how much you want to highlight your mental health background, depending on what type of consulting you will be doing, your client base, the company culture, and your own opinion and comfort level.

TYPES OF CORPORATE CONSULTATION

Businesses hire consultants for many different reasons. Just as they hire technology consultants to improve their IT departments, they hire psychological consultants to improve their most critical resource: their people. Some areas that are well suited to psychological or behavioral health consultation include:

- Human resources consulting
- Executive training and development
- Emotional intelligence
- Team building and leadership development
- Stress management
- Multiculturalism and diversity issues
- Assertiveness training
- Sexual harassment
- Interpersonal effectiveness and communications skills
- Conflict resolution, negotiation and mediation
- Multidisciplinary collaboration

As you can see, there are many areas in which therapists can become excellent resources to corporations. Businesses today are recognizing more and more that their most valuable resource is the people who work within their organizations. They are hiring consultants to improve the functioning of their human resources on several levels. One of the most valuable ways is by having consultants provide trainings for upper-level executives, who then lead and manage people more effectively. Another way is by having consultants come in and provide workshops, seminars, or trainings for employees.

HOW TO GET STARTED IN CORPORATE CONSULTING

If the world of consulting sounds intriguing to you, you are probably wondering how to get started. This section will give you some ideas to get you on your way.

Training

If you do not have experience in the business world or as a consultant, you will want to receive some training before trying to market yourself as a business consultant. You have several options for training. Besides enrolling in a professional training program, you could do a combination of teaching yourself by reading the literature and learning about the practical side by hiring a mentor, supervisor, or consultant to show you the ropes.

There are training programs available that can show you how to do corporate consulting. A formal education program, such as an MBA or a certificate program within an MBA, can prepare you to be a consultant. Many MBA graduates (without training in psychology or counseling) go into corporate consulting and consult on strategy and human resources. You do not have to complete an entire master's degree to gain some practical knowledge and experience. You can select some courses, focusing on those that provide you with hands-on experience. Several of my MBA courses focused on working with businesses, both for-profits and nonprofits, as a consultant.

You can also find training programs that are not affiliated with universities. For example, the Global Consulting Partnership's (GCP) Professional Executive Coaching Certificate Program (www.clinical-to-consulting.com) shows you how to most effectively use your advanced degree without turning businesspeople off by having them think of you solely as a therapist. According to Mark Brenner, PhD, chairman of GCP, therapists who are considering the transition into consulting face two psychological hurdles. The first is their own skewed view of the business world, seeing it as cold or unconcerned with human feelings and behaviors. A program such as GCP's can help you to learn that some of the most humanistic programs are occurring within corporate settings, such as adult learning and diversity initiatives. The other hurdle that therapists face is marketing and selling.

Another option is to be trained by someone who does corporate consulting work. You can hire someone to teach you how to transition from therapy to consulting. This person can serve as a mentor, so select someone whose career you would like to emulate. Your trainer/mentor can also provide you with consultation on your consulting work, once you begin to provide your services to various organizations.

GAINING EXPERIENCE

There are three important considerations in beginning or building your work as a consultant. You need to decide what kind of consulting you will do, for whom you are going to consult, and how you will gain experience and generate leads.

The answers to the first and second questions depend greatly on your interests, background, and experiences. If you have never done business work but you have worked in many multidisciplinary teams and helped those teams to function effectively, then you may be most prepared to do team building. If you are not interested in working with large groups but would like to work one-on-one with business leaders, you may prefer executive development. If you have a good deal of training in multicultural psychology or assessment and have worked with many diverse populations or are of a diverse background yourself, you may enjoy conducting diversity, culture, or multiculturalism assessments or consultations.

The types of organizations you will be a consultant for will be dictated by your experience and your marketing abilities. Generally speaking, it is difficult for someone without a good deal of experience consulting to Fortune 500 companies to get hired by a Fortune 500 company. It is much more feasible to start with a local business or organization and work your way up, if you are interested in ultimately working with larger corporations. Gaining experience in consultation is definitely possible either during or after graduate school. By being proactive, you can seek out or create organizational consultation experience during a practicum, internship, or clinical position. You can create your own program and then deliver it to various departments or organizations. It may not be easy to get business consulting experience, but you can certainly gain experience with providing consultation to various programs, departments, individuals, or teams. Your consulting experience does not have to be in the business world for it to prepare you for corporate consulting. You can create and hone your area of consulting expertise within clinical or counseling settings and then apply it to businesses if that interests you. If you cannot think of any kind of consulting you can offer right away, here are some ideas:

- Eating disorder education for college dormitories and residence halls.
- Consultation hours for psychiatry residents to discuss their cases with you.

- Performance improvement consultation to university sports teams.
- Running a case consultation group for a community mental health program.
- Behavioral health consulting to different departments in a hospital, such as gynecology, oncology, or cardiology.
- Stress management for local nonprofit organizations.
- Cultural assessments of various organizational cultures.
- Communications evaluation for local small businesses.

Another way to get some experience is to work for a busy consultant and take a small portion of the fees charged. For instance, you will earn 25 percent of what you bring in and the consultant will earn 75 percent. This is a win-win scenario for you and the consultant who is helping you get in front of clients. You will make some money, but more important, you will gain real-world experience that can be difficult to come by. Since there is a catch-22 when it comes to getting experience (no one wants to hire you until you have experience, but you can't get experience until someone will hire you), this type of setup would be perfect. To locate a consultant for this kind of arrangement, look for a local business consultant in your area, preferably from a mental health background. Offer to take them out to lunch or dinner to learn about their work. If you build a connection with a particular consultant, you can propose a training setup with them.

Most graduate school training programs do not offer business consultation as potential practicum or training options, but do not let this limit you. For example, Dr. Dante Capitano, the managing director for RHR International, created his own consultation company before going to RHR International, the largest corporate psychology consultation firm in the world.

Interview with Dante Capitano, PsyD

Dr. Capitano is the managing director of the Philadelphia office of RHR International and a trusted advisor to CEOs and presidents of large organizations. RHR International Company advises senior management on culture, people, and process issues through the development of high potential talent and aligning behaviors around new strategies. Visit www.rhrinternational.com.

**You came from a clinical background. Can you tell us
how you got into consulting?**

I went into graduate school knowing that I wanted the practical, interpersonal, and diagnostic training necessary to be an effective business consultant. I chose the clinical degree because it provided me with many more career opportunities. I felt at the time that industrial and organizational (I/O) route was more restrictive. The PsyD degree proved to be an extremely practical degree that prepared me well for working in an applied setting. I then leveraged that training to secure a postdoctoral position with the Center of Cognitive Therapy (CCT) at the University of Pennsylvania. During my second year at Penn, I built a business case and a business plan to start up a part-time consulting practice within the CCT. We provided workshops, executive assessment, and general team process consultation to pharmaceutical companies and health care systems. After two years with Penn, I joined RHR.

What types of clinical skills did you find transferable?

Transferable skills include relationship and interpersonal skills, professionalism, psychological assessment, and credibility building. The main difference is that when you are consulting to large organizations you are not using a pathology-based model. You rarely see someone with a clinical diagnosis. In general, these are healthy, driven, motivated individuals who are looking to become stronger, more effective leaders.

Many therapists transitioning over to consulting also need to develop better business acumen. You will need to learn basic finance, marketing, and competitive dynamics that affect a specific industry. Moreover, you need to recognize what is important to business leaders—for example, the financial indicators, employee issues, the board of directors, the stockholders. You will need to attend workshops, classes, and read business books (like *The Leadership Pipeline*, by Charan et al.), magazines, and newspapers (like the *Wall Street Journal*) to help you acquire this knowledge. These issues are generally not covered in traditional psychology programs.

**How does working with a firm like RHR differ from
working with other major firms as a consultant?**

The large management consulting firms like McKinsey and Accenture are primarily strategy firms. They are very good at what they do. Their consultants come in and help organizations develop major strategy/

change initiatives that will ultimately help the business become success-ful. RHR tends to come in after the strategy is created to help translate the strategy into behavior (help realize the value of the established vision/strategy). With a company like RHR, keen psychological insights and penetrating feedback and counsel are where value is added. In other words, RHR consultants are generally the tool. This is more labor intensive for the consultant but creates a customized program for senior level executives in organizations. There are other consulting companies that use more of a tools-based approach, which can be seen as less customized and flexible.

What is the necessity or utility of having an MBA for this type of work?

An MBA can be helpful but it's not necessary. Experience is better. When I am recruiting for RHR, I look for candidates who have worked at least three to five years in a business environment. The MBA certainly helps at a practical level as you are transitioning into business consultation because it gives credibility and will help you understand the business jargon and speak the language.

What are some of the different consulting activities psychologists do?

We provide a range of services, including:

- Executive assessment for selection and development of executives.
- Executive integration—creating a plan for the first year in an organization, helping executives to integrate successfully, and accelerating credibility and alignment with the team/organization.
- Team development.
- Trusted advisers to CEOs, presidents, senior management.
- Merger acquisition, assisting two corporate cultures to come together.
- Succession planning.
- Executive education.

What are the core competencies in a job like this? What types of skills?

I recommend that a person have skill in these seven areas:

1. Strong interpersonal skills.
2. Flexibility and the ability to work with diverse populations.

3. Must project honesty, trust, and credibility instantaneously.
4. Articulate, concise, and solution-oriented communication.
5. Proactive, able to think ahead of and anticipate needs of your client.
6. Quick, strategic mind.
7. Comfortable in an upper-level executive climate. Must be comfortable presenting in the executive suite.

**What types of personality traits are consistent
with successful consultants?**
I can think of four essential traits:

1. Independence and entrepreneurial spirit.
2. Tolerance for ambiguity.
3. Willingness to put your reward and compensation at risk based on your performance.
4. Emotional stamina—ability to tolerate long days and demanding clients while staying poised and not becoming overwhelmed.

**What would make a psychologist competitive for a
consulting position at a company such as RHR?**
In addition to the characteristics I've already described, someone who can manage the ebbs and flows of the workload (from not being busy to feeling overwhelmed); who can establish strong, lasting, value-add client relationships; and who possesses the ability to develop new business for the firm, would be quite competitive.

What is the salary range for consulting psychologists?
Compensation varies greatly depending on the specific firm and the individual's performance level. In general, a first-year consultant could expect to make approximately $70,000 to $100,000. In the next two to five years, you could see a range from around $120,000 to $200,000. Again, earning potential could be higher depending on the aforementioned variables.

(Author's note: These salaries reflect ranges in the field, and Dr. Capitano is not describing salaries specific to RHR.)

What is the lifestyle like? Is there a lot of traveling?
As I am sure everyone has heard, consulting is not a 9-to-5 job, and it does involve travel because we go to the client's site. In my experience, your consulting work is a lifestyle and not necessarily separate from your

family life. It sort of all mingles together, hopefully in a healthy way. Consulting will also stretch your ability to be flexible and balance multiple competing priorities (within work and home life) on a weekly basis. There are many exciting 15-hour days with multiple challenges and multiple clients. For me, the rewards of this work have significantly outweighed the downsides.

What would you recommend to graduate students or therapists who are thinking about getting into consulting psychology?

Overall, clinical and counseling degrees prepare you very well to interact with people, conduct assessments, and provide insights to others. In addition, you can take business classes to increase your knowledge and also show your motivation and interest.

Developing your entrepreneurial spirit and taking some risks will also serve you well. Unfortunately, there are not many internships or postdocs available that provide an opportunity for this type of work. Two options that are immediately available to transitioning psychologists are working for a very small practice (one or two local business consultants) or going out on your own.

If you do decide to venture out on your own, start something of small proportion that is reasonable to demonstrate your passion and willingness to take some risks to get out there. Establishing small wins and demonstrating ongoing consulting experience will also be very attractive to larger consulting firms. Developing a workshop or training and offering it through your university or agency is another way to build your reputation.

Do you have any thoughts about seasoned practicing therapists looking to transition their careers into consulting?

I have seen some seasoned therapists transition successfully. However, this can be a very difficult transition for others. Changing gears in mid career is not an insignificant step. Although some of the base competencies will transfer fairly well, there will be a number of things that the seasoned therapist will have to unlearn. Stepping back into a learning phase in order to be an effective business consultant can be a very frustrating experience for a seasoned therapist. In my experience, most seasoned therapists do not have the energy or want to spend the time to make this transition. Understanding what is motivating you to make the change is very important. When the motivation to get into consulting is primarily financial, it is not usually a good fit. Ask yourself why you want to do business consulting. Do not underestimate the sacrifice it will take to adapt into a consulting firm that has a structure, hierarchy, and bureaucracy (as opposed to running your own practice or working in a smaller agency).

Consulting to Family Businesses

Family businesses combine two distinct realms: family life and the business world. Business highs and lows can affect the family, and family joys or challenges can affect the business. Family businesses often have their fair share of drama and disagreements.

Family therapists can utilize their skills in family counseling in a new setting: family businesses. Your skills as a family therapist will directly apply because as a family business consultant, you will:

- Assess the family dynamics and conceptualize the situation from a systems approach.
- Examine multigenerational family issues, particularly as they apply to succession planning (having the next generation take over the family business).
- Consider how family members who are not present (extended family, etc.) are actually playing a role in the current family dynamics.
- Understand how roles from the family unit are acted out within the business.
- Manage the intense emotions that the family culture, history, and issues can raise.
- Help family members to better understand and communicate with one another.

Despite all of these similarities and interchangeable skill sets, family business consultation is *not* the same as family therapy. In fact, it is very different. The goal of the consultation is a business goal, not a family goal. While family communications and relationships can certainly improve as a direct result of your consultation, that is not the aim of the work.

It is not uncommon for family business consultants to refer families for family therapy as well. Family therapy can be concurrent with the consulting or may be recommended as a precursor to the consultation so the family can work through underlying family issues that could interfere with the effectiveness of the consultation.

In family business consultation, the goals are to improve some level (or multiple levels) of business functioning. Some examples of these goals include:

- Plan for the daughter to take over her father's business when he retires.
- Structure a partnership agreement between family members.
- Create clear roles and titles for family members within the company.
- Reduce sibling rivalry regarding signing new accounts to the business.
- Resolve family members' contrasting views on how the business should be run.
- Create an agreement regarding the level of risk to be assumed by the company when the risk-averse father disagrees with the risk-seeking son.
- Resolve family disputes regarding work hours and dedication to the business.

ADVISING FAMILY BUSINESSES

In this section, we will look at the process of family business consulting to help you have an idea of how it works.

DEFINING THE CLIENT

One of the most important initial steps in consulting with a family business is defining who the client is. It is important for the consultant to always ask herself and keep in mind, "Who exactly is the client?" In a family business, the client could be an individual (the owner, the person who hired you, the future successor), the management team, or the entire family business. It is also important that you, the consultant, recognize the impact of the entire family system and interacting systems on the family.

ENGAGEMENT AND GOAL SETTING

It is crucial that the family business consultant establish clear engagement rules up front because family business advising can mean many different things to different people. I recommend beginning by negotiating a contract. It is beneficial to create a written contract that outlines the clients' goals and objectives, a timeline for achieving those objectives, and rules or procedures for the consultation.

Toward the beginning of the consultation work, you will want to conduct a systems assessment to determine how everything is currently running. You can conduct your assessment by meeting one-on-one with the family members for confidential interviews. Many advisers elect to use the data collected from these interviews to prepare a formal report to present to the family. If you choose to do this, be sure that the individuals are aware of what you will be reporting. The assessment is valuable in giving you a complete picture of the functioning of the family and the business. You will want to obtain information regarding the history of the family business, the roles of the family members in the business, motivation and skill level of the individuals, compensation issues, legal issues, financial status (profits, growth, goals), business strategy (including marketing plans), and the management team (Bork, Jaffe, Lane, Dashew, & Heisler, 1996).

It is very easy to make and act on assumptions when working with a family business. You may assume that the family's goal is to get along better, or that the fundamental goal is to increase sales. Be careful not to rely on assumptions when defining the goals. One way to be sure you are not doing this is by outlining the goals for the consultation with all of the family members who will be involved in the process. The family and consultant can collectively identify the specific goals for the work.

THE PROCESS OF THE CONSULTATION

There are several models for working with family businesses, a good one being *process consultation*. This approach is laid out in *Working with Family Businesses: A Guide for Professionals* (Bork, Jaffe, Lane, Dashew, & Heisler, 1996). In this approach, you perform six functions:

1. Work with the entire system using an open-systems perspective.
2. Balance the needs of the family and all business stakeholders.
3. Improve communication skills.
4. Develop business and personal structures and boundaries.
5. Assist in the evolution and growth of the family business.
6. Collaborate with other professionals as part of a team.

Throughout the process of consultation, you use your knowledge of family systems and developmental life cycles and match those variables up against the characteristics of the businesses system to see how each interacts with the other. Business life cycles tend to show a beginning; a growth period; a period of thriving, expansion, or renewal; and a period of decline or plateau. These stages may repeat many times throughout life cycle of the business. As a therapist, you can also use your knowledge of individual stages of development, challenges, and growth (with models such as Erickson's or Levinson's).

The intervention strategies that you utilize will be specific to the goals of the intervention and the business. For example, you will rely on various techniques for helping a family overcome conflict, plan for succession, improve profitability, enhance employee relations, or manage wealth. This is a lot of information to integrate and think about, which is part of why consulting to family businesses can be so challenging and so interesting.

A Team Approach

Ideally, the family businesses consultant works with other family business advisers and specialists. With your mental health background, you will likely be working on role conflicts, communications, issues, and relationships as they relate to the functioning of the business.

Collaboration with Other Professionals

The family business likely has many other professionals and consultants who advise them on other matters. The business is likely to most benefit when the family business's entire team is aligned to help the family. This is similar to working with a child and involving many members of the child's system, including his parents or guardian, teachers, counselors, and education specialists. With the family business, this team is likely to consist of attorneys, strategy or marketing advisers, bankers, investors, accountants, financial planners, and management development specialists. Of course you want to discuss confidentiality with your family consultees and decide which aspects of your consultation work with them you will share with the other professionals.

251

Family Therapy Referrals

As a family business consultant with a behavioral health background, it is important that you keep your consultation separate from your clinical expertise. This can be a challenge, especially when the family you are working with begins to show signs of considerable family dysfunction. It is important to know when to refer them out for family therapy. One of the best indicators of the need for such a referral is how you are feeling. When you find that you are beginning to wear your therapy hat or feel pulled to put it on, then outside therapy may be a good idea. If you find that the work is starting to focus on emotional issues, factors from the family members' pasts, or intense dysfunction, a referral is probably a good idea.

You will need to use your judgment regarding whether it would be better to have the family work on some issues before beginning or continuing with the consultation. It is often possible to have the family see a therapist and see you as a consultant at the same time. You and the therapist will need to be explicitly aware of issues of confidentiality and have clear releases of information signed so you can communicate. Collaboration between you, as the consultant, and the family therapist can be very useful.

How to Get Started in Family Business Consulting

If you do not yet have experience with family therapy, gaining theoretical knowledge and practical experience with family work is a great starting point. Take courses in family therapy and systems theory, read as many books and articles as you can, and gain clinical experience with families. If your job or practicum does not offer family work, you can find appropriate supervision and seek out family counseling experiences. Family therapy orientations such as solutions-focused therapy, which focuses more on the present and on results or resolutions, are the most amenable to family business consulting.

If you already have experience with family therapy, the next step is to start gaining some consulting experience to begin conceptualizing the situation differently. Systems-based consulting experiences are the best. You can offer organizational or team assessments within nonprofit or for-profit agencies. If you are not experienced with consulting interventions, assessment is a good place to begin. Family business consulting usually begins with a team meeting in which business goals are discussed and framed. Then compare how the results are similar to or different from ideal functioning. Request supervision on these assessments from a psychologist familiar with organizational assessment or a family business consultant.

Until you have enough experience to ethically and effectively market yourself, focus on gaining supervised experience. Once you have sufficient experience to begin looking for clients, one of the best ways to find them is through strategic referral partners. Optimal referral partners are other professionals who have family businesses as a significant part of their client base. Often these professionals find that the families are turning to them for consulting around family issues that relate to the business. These professionals are not qualified for or interested in conducting this type of consultation. They are happy to refer to an expert in family business consulting. Some of these types of professionals include:

- Small business and estate attorneys
- Consultants for business development, marketing, and strategy
- Small business loan bankers and lenders
- Small business accountants

EDUCATIONAL CONSULTING

Consulting within the school systems or regarding education is an excellent opportunity for mental health professionals.

EDUCATIONAL CONSULTING MODELS

In the 1970s, *resource consultants* began consulting with special education teachers to help improve their teaching processes and the education of their students. McKenzie (1972) put forth a model, often referred to as the Vermont Consulting Teacher Model, in which a consultant helps a classroom teacher to understand diagnoses and assist in the children's education (Brown, Pryzwansky, & Schulte, 2001). The consultant is an applied behavioral analysis expert who trains the teachers and facilitates the teachers' work with the students.

Behavioral consultation is a term created in 1983 by Bergan and Schnaps to describe the process in which a consultant helps a teacher to change his or her behavior. The classroom teacher in this model is the consultee. This type of approach is classified as instructional consulting and is based on a collaborative relationship between the consultant and the consultee or teacher (Brown, Pryzwanksy, & Schulte, 2001).

There are also group consultation models for school consulting. The group is typically a group of teachers who work with similar students or types of classes. These group consultation sessions are often used to provide support, to problem-solve work-related issues, and to gain ideas from the solutions of others in the group. Consultation groups may be *case-centered*, meaning based on specific case-consultations. Case-centered groups are led by one or two consultants and can be particularly effective at improving the professional development of new teachers. A *C-Group* is a similar type of group which has the 11 Cs as its goal: collaborating, consulting, clarifying, communicating, cohesiveness, confronting, concern, caring, confidential, commitment, and change-focused (Brown, Pryzwanksy, & Schulte, 2001).

Through my executive coaching work, I have been learning more about *consulting to parents*. Many of my executive coaching clients are hiring educational consultants to help them make the right choices for their children's education. Parents want the best education for their children but may not know how to find it, so they seek consultation in this matter. This is particularly true for the middle- to upper-class parents who have flexibility in educational options. Some parents may value public education but wonder how they should supplement it to ensure that their children receive the best education possible. Other parents debate whether they should move to a new school district that is reputed to offer better education. Since moving would be a major undertaking, it is useful to gain consultation from a child development and education specialist before putting their house on the market.

Educational consultants can also *consult to principals and administrators*. Some aspects of this type of consultation may be similar to corporate or executive consultation with a focus on improving organizational effectiveness, efficiency, or health. The consultant may work with the principal and school administrators to help them improve their leadership or communication skills. The consultant may also help the administrator strategize regarding the best way to deal with problematic students, parents, or teachers.

Who Is Doing Educational Consulting?

School psychologists, child and adolescent psychotherapists, family therapists, child assessment specialists, parenting training counselors, and other therapists who work with children and school systems may choose to consider the educational consulting field.

Consultants to school systems use various titles such as: school psychology consultants, educational consultants, child behavior specialists, parenting and educational advisers, or consultant to school systems.

How to Get Started in Educational Consulting

If you have extensive training and education in childhood development, education, applied behavioral analysis, learning disabilities, systems theory, and parenting, you will be ahead of the game and may be well prepared to get into educational consulting. If you have not taken courses in these areas, decide what type of educational consulting you are most interested and take courses for credit or continuing education classes in those areas.

The Independent Educational Consultants Association (IECA) is a great resource for obtaining training in educational consulting. This is a nonprofit, international professional association that represents full-time, experienced, independent educational consultants and advisers and is headquarted in the Washington, D.C. area. It ensures that those in the educational consulting profession adhere to the highest ethical and business standards. You can find excellent professional training institutes, workshops, and conferences through the IECA. They publish a directory of consultants in which you may want to be listed once you are a qualified consultant.

When you have the appropriate knowledge of educational consulting, you can develop a program and begin offering it to schools. Offering your program for free at first, to gather data on its effectiveness and the areas in which it helps the schools, students, or parents. As your program improves and becomes successful, you can begin to charge for it. Research the market rate for similar services in your area and in similar school systems since rates will vary widely by location. As you will see in the following interview, schools are looking for creative, educational, thought-provoking, and informative programs for their students, and they are willing to pay for high-quality consultation. Many schools and their teachers are in need of process improvement. By consulting to schools, you can benefit hundreds of students through your services.

Interview with Dr. Michael Fowlin

Michael Fowlin combines his interests in acting and psychology into work that includes peer mediation, diversity workshops, violence prevention, and gender sensitivity training. His web site is www.michaelfowlin.com, and he can be reached at by telephone at (973) 326-9838.

How are you involved with school or educational consulting?
Currently, I am contracted by schools to put on motivational presentations for students and staff. The presentations address a wide range of diversity topics, including race relations, gender equity, sexual orientation inclusiveness, and the needs of special education children. The presentation mixes psychological training with traditional theater and speech techniques. My performance/presentation is about 75 minutes long, with questions and comments that follow. In some schools, I am asked to assist in follow-up activities.

How did you get started?
The genesis of my productions started in a graduate class in the spring semester of 1995. I was taking a class called "Adolescent Theory and Therapy." Each student was required to make a presentation on a topic in the subject area. My topic was adolescent sexuality. Now, it is important to know that I've always hated doing strict didactic presentations. My personality always needs to spice things up a little. So that's what I did. Before getting into the didactic piece of my presentation, I opened up with a 15-minute mini one-man show, highlighting various characters addressing a plethora of areas within adolescent sexuality.

The main reason I chose to open up my presentation in this format was to escape the drab routine of reciting endless statistics. Little did I know that within a few months of that class I would be called on to put together a similar show for delegates attending a diversity camp called Anytown. It was at this camp where I was discovered. Students saw me perform and they were overwhelmed, to say the least. They wondered why there weren't assemblies in their schools that addressed the topics I covered. They wanted to know if I would be willing to perform at their schools. I thought, "Sure, it would be great to be able to act a little while I'm in graduate school." I knew with my graduate school demands I could only do a few shows a year, and that's what happened . . . in the first couple of years. However, as each year progressed, I ended up doing more shows. I started with four shows a year. Now, almost 10 years later, and with five separate presentations, I do between 340 and 370 shows/presentations a year.

What are some of the rewarding aspects of this type of work?
For the most part, the entire package of presenting at schools is extremely rewarding. Being on stage in front of an entire school, making people laugh, cry, and think is magical. I specifically enjoy knowing that I am saving lives. The stories that people share with me after my presentations are deeply touching. Knowing that I can incorporate my psychological training to help people in their moment of crisis is a powerful responsibility and challenge. I've seen people on the brink of death via suicide or illness finding some peace through my presentation.

I recall one evening, in the latter part of 2003, a man came up to me after my presentation at a northern New Jersey high school. He looked to be in his mid to late 20s. He stated that he had seen me perform at his high school back in 1995 when he was a senior. On the day I presented at his school, he was thinking about suicide. Fortunately, after my show, he felt no such urge to end his life. He was deeply affected by my presentation, desirous to make his life count for a greater purpose. He then went on to say, "I stand before you today as president of this board of education, because you saved my life." I was speechless. He was just one of many individuals who have shared the impact of my presentation on their lives.

Another enjoyable aspect of my work is definitely the fact that I'm my own boss. There is nothing more satisfying to my spirit than waking up knowing that I do not have to report to any boss. I would not like the idea of reporting to someone in the line of work that I'm in—it would cause me great distress.

What are your top 5 to 10 recommendations for therapists who want to begin an educational consulting type of program?

1. Be creative.
2. Find your own angle.
3. Be engaging and entertaining.

4. Be financially reasonable, but not inexpensive. Inexpensive is associated with cheap. Cheap is associated with "not very good."
5. Put together a press kit.
6. Be flexible. Have themes that can adapt to a variety of topics or concerns.
7. Know your limits.
8. Be willing to say no.
9. Make sure that your presentation is a passion, not just an income maker.
10. Connect. Connect. Connect.

RESOURCES

BOOKS

Beer, M. (1980). *Organizational change and development: A systems view*. Santa Monica, CA: Goodyear.

Bork, D., Jaffe, D. T., Lane, S. H., Dashew, L., & Heisler, Q. G. (1996). *Working with family businesses: A guide for professionals*. San Francisco: Jossey-Bass.

Brown, D., Pryzwanksy, W. B. & Schulte, A.C. (2001). *Psychological consultation: Introduction to theory and practice*. Needham Heights, MA: Allyn & Bacon.

Buckingham, M., & Coffman, C. (1999). *First, break all the rules: What the world's greatest managers do differently* (1st ed.). New York: Simon & Schuster.

Charan, R., Drotter, S., & Noel, J. (2000). *The leadership pipeline: How to build the leadership powered company*. San Francisco: Jossey-Bass.

Conger, J. A., & Benjamin, B. (1999). *Building leaders: How successful companies develop the next generation* (Jossey Bass Business and Management Series). San Francisco: Jossey-Bass.

Drucker, P. F. (2002). *The effective executive revised* (1st ed.). New York: HarperBusiness.

Dehni, J., Harvard University Business School, and Harvard Business School Management Consulting Club (2000). *The Harvard Business School guide to careers in management consulting*. Cambridge, MA: Harvard Business School Press.

Goleman, D., McKee, A., & Boyatzis, R. E. (2002). *Primal leadership: Realizing the power of emotional intelligence* (1st ed.). Cambridge, MA: Harvard Business School Press.

G. Caplan & R. B. Caplan (1999). *Mental health consultation and collaboration*. Long Grove, IL: Waveland Pr Inc.

Katz, D., & Kane, R. L. (1978). *The social psychology of organizations*. New York: John Wiley & Sons, Inc.

Lowman, R. L., California School of Organizational Studies, & Alliant International University (2002). *The California School of Organizational Studies handbook of organizational consulting psychology: A comprehensive guide to theory, skills, and techniques*. San Francisco: Jossey-Bass.

Martin, I. (1996). *From couch to corporation: Becoming a successful corporate therapist* (1st ed.). New York: John Wiley & Sons, Inc.

Rothwell, W. J., Sullivan, R., & McLean, G. N. (1995). *Practicing organizational development: A guide for consultants*. San Francisco: Jossey-Bass.

Weiss, A. (2002.) *Million dollar consulting: The professional's guide to growing a practice* (3rd ed.). New York: McGraw-Hill.

WEB SITES

American Association for Marriage and Family Therapy:

www.aamft.org/index_nm.asp

APA's Division 13—Society of Consulting Psychology:

www.apa.org/about/division/div13.html

APA's Division 14—Society for Industrial and Organizational Psychology:

www.apa.org/about/division/div14.html

Independent Educational Consultants Association:

www.educationalconsulting.org

Global Consulting Partnership's Professional Executive Coaching Certificate Program:

www.clinical-to-consulting.com

The Family Business Consulting Group:

www.efamilybusiness.com

RHR International:

www.rhrinternational.com

The Family Firm Institute (FFI) — an international professional membership organization for the family business field:

www.ffi.org

Resource for family business owners:

www.fambiz.com

Become listed as a consultant:

www.prosavvy.com

TERMINOLOGY

consultant   One who provides professional advice, information, and
consulting services.

educational consulting   A process by which a consultant with expertise
in human behavior, education, or teaching enters the school system with
the goal of creating an optimal and most effective educational system for
the students.

executive integration   The process by which an executive assimilates
into a new corporation, which can be facilitated and assisted with
consultation.

family business consultation   A consulting process in which an expert
in human behavior, family business, or business development works with
family business owners (and at times the business's employees) to promote optimal business performance.

Fortune 500 companies   The 500 companies with the highest annual
revenues as reported in *Fortune* magazine. All companies who make the
list publish financial data and must report part or all of their financial figures to a government agency.

human resources   The department or division within an organization concerned with employees and personnel.

open system   In systems theory, a system that receives information from outside of the system, is affected by information outside of the system, sends information outside of the system, and has an impact on factors outside of the system.

organization development   A consultation process that identifies and develops strengths in a company's human resources to increase problem-solving skills, team performance, and overall effectiveness of the organization.

succession planning   The plan that is set in place for the business to switch hands from the current owner or president to the next. In a family business, this means planning for the next generation to take over the business.

Academia and Teaching

Thought flows in terms of stories —stories about events, stories about people, and stories about intentions and achievements. The best teachers are the best storytellers. We learn in the form of stories.

Frank Smith

Professors known as outstanding lecturers do two things; they use a simple plan and many examples.

W. McKeachie

TO TEACH, CONDUCT RESEARCH, OR DO BOTH?

Therapists have very different reasons for choosing to get into the academic world. One of the chief distinctions is whether you want to be primarily involved with teaching or researching. Typically, if you are interested in pursuing an academic tenure-track faculty position at a university, you will need to be proficient and prolific with your research activities. You are likely to be recruited or competitive for academic positions based on your areas of research interest, experience, and publications.

If you know that you love to teach but are not very much into research, you have several options. One option is to teach as an adjunct professor or to teach within a department that is more practice-based and less research-based. For instance, you could look into teaching an organizational psychology, human behavior and motivation, or systems theory course within an MBA program. Another option is to teach as a core faculty member within a program that does not require a good deal of research. Many doctor of psychology (PsyD) and master's of social work (MSW) programs do not entail a high degree of research. While many professors in these programs conduct empirical research, some do not.

THE ACADEMIC WORLD

Roediger (in Sternberg, 1999) makes the noteworthy point that academia is not homogenous. A professor position at a small liberal arts college may focus on teaching, whereas faculty at large universities are likely to devote a large amount of time to research. Among professors at large universities, some may teach two or three courses per semester while others teach two courses per year. The setting in which you choose to work is going to define, to a large extent, the requirements, activities, and expectations for you.

Academic positions are typically well suited for those who are interested in some combination of research, teaching, and clinical work. Academic positions tend to lend themselves well to some of the diversified career options we have discussed, such as writing or public speaking in addition to one's regular position. A university affiliation, particularly a professorship position, can help you gain more media attention.

PUBLISH OR PERISH

As most people know, the academic world is very much driven by numbers—the number of publications produced. For those who enjoy research, data analysis, and writing, the push for publishing can feel challenging and motivating. When you know exactly what is expected of you in terms of publications, you can use that as a goal to produce articles.

Writing and publishing can be enormously professionally fulfilling and can help you to network with interesting colleagues across the globe. When people see your name on an article similar to their research area, they may contact you for collaboration, and vice versa. You can eventually use your publications as a platform for obtaining tenure, asking for raises, getting grant funding, and getting a book deal.

For those who do not take pleasure in research activities, the pressures to publish can feel overwhelming and frustrating. Like any job activity, when you must do a lot of something that you do not really enjoy, you can feel resentful and feel like you are constantly being pushed to do something rather than being pulled toward it. When research is not consistent with your career vision, you will feel like you are being dragged, rather than experiencing our goal for you, which is to feel drawn toward the activity like a magnet. The quantity and quality of expected publications varies greatly by university, college, department, job position, and whether you are on a tenure track. Think about what level of research you would like to be involved with, and then find academic positions that are in line with that goal. If you know that you are not very interested in research, look into adjunct and instructor positions that may not require research.

Doing Two (or Three or Four) Things at Once

The ability to manage your time in academia is critical to your success. Most academic positions require a juggling act between reading and preparation for courses and research, grant writing, collaborating with other faculty, grading essays and examinations, meeting with students, writing papers and books, attending faculty and committee meetings, attending conferences and professional meetings, lecturing in different locales, consulting, and editing manuscripts. An academic career requires excellent time management skills and the ability to handle multiple demands.

Many professors lament their lack of dedicated time to conduct research. For those who go into academia primarily as researchers, it is frustrating not to have time to do it. The primary piece of advice from professors who do find time to research is to learn how to prioritize and schedule. You may look for strategic ways to make your schedule work for you. For example, if you know that you do your best research when you have a whole day to dedicate to it, stack your courses together on specific days. You could teach on Mondays and then dedicate the other days to your research activities. To be successful in academia, you will need to learn how to filter out distractions and keep your eye on where you need to be going at all times.

Another solution to the problem of multiple activities and demands is to get creative and look for opportunities wherever you can. Martin Franklin, PhD, associate professor of clinical psychology in psychiatry at the University of Pennsylvania School of Medicine, has some excellent advice for how to succeed in academia. One of his recommendations is to try to get two birds with one stone whenever you can. For example, if you are working in a clinical setting and would like to build up the research component of your curriculum vitae, you can collect data within the clinical setting. Integrating research into clinical practice allows you to keep your hands in both worlds and thereby maintain maximum flexibility. It also allows you to examine different kinds of questions outside the context of the randomized controlled trial, and gives you something else to do while your trials are baking—which usually takes five to seven years from the entry of the first patient until the publication of the main findings, at least with the big multicenter trials. You can get some great data on treatment effectiveness and generalizability. You can also look at therapist effects, such as the differences in treatment outcomes with treatment conducted by interns versus experienced licensed clinicians.

Dr. Franklin, along with Dr. Jonathan Abramowitz and colleagues, published eight papers from data collected in the open clinic of the Center for Treatment and Study of Anxiety. He suggests using the data collected in a clinic as an opportunity to answer some questions and then submitting a grant request to fund the next step of ideas that follow from this data. One of their recent articles based on clinic data that compared the effectiveness of exposure and ritual prevention for obsessive-compulsive disorder in randomized and non-randomized samples was published in *The Journal of Consulting and Clinical Psychology* (JCCP) (Franklin et al., 2000). Their studies are acknowledged to be open trial data with no follow-up and no truly independent assessments, yet all eight were published in good journals, for the most part, including four into APA journals and three into JCCP, which is reputed to be the top tier journal in this field.

Another recommendation from Dr. Franklin is to consider research opportunities within the context of your position. If you are in an administrative position and you have access to large lists of psychologists, you can find out what people are really using for treatments. If you want to disseminate an empirically supported treatment, you can first use this data to show whether therapists in the community are actually using empirically supported treatments, and whether a need for treatment dissemination exists.

Along with the multiple demands in academia often comes a wonderful benefit: flexibility. Much of your time is yours to schedule. Roediger states that in his experience, a nice benefit is the independence and flexibility to write when you want to write, and read when you want to read. If he spends a day attending a parent-teacher conference for his child, he is able to do some work when he gets home in the evening (Sternberg, 1999).

NEGOTIATING YOUR SALARY AND CONTRACT

In an article by Tori DeAngelis in a recent issue of the APA's *Monitor on Psychology*, several issues for new psychologists were addressed. One of the recommendations was to negotiate your salary. DeAngelis cited Dr. Karen Gasper as saying that it is particularly important in academia to negotiate your salary because of the wide variation in starting salaries. Your first salary sets an anchor for all of your later salaries, and if it is set too low it will be hard to bring it up later. You can use other offers to negotiate your salary.

Remember that the key to effective negotiation skills is to have in mind both your ideal outcome and your satisfactory outcome. Anywhere in the window between them is an offer that you would accept, but you will try to secure a salary in the higher end of that range; an offer below that range will be unacceptable. To help you set your range, find out what faculty and instructors in similar positions are earning. Then you can objectively compare your ideal salary to what others are earning to be sure that it is reasonable. Review your contract with a fine-tooth comb and have your attorney review it as well. Adopt a future-oriented view and ask yourself, "Would this work for me five, ten, fifteen years down the line as well as right now?" Do not jump into something just because you are excited about the prestige of working at a particular university or feel like you really need a job right then.

Be alert to items like noncompete agreements. Some departments will require that you sign a noncompete agreement, stating that you will not engage in outside work that can be seen as in direct competition to your department, center, or university. This type of agreement may limit you from seeing clients in private practice. If you know that you are interested in seeing clients in private practice, you should negotiate this point. You can negotiate to see clients that would not otherwise be seen at your center so a mutually beneficial situation (not a competitive situation) is created. For instance, if you are working in a depression research center that conducts research and provides treatment for individuals, you can negotiate to see couples and families in private practice. Universities may also require that you give them a portion of what you earn in private practice. This percentage can be negotiated as well. If your university has a strict, no-negotiation policy on these noncompete matters, you can use that to negotiate a higher salary by saying something like, "I was planning to see private clients to supplement my salary. If that is not a possibility, I would be willing to consider the position if my salary offer was increased by five percent."

FIND A MENTOR

A wonderful mentor can make a world of difference for your success and satisfaction in academia. Such an individual can teach you a great deal, introduce you to great networks, and use his or her resources to help you get your own grants and publications. Likewise, the chair or director of your department can have an effect on the tone of your career. The tone and climate of your department in academia can make a significant difference in your happiness and ability to succeed there. Consider whether the tone of the department is competitive, supportive, collaborative, intellectually rewarding, creative, research-focused, treatment-focused, helpful, enjoyable, casual, formal, or independent. Some of these qualities are great if they are not taken to an extreme. Having some independence, for instance, is ideal, but if the overall tone is completely independent then you may miss opportunities to collaborate with and learn from your colleagues.

Here are some qualities to look for in selecting an ideal mentor:

Availability. This person makes himself available to you for questions and collaboration. While many prominent psychologists are well known and in high demand all over the world, and therefore are out of town a great deal, you want to look for someone who is readily available when she is around. Consider the trade-off between prominence and availability. It may be a better choice to work with a mentor whose research is not quite as well known, but who is more frequently available to you.

Empowerment. Remember our discussion of effective organizational leaders in Chapter 6? One of the most critical qualities of a great leader or mentor is her ability to empower others. This means that she will give you the resources you need to do your job exceptionally well *and* will give you the freedom and independence to make it on your own. The best mentors are those who truly want to see their junior faculty getting large grants and many publications, and who will help you learn how to do so on your own.

Flexibility. You want the senior faculty who you work under to be flexible and open-minded enough to hear your views and thoughtfully consider your suggestions and ideas. You want to feel that you can positively make a difference and influence your department, not that you are just a sheep following the herd.

Independence. A good mentor is like a good parent. The parent lets the child try new things and perhaps make some mistakes on his own. This is how the child learns and grows. If a mentor is constantly asking you to do things for him and under his direct guidance, you will not have the independence to make it on your own. Independence goes hand in hand with empowerment. From the experience of independence, you learn how to be empowered. It will be much more difficult to find success without this quality — it is possible, but it can feel like an uphill battle.

Loyalty. You want to feel that the senior faculty or your mentor will be there for you. You want to know that they will defend you (unless, of course, you do something egregious). It would be horrible to worry about your colleagues talking about you behind your back or dismissing your ideas and contributions. Ideally, your mentor and department chairs will be highly supportive of you, even when they are not personally interested in your research topic.

Similar Values. An ideal mentor or chair is someone who supports your value system. If, for example, you know that you want to have a child in the next few years and that you would like to reduce your work to 60 percent of your full-time requirements, it is helpful if your mentor or department chair will be supportive. When your value system is in opposition to that of your supervisor, boss, mentor, or chair, you may find yourself frequently frustrated and dissatisfied.

WHAT YOU REALLY NEED TO KNOW AND DO TO GET AHEAD IN ACADEMIA

According to Marty Franklin, what you need to know and do depends in part on your academic track and on the degree of research focus in your department. He recommends that you clearly know what track you're on and what is expected from you within that track. If, for instance, you are on a purely research track, then you should focus your time and energy on publishing papers in peer-reviewed journals, almost to the exclusion of other projects. If you are on a clinical-educator track, books and book chapters can also count toward promotion and thus benefit your career.

While you still want to focus most of your attention on your articles and papers, books and chapters may count toward the requirements and expectations the institution has for you.

In academia, according to Dr. Franklin, it is critical to be practical and discerning about every project that you take on. If you know that you will be evaluated in five years, it may not be a good idea to run a study looking only at longitudinal data that will not be mined for seven years. Ask yourself whether you could do a shorter project or experiment to collect data that you could analyze after one year.

In summary, he says, "Keep your eye on the pragmatic outcomes. Know the dependent measures by which you will be evaluated up front." If you know that you will be expected to produce six to eight papers per year, you can calculate how many you need to *submit* per year, or even per month, to achieve your goal. You will benefit your career and please your department or university when you are achieving your goals.

Roediger states that in his opinion, the two factors that predict success in the academic world are achievement motivation and persistence. He says that achievement motivation entails how much you want to do and how hard you are willing to work to do it. Many universities require a great deal from their professors in terms of publications, grant funding, and the like, and you need to be internally motivated to live up to these expectations (Sternberg, 1999).

Persistence is important in academia because there are many times when you will need to try and try again despite rejection. Many grant proposals need to be resubmitted several times and can take months or years to get funded. Because of this, I will add patience and acceptance to Roediger's list. You must first be patient about the timeline that research and grant submissions often entail. You must also accept the fact that some things are beyond your control, and know when to abandon an idea that is not working in favor of an alternative plan.

Do not be afraid to ask questions and continue asking them until you get answers. This is the time to be the CEO of your career and be proactive. If you know that six to eight papers per year will be expected of you, find out all the details. Ask how many of those papers you are expected to be first author on. Find out whether the order of authorship matters. Learn whether book chapters count and how they are weighed.

When authorship order on your papers matters, Dr. Franklin recommends that you have a very clear and open conversation with colleagues about the order of authorship *before* any work is begun, and document the decisions from this conversation in writing. You will need to be assertive about your goals for the authorship order and make a plan for what each author (and their respective position) will contribute to the project. It is not a good idea to wait and see how much work everyone does. It is a good idea to re-evaluate people's time investments as you go along to be sure that authorship order corresponds with work.

Your selection of a mentor is another important area that can help you to succeed in academia. As discussed previously, you should find a mentor with whom you feel comfortable, who is supportive, and who fosters your professional development. Dr. Franklin recommends that you select a mentor who is currently publishing a good amount in your field. For those who are still students, it is a good idea to find out about a potential mentor or dissertation chair's policies for letting students work with them, and also what their previous students are doing now. If they are out doing what you want to be doing, that is a great sign.

It is also a good idea to look at the projects you take on and your internship and training experiences in this way. If you do your internship at a place where no one is conducting research and publishing, this could hurt you. If you have a very strong research background going into an internship or a postdoc, then research during that year may be less important. For those who have not yet begun or completed dissertation work, pick something doable. Academia does not view dissertation as your life's work. Instead of planning to do something grandiose, plan to do something that you are interested in and can finish on time. You can always do larger-scale research projects down the line when you are getting paid for your work.

The final point to make here about how to really succeed in academia is the idea of having balance in your life. Most academicians do not work 9 to 5, 40 hours a week. On the other hand, you need to consider what you really want to do in your career and your life. You may be able to limit yourself to 55 total hours of work per week and still advance your career and see your family. Dr. Franklin said that many in academia struggle with the feeling of never being caught up and never having a clean desk. The best approach, he says, is to accept that this is a fact of academic life. There is not time to be perfectionistic and do everything just right in the academic world, at least not if you want to work less than 80 hours per week. This is where being strategic about what you take on and how you allocate your time comes back into play. If you create one perfect paper, you may be forsaking six good papers. When your grant proposal or your CV is reviewed, people will see one versus six publications, and they are unlikely to read that perfect paper anyway. If you have a tendency toward perfectionism, remember that it may cost you in both your personal and professional life. If you set the precedent of working 85 hours a week, or getting mired in details and obsessions, this may hinder you from meeting many of your goals.

TEACHING AS THE PRIMARY CAREER PATH

Teaching can be an immensely rewarding way to spend your professional career or an enjoyable adjunct to your other career activities.

THE JOYS AND BENEFITS OF TEACHING

Many who teach say that they learn more from teaching than they ever would from other activities. Many therapists also feel that teaching is a nice way to help a lot of people (students) without some of the burnout issues that can come with full-time clinical work.

Super and Super (2001) state that a key benefit of teaching at the university level is the prestige it offers you. They state that a teaching assignment gives you credibility and is a sign of attainment. This makes sense intuitively, because one would assume that if you are teaching something, then you are an expert in it. You are able to make yourself known to a wider audience and enjoy sharing your knowledge. This prestige from university connections is an incentive to teach part-time. It can help you to make connections and advance your career.

Depending on the type of setting you teach in, teaching may not be the most lucrative professional activity. For instance, one of my colleagues recently told me that he was offered an instructor position at a university to teach a class. The entire course paid $2,000, which is what he typically charged for one or two days of consulting work. Because the topic was one that he had lectured on in the past, the course would not require a great deal of preparation, so the amount paid was fine. His interest in teaching was not for the extra income as much as for the enjoyment, credibility, and fulfillment. He believed that teaching is one of the best ways to give back. We have all had professors who have literally changed the course of our careers and our lives. As a professor or teacher, the difference that you can make in the lives of your students can be profound.

Another great reason to teach is to get you thinking. Teaching can also inspire and satisfy you. Many top writers say that they came up with book ideas while they were teaching or during conversations with students or colleagues. You learn something best when you teach it, and you begin to think in new ways about all the things you already know. To teach, you need to be up on the latest research, data, and information. Good teachers continually learn more about their subject matter.

Teaching can also help you with developing lectures and speaking programs. You can look at it as a paid opportunity to develop and practice lectures that you can later modify and promote independently. Before delivering and charging for your services as a professional speaker, it is a great idea to have some practice with student audiences. Both your confidence and the quality of your program will improve. Super and Super (2005) point out that by teaching in a classroom, you will develop and refine your abilities to synthesize and present information. You can then apply these skills to professional speaking engagements.

Another great reason to teach is to hone your communication skills. Anxiety or apprehension about public speaking is more the norm than the exception for most professionals, therapists included. Public speaking generally requires a good deal of experience before you can really become comfortable at it. By teaching a course or a full course load, you can greatly improve your public speaking abilities and be in a better position later to do professional speaking, which is a highly lucrative field.

TEACHING IN VARIOUS SETTINGS

If you are interested in teaching at the university level, you have several options. The first consideration is whether you also want to do something else part-time, such as work at an agency, a part-time private practice, or part-time writing or professional speaking. If you want to do something else part-time and teach part-time, you can teach in a variety of settings as an instructor or adjunct professor. Some examples include:

- Teach a class at a community college.
- Teach a class at a high school, such as an advanced placement class.

- Train medical students or residents by teaching seminars on clinical issues.
- Teach a class in a clinical psychology program (such as a PsyD program).
- Teach a class in a social work program (such as an MSW program).

TEACHING WITH A MASTER'S DEGREE VERSUS A DOCTORATE

It is certainly possible to find great teaching positions with a master's-level degree. If you have a master's and are not interested in pursuing a doctorate, it may be best to look into teaching positions at two-year colleges and community colleges. While these institutions do not offer the same degree of name recognition and prestige that four-year schools and large universities do, they offer many excellent opportunities. You can play a role in preparing students to go on to four-year colleges and even advanced degrees. A friend from my undergraduate university completed two years at a community college before transferring to Cornell. He described some fantastic teachers at the community college who prepared him well to transition into an Ivy League school. He later went on to a PhD program in developmental psychology and has excelled across the board.

Teaching in a two-year college or community college can also be a better match for you if you are not as interested in running research protocols or writing grants as you are in working directly with students. You are less likely to experience the types of pressure that professors in large universities have. There are also jobs for master's-level therapists in four-year colleges and universities. You may look into adjunct teacher and instructor positions. A doctorate degree will open more doors for you if your goal is to obtain a faculty position at a major university.

The "all but dissertation" (ABD) designation may make it more difficult for you to obtain a faculty position. Even though you are so close to completing your degree, many universities will view the ABD as a negative because you will need to spend time completing your dissertation. Faculty positions are highly competitive and many programs look for the most highly skilled and credentialed candidate they can find. Another problem with ABD is that you are likely to get paid significantly less. You may set yourself up to make less than you are worth for many years into your career if you initially take an ABD position.

TEACHING AND OTHER WORK AT ONCE

Many professors and instructors enjoy having a small private practice in which they see patients, conduct assessments, provide consultations, or do private lectures and workshops. This allows you to diversify your services, earn supplemental income, and stay involved with different areas of professional practice. As mentioned earlier, in many faculty positions you either cannot do some of these additional services or you can keep only a percentage of your income earned with them. There may be different regulations, based on your university's policies, for different private services provided. If you are interviewing for teaching or faculty positions, these are important matters to be aware of, preferably before signing the contract.

Creating marketable programs from your lectures is relatively easy. Take a few of your more popular or interesting lectures and think about who else would like to hear them. Write a list of potential target audiences and select the best one (biggest, most well defined, most approachable, and those who can afford to attend your programs) to begin with. Then begin to modify your lecture so that it fits your new audience. Consider whether it would work best as a lecture, workshop, or seminar. Develop it, price it, and begin marketing it.

Similarly, you can build a small clinical or consulting practice while you are teaching. The key is to decide on a realistic goal for the number of clients or consultations that you want to do. Make sure that doing so in no way competes with your work at the university, if that is an issue. Ask your colleagues, talk to supervisors, directors, and department chairs to be sure what your guidelines are, and then begin developing your small practice.

Interview with Robert A. Rando, PhD

Dr. Robert Rando is the director of the Center for Psychological Services and an associate professor in the school of professional psychology at Wright State University in Dayton, Ohio. He can be reached via the counseling center's web site, www.wright-counseling.com.

What are some of the most enjoyable aspects of teaching?
One of the most enjoyable aspects of teaching is being able to participate in the professional development of the students. I have also never taught a

class, provided supervision, or provided therapy and not learned something. Teaching is a mutual process. I enjoy the mutuality and the growth that I am able to participate in.

In your opinion, is it rewarding to teach in combination with doing other professional activities?
It is very rewarding to teach in combination with my administrative and clinical activities, when I have the time. When my administrative duties are intense, it is more difficult for me to enjoy teaching—everything feels rushed and I don't enjoy the process to the same degree.

How can a student or therapist gain experience with teaching?
Some programs offer teaching assistant positions, fellowships, or graduate assistantships as a means for students to gain experience. Some academic programs in psychology have courses on teaching that can be very beneficial. I also think that students and therapists should explore neighboring colleges—quite often part-time teaching positions are available.

APPLICATION FOR TEACHING OR ACADEMIC FACULTY POSITIONS

When you know that you want a teaching or a faculty position, the first step is to identify some settings where you would like to teach. Factors to consider include:

- Geographic location.
- Salary and compensation packages.
- Student populations (i.e., undergraduate, graduate).
- Types of courses and course subject matter (i.e., large lecture courses versus seminars or experiential courses).
- Colleagues—backgrounds, areas of research, and teaching interests.
- Climate or culture of the department.
- Funding for research activities; support for grant writing and submission.
- Research expectations and requirements.
- Reputation of the university or college.
- Whether they have your ideal position (i.e., tenure-track faculty, clinical faculty, staff psychologist, instructor, etc.).

- Whether the site is affiliated with a clinical program such as a university counseling center, hospital, or clinic.
- Dedication to promoting a diverse professional climate by hiring (and promoting) women and people with various ethnic, racial, and cultural backgrounds.

Once you have identified some settings that meet your criteria, you can inquire whether they are hiring. Conversely, you can research places that are currently hiring to determine whether those places meet your needs. To begin application, you will need to request letters of recommendation. Most sites require three letters, but this can vary. It is typically a good idea to get at least one or two letters from people in positions similar to the type of position you are applying for. For example, if you are applying for a primarily research-based academic position, you would want letters from reputable researchers.

You will then need to write a letter of interest. Think of this letter as a marketing tool. You are essentially marketing yourself and describing why you are a person they should hire and would want to work with. Do not be overly modest about your accomplishments or they will not know how great you would be in that position. Always keep in mind one of the fundamental rules of marketing: to answer the question, "What's in it for me?" The people who are reviewing your materials will be asking themselves the question, "How would I, my organization, or my department benefit from hiring this person?" Highlight the specific potential benefits you would bring by focusing on your areas of expertise, skills, and unique attributes that can help them meet their strategic goals. Get feedback on your letter—ask several colleagues and supervisors to review it. You could also contact the faculty development department at the university from which you graduated. They are often able to provide in-discipline samples of other letters of interest or intent and offer feedback on your letter.

Interview with Indira Paharia, PsyD

Dr. Paharia is a licensed clinical psychologist and serves as both assistant professor and assistant director of the Institute for Graduate Clinical Psychology at Widener University in Wilmington, Delaware. Her specialty is health psychology.

What is it like to do a few different avenues of mental health work?

I am a core faculty member at the assistant professor level and teach a full doctoral level course load each semester. It is often challenging to balance my role as part of the faculty and my role as part of the administration. I have to maintain clear boundaries in order not to jeopardize my administrative position, while simultaneously building strong relationships with fellow professors. It is also challenging to balance all the responsibilities of administration, teaching, and research at once. It is a juggling act that requires a lot of organization and prioritizing.

What is one piece of career advice that you wish someone had told you as you were getting started?

How difficult it would be to pay off student loans as a psychologist. Also how sexist most professional environments continue to be.

How might practicing therapists get involved with teaching, either part-time or full-time?

Publish in local journals; conduct continuing education workshops; attend university-sponsored events to network with the faculty; find out what a program is searching for and contact the dean with a proposal; get a reference from an alumnus of the program; take a visiting professor or adjunct position.

How do you believe the field of mental health will change in the next five or ten years?

Mental health will likely change in parallel to changes seen in medicine within the last 10 years. Therefore, there will be a greater push for specialization within psychology, and health psychology will move to the forefront of mental health as further integration between medicine and psychology is realized. We may also see increased reimbursement for our services as managed care is forced to expand coverage.

Interview with Martin M. Antony, PhD, ABPP

Martin Antony is a professor in the department of psychiatry and behavioural neurosciences at McMaster University in Hamilton, Ontario, and is the psychologist-in-chief and director of the Anxiety Treatment and Research Centre at St. Joseph's Healthcare in

Hamilton. To learn more about Dr. Antony and his work, visit www.martinantony.com.

You are successful in many areas, including research, teaching, clinical work, and writing. How has this level of diversification benefited your career?

The more different types of things I do, the more people become aware of my work and the more opportunities arise. It's not necessarily always a good thing. In academia, value is placed on specific research in a focused area, while my research is broader. There are always costs and benefits, which depend on the setting and the people around. Some programs would look at my CV and think it is too broad, while others may think it is great. I choose to do what I enjoy. I like doing a lot of different things, so that keeps it interesting for me.

What are some ways that you are involved with teaching?

I do a lot of clinical teaching and supervision. I do some lectures for psychiatry and psychology residents. Continuing education classes and workshops provide opportunities for another type of teaching. I also teach and supervise within the psychology internship program here at St. Joseph's Healthcare. I began this internship program and we're undergoing accreditation now. In the past, when I was at the University of Toronto, I taught lecture style courses, like abnormal psychology.

How could someone who is interested in teaching courses or running workshops get started?

To find opportunities to teach formal courses, the best thing to do is to contact departments where courses are being taught. For example, at the University of Toronto, I had a faculty appointment in the department of psychiatry, but I wanted to teach a course in the department of psychology. I was able to arrange it with a phone call. Fortunately, they had a course that needed to be taught, and none of their own faculty were able to teach it.

For opportunities to teach workshops, the first thing you need to do is make sure you have done something that would make people want to attend a workshop you are giving. Being associated with an academic center is one way to gain credibility, but it is certainly not necessary by any means. Having had special training and expertise will make you attractive as a workshop presenter. In my case, one of the biggest things that has been useful is having written books. A lot of times the people who go to workshops are clinicians who know about the books. You also need to make sure that you do good workshops. A lot of my workshop opportunities have come as a result of word of mouth.

I've also done a bit of marketing. I will occasionally write to sponsors of other workshops with a description of my workshops, and I also have a web site. Another option is putting on your own workshops, rather than going through a sponsor. There are companies who will organize everything for you, like brochures, mailing lists, and catering, or you can save money and do it yourself. If you are new to giving workshops, consider giving some for free. I once heard Christine Padesky mention that she got her start that way. Now she is a very successful author and workshop presenter, as well as a psychologist who runs a successful private practice.

How can professors market themselves within their universities?

At my university and hospital, I make a point of doing lectures and clinical workshops for free from time to time. For me, it is important to be marketing myself both outside and within the institution. In my setting, many of the departments do not know about the research I do, so it is up to me to show them. For example, whenever I publish a paper, I send a copy to our psychiatrist-in-chief and the chair of my academic department, as well as several administrative directors, our hospital CEO, and the head of our hospital's marketing department. I do this with my books, too. I also make a point of getting onto committees so people know who I am and what I am doing.

I make sure that any news about our Centre gets posted in the hospital's newsletter and on the university's web site. For example, if a staff member wins an award or publishes a new book, we make sure that the news gets out there. Our staff are encouraged to get involved in community lectures and to get their names out there as much as possible. A number of us do a lot of media interviews (TV, radio) as well.

One of the things I like about my setting is that I have independence. This is, in part, because I let people know what I am getting done. I sometimes work from home and I can accomplish a lot from there. Making sure the hospital knows what I am doing is helpful in gaining flexibility and space as needed.

How does your writing and lecturing tie in to your academic and research work?

Everything mutually enhances the others. For example, we studied perfectionism across anxiety disorders and presented the findings at the annual Association for Advancement of Behavior Therapy (AABT) meeting. New Harbinger then asked me to do a book on perfectionism, based on the poster.

In other cases, the books have influenced the research. Now we have a postdoc looking at the effectiveness of one of my self-help books for social phobia versus standard therapist-assisted therapy. I recently got an e-mail from a student in Australia who is using the perfectionism self-help book as part of a research study. It can happen in either direction.

What are some tips to help professionals survive and thrive in academia?

It is probably hard to succeed in academia without working hard. It is unusual to have 9 to 5 type hours. It is easier to do a job you don't enjoy if you're working only 35 hours a week. However, if you are working 50 or 60 hours each week, make sure you like what you are doing.

There are a lot of ways to measure what is a good job. Some high-profile departments and universities may not be great to work in. Other settings can be more friendly and flexible but may not have the reputation. It comes back to your own needs and wants. In selecting a position, consider factors like the quality of your professional relationships, the research possibilities, the salary, the geography, and so on. You'll need to weigh the different aspects against each other.

For me, the freedom that I have is very important. I like writing and editing books, and my department is very happy to have me do that. However, I know that some other university departments frown on their faculty spending time on books and do not place the same value on them as empirical papers. It's too bad, because the impact of a book on mental health can often be substantial, just as substantial as the impact of empirical research. There are many pathways to success and the world needs lots of different kinds of people. Some will be outstanding researchers, others will excel in their clinical work, some will be incredible teachers.

While you can look for a setting that matches your interests, remember that you are going to have an impact on the setting as well. A setting changes when a new person arrives, and you will have an impact on the program. You can change the environment. At my hospital where I am chief psychologist, there was nothing going on in the area of anxiety disorders (my area of interest) when I arrived, and there was no teaching happening in psychology. I saw that as a challenge rather than a deterrent. We now have a thriving anxiety disorders program and a new funded psychology residency program.

So recognize that you are not going into a static system; when deciding whether to take a job, ask yourself if you can turn the setting into what you want it to be. By talking with people who work there, you can get a feel for how flexible the setting may be. Remember, too, that no decision is permanent. You can always leave if the position isn't what you had hoped it would be. Also, I recommend applying for positions in a wide range of places so you have more options.

RESOURCES

BOOKS AND ARTICLES

Abramowitz, J. S., Franklin, M. E., Kalsy, S., & Furr, J. (2003). Symptom presentation and outcome of cognitive-behavior therapy for obsessive-compulsive disorder. *Journal of Consulting and Clinical Psychology*, 71 (6), 1049–1057.

Abramowitz, J. S., Franklin, M. E., Zoellner, L. A., & DiBernardo, C. (2002). Treatment compliance and outcome of cognitive-behavioral therapy for obsessive compulsive disorder. *Behavior Modification*, 26 (4), 447–463.

Bolles, R.N. (1995). *The 1995 what color is your parachute? A practical manual for job-hunters and career-changers*. Berkeley, CA: Ten Speed Press.

Boice, R. (2000). *Advice for new faculty members* (1st ed.). Needham Heights, MA: Allyn & Bacon.

Brems, C., Lampman, C., & Johnson, M. E. (1995). Preparation of applications for academic positions in psychology. *American Psychologist*, 50 (7), 533–537.

Davis, B. G. (1993). *Tools for teaching* (1st ed.). San Francisco: Jossey-Bass (Jossey Bass Higher and Adult Education Series).

DeAngelis, T. (2005). Things I wish I'd learned in grad school: Experts advise new psychologists on finances, office politics, and professional growth. *American Psychological Association Monitor on Psychology*, 36 (1), 54–57.

Franklin, M. E., Abramowitz, J. S., Furr, J., Kalsy, S., & Riggs, D. S. (2003). A naturalistic examination of therapist experience and outcome of exposure and ritual prevention for OCD. *Psychotherapy Research*, 13 (2), 153–167.

Franklin, M. E., Abramowitz, J. S., Kozak, M. J., Levitt, J., & Foa, E. B. (2000). Effectiveness of exposure and ritual prevention for obsessive-compulsive disorder: Randomized compared with non-randomized samples. *Journal of Consulting and Clinical Psychology*, 68 (4), 594–602.

Heiberfger, M. M., & Vick, J. M. (2001). *The academic job search handbook* (3rd ed.). Philadelphia, PA: University of Pennsylvania Press.

Kennedy, J. L., & Laramore, D. (1993) *Joyce Lain Kennedy's career book*. Lincolnwood, IL: VGM Career Horizons.

Keller, P. A. (1994). *Academic paths: Career decisions and experiences of psychologists*. Mahwah, NJ: Lawrence Erlbaum Associates.

McKeachie, W. J., & Hofer, B. K. (2001). *McKeachie's teaching tips: Strategies, research, and theory for college and university teachers* (11th ed.). Boston, MA: Houghton Mifflin Company.

Newbern, D. (1993). A guide to the academic job search: Part 3: The academic job interview. *APS Observer*, 6(6), 26–28.

Reingold, H. (1994). *The psychologist's guide to an academic career*. Washington, DC: American Psychological Association.

Sternberg, R. J. (Ed.) (2000). *Guide to publishing in psychology journals*. Cambridge, MA: Cambridge University Press.

Sternberg, R. J. (Ed.) (1999). *Career paths in psychology: Where your degree can take you*. Washington, DC: American Psychological Association.

Super, C. M., & Super, D. E. (2001). *Opportunities in psychology careers*. Lincolnwood, IL: VGM Career Horizons.

Darley, J. M., Zanna, M. P., Roediger, H. L. (2003). *The Compleat Academic: A Career Guide* (2nd ed.). Washington, DC: American Psychological Assocation.

Web Sites

NIH page for National Research Service Awards (F32s):

http://grants1.nih.gov/training/nrsa.htm

NIH page for small pilot study grants aimed at new investigators:

http://grants.nih.gov/grants/guide/pa-files/PAR-00-119.html

"K Awards" for early career psychologists:

http://grants.nih.gov/training/careerdevelopmentawards.htm

Web site listing faculty and teaching positions:

www.psyccareers.com

Internet listserv with discussions about academia and teaching, and postings of academic job openings:

http://health.groups.yahoo.com/group/NewPsychList/

(Or join by sending a blank email to: newpsychlist-subscribe@yahoogroups.com.)

APA's page for early-career psychologists who may want to get into academia:

www.apa.org/earlycareer

International Schools Services—international teaching positions:

www.iss.edu

Carney, Sandoe & Associates—recruiters of teachers and administrators for secondary schools:

www.carneysandoe.com

Educational Resources Group—recruiters of teachers and administrators:

www.ergteach.com

Site with many references for entering academia:

www.psychgrad.org/aftergrad.html

Site on teaching clinical psychology:

www.rider.edu/~suler/tcp.html

The Riley Guide—employment opportunities and job resources on the Internet (has strategies for salary negotiation and other helpful tips):

www.rileyguide.com

TERMINOLOGY

Assistant Professor   The next level above an instructor position in a university. Professors are typically in this position for five to seven years, sometimes longer in certain departments, and this is the major hurdle to pass to get to associate professor.

associate professor The professor title after assistant professor. You typically have more job stability when you reach this level.

authorship order The order in which the authors are given credit on any written or verbal representation of their work, including presentations, papers, books, and posters. The first author is typically the one who did the greatest amount of work and who receives a greater amount of credit on the project.

clinician-educator track A non–tenure track in academia in which your duties are split between teaching, research, and clinical work. It can be assumed that roughly half of your time will be spent conducting clinical treatment in this track.

clinical research Clinical research on treatments and outcomes which may or may not be within a randomized clinical trial.

contract negotiation The process during which, after you have been offered a position, you state your goals and requests and negotiate for them to be included in your contract. You may choose to involve an attorney, particularly when the implications of aspects of your contract are not entirely clear to you.

empirically supported treatments (ESTs) Clinical treatments whose validity and efficacy have been established through randomized clinical trials. ESTs include treatments such as interpersonal psychotherapy and cognitive behavioral therapy. These are standards of evidence that can be brought to bear when treating DSM-IV disorders.

instructor An entry-level faculty position. Depending on the department, you may be involved in a combination of teaching, research, and clinical activities.

professor The designation of professor means that you have achieved full professorship. Some departments do not require that associate professors ever work toward becoming a full professor, while other departments do.

randomized clinical trials (RCTs) Empirical research in which subjects are randomly assigned to a treatment condition. This method is thought to eliminate problems such as selection bias, and can raise questions regarding generalizability.

tenure The status of having a permanent position without periodic contract renewals. If you achieve tenure, you are guaranteed a portion of your salary. In some departments, if you do not earn your full salary by bringing in grants, you will earn less than your full salary, possibly only the portion that you are guaranteed. This arrangement may make it financially difficult for you to stay. Tenure guarantees your position and some salary but does not necessarily guarantee a job because you may not be able to earn enough to stay.

tenure-track The type of faculty positions that are geared toward achieving tenure.

CHAPTER 13

Administration and Supervision

Whatever you can do, or dream you can, begin it. Boldness has genius, power and magic in it.

W. H. Murray (often attributed to Goethe)

Plans are only good intentions unless they immediately degenerate into hard work.

Peter F. Drucker

WHAT IS ADMINISTRATION?

Administrating and directing involve running some type of program and overseeing the operations. There are various levels of administration, and sometimes the top administrator in an organization is akin to a CEO or COO. Administration often entails coordinating personnel and staffing issues, managing information technology, supervising staff members, overseeing budgeting and financial considerations, tackling managed care issues, organizing agency initiatives, and/or creating training or consultation programs.

Mental health care administration is a growing field and is a natural transition for some therapists after clinical work. Therapists who want a break from clinical work and are interested in management or the business of behavioral healthcare, and who have education in directing groups or organizations, may be well suited to administrative work. Those who move into administration simply as a break from clinical work tend to be less happy than those who are genuinely interested in supervisory or administrative work. Many therapists who are interested in administrative work obtain management experience and education in health care policy or administration.

IS ADMINISTRATION FOR ME?

Because administrative work is so different from clinical work, see whether you have the personality, abilities, and interests necessary to make you a good administrator. Complete the questionnaire provided here to get an idea about whether you may be a good administrator, supervisor, or director.

Answer all questions on a scale from 0 (not at all true for you) to 5 (very true for you).

1. I have been told that I have strong leadership skills. _____

2. When I am involved in a project, I almost always enjoy serving as the team leader or project manager. _____

3. Teachers and professors have told me that I have a unique ability to gather people and encourage them to get involved with various projects. _____

4. I greatly enjoy supervising others. _____

5. When I think about my career path, one of my primary goals has always been to obtain a leadership position or direct a program. _____

6. People have often told me that I am able to get team members committed and energized for new projects. _____

7. I tend to be highly organized in my work. _____

8. I have some great ideas about companies or businesses in my field. _____

9. I am someone who learns a great deal from supervising others. _____

10. I have no problem delegating work and letting people know what I expect from them. _____

11. I would enjoy moving away from direct clinical care and toward administration. _____

12. Others have told me that I would make a great director. _____

13. My personality seems better suited to administration and supervising than to other areas in behavioral health. _____

14. I have strong skills in scheduling and planning. _____

15. I am good with numbers and I understand financial planning pretty well. _____

16. My interpersonal skills are excellent. _____

17. I would feel comfortable running a meeting or supervision group. _____

18. People have told me that I am able to motivate and inspire others. _____

19. I would enjoy developing the strategic planning for an organization. _____

20. I have aspired to create and direct a program. _____

Please note that this questionnaire is not an empirically validated measure and is intended solely to provide some general information and considerations. If you scored around 60 or above, you are likely to be someone who has strong leadership potential as an administrator. A score above 80 indicates even stronger potential. If you scored below 60, you may want to consider whether it is because of lack of interest or lack or experience.

An Administrative Career

Therapists can make great administrators because they know firsthand the work done within the organization. Think about all that you have learned about the functioning of different organizations when you worked in them. You can probably immediately call to mind what worked and what did not work so well. You likely learned by observing the actions of your own supervisors or administrators and noticing what they did that was effective or ineffective.

Several therapists-turned-administrators with whom I spoke said that they were not content in their clinical positions because of the lack of opportunities for upward growth. These therapists stated that they found they had a desire to influence a greater number of people, including both clients and other therapists. They wanted to play a greater role in their organizations and affect the policies that can influence the functioning of their agencies and the impact on future generations. If you share some of these feelings, then you may truly enjoy an administrative role.

There are many different administrative positions within hospitals, universities, community mental health centers, other community agencies, counseling centers, medical clinics, businesses, nonprofit organizations, and training programs. Some examples of administrative work for therapists include:

- Health care human resources manager
- Supervisor of clinical work in an organization
- Financial manager of health care services
- Hospital administrator
- Counseling center director
- Nonprofit administrator or board member
- Director of a clinical or training program
- Dean of student services or academic programs
- Director of a program or center that you created

ACTIVITIES

Administration is a very different type of work from direct patient care and includes many areas of responsibility: financial, human resources, planning, supervision, work processes, and communications. Some of the activities in which a behavioral health care administrator may be involved include these:

Financial

- Setting objectives and measuring actual fiscal figures
- Determining client hours necessary for clinicians
- Making sure that clinicians meet required hours
- Ensuring proper financial resource distribution

Personnel and Human Resources

- Delegating work among employees and overseeing performance
- Addressing conflicts and disciplinary issues and improving communication channels
- Maintaining staff morale, incentives, and motivation
- Conducting employee performance appraisals

Planning

- Determining strategic organizational direction
- Scheduling employees' activities and requirements
- Developing and implementing new programs
- Scheduling programs, groups, and other activities
- Preparing for fluctuations in client and staff needs
- Forecasting future growth and developments

Supervision and Leadership

- Overseeing staff assignment to supervisors
- Running meetings and supervision groups
- Directly supervising staff, therapists, or other team members
- Ensuring that all employees have the necessary support for optimal work

Processes

- Assuring adherence to strict ethical standards and guidelines
- Undertaking quality assurance efforts
- Implementing company objectives and goals
- Creating and evaluating programs
- Monitoring and insuring optimal considerations and use of issues of diversity and multiculturalism
- Collecting and analyzing data on various organizational activities

Communications

- Communicating with different disciplines or departments
- Improving multidisciplinary team performance
- Obtaining necessary information to answer questions of staff members
- Ensuring that staff has a means of airing any grievances

Activities and Experience

List your relevant leadership experience. Think through your experiences in administrative, supervisory, or directorial roles. Use the preceding lists of activities to help frame some of your ideas: _____

_____

_____

_____

_____

_____

_____

_____

_____

_____

_____

_____

GET THE NECESSARY EXPERIENCE

Use the list of experiences you created here to identify areas in which you require further experience. It can be difficult to gain direct administration experience until you have developed the repertoire of leadership and administrative skills necessary to be competitive for a directorial role. Because management is quite different from clinical work, you will be more qualified if you have leadership experience.

FINANCIAL

If you work as a therapist in a behavioral health care or counseling organization, you can increase your awareness of the financial functioning of the organization. At minimum, you can keep track of your own financial performance by tracking your client hours and your fees per client hour. Another option is to find out who the financial administrators are and ask them whether you can do an apprenticeship, or volunteer to help them out on your own time.

It is unlikely that this type of work is part of your current job description. You will, therefore, need to explain that you want to learn more about the financial aspects of mental health care administration and that you are willing to do this work on your own time. You can request to sit in on meetings; shadow directors, executives, or administrators; and perform appropriate aspects of the work.

PERSONNEL AND HUMAN RESOURCES

If you are a staff psychologist or therapist in an organization, you can become involved with interviewing practicum students, interns, and other staff members. Take it upon yourself to post job descriptions; go through applications, CVs, and resumes; select a group of interviewees; and coordinate the interview process. You could also assist the director of training with hiring and managing personnel.

If you are an intern or student in an organization, initiate activities designed to improve employee morale, motivation, and communication. For instance, you can begin an employee spotlight program where each month, certain employees are awarded a free lunch (be sure that all employees receive this once over the year); a celebration of birthdays each month where everyone gets together for cake; or a work-free meeting once a month that is scheduled during a regular meeting time but used to discuss cases, work culture, climate issues, or whatever else is on people's minds.

PLANNING

To gain experience with planning activities, offer to coordinate a program or specific activity. For instance, take an occasion like National Depression Awareness Day and develop screening and psychoeducational activities. Plan what different people will do during various parts of the day or week, and schedule all of your priority tasks.

Let your current supervisors or bosses know that you are interested in becoming involved with strategic planning in any way that would be feasible and appropriate. Perhaps they will invite you to sit in on board meetings, or you can take it upon yourself to plan a specific activity for the organization. If members of your agency have been talking for some time about beginning a crisis walk-in service, offer to begin planning for this activity. Designate a specific time during the week that it will occur, and begin scheduling staff to cover the service.

SUPERVISION AND LEADERSHIP

In your current job, you can gain experience by supervising other therapists if you are at the proper level of training yourself. Supervising can give you direct experience with some of the activities and skills previously described. Offer to run meetings and a group supervision session.

If you are a student and cannot yet supervise, make a point to learn from your supervisors, not only in terms of clinical content but in terms of process. Keep a supervision journal and make notes of what you find to be more or less effective. For instance, jot down how you found it useful when your supervisor shared his own struggles with a similar presenting problem, or how one supervisor helped you discover your own strengths as a therapist. If you are in group supervision, observe how group members respond to the supervisor's style and facilitation of supervision.

PROCESSES

There are many opportunities at any job to gain experience with work processes. For example, you could create some quality assurance programs and organize regular chart reviews and case discussions. You can develop a program and begin marketing it and running it. You can then collect data on your program and present it to your group.

Since adherence to professional ethics guidelines is an important part of organizational processes, you can begin a monthly ethics discussion group in which therapists at your work take turns presenting a case and discussing ethical considerations. You can begin the same type of case consultation and quality assurance in regard to client multiculturalism.

COMMUNICATIONS

At your workplace, if there is no means of communicating employee feedback, you can initiate an anonymous feedback box or meeting to discuss issues at hand. Since interdisciplinary or interdepartmental communication can be important in administration, try to gain as much experience as possible in serving on a team and, better yet, working as a leader on various teams. Leading meetings can be a great way to gain this experience. Serving as an interteam liaison is another excellent way to learn the communication skills of an administrator. If opportunities are not apparent and readily available, look into collaborating with a different department on a project so you can gain experience with interdisciplinary communication.

IN THE CLASSROOM

Formal education can be an enormous asset in increasing your knowledge base and in making you more competitive for administrative positions. Do not feel that this section applies to you only if you are currently a graduate student. There are always opportunities for further learning and education at any point in your career.

FINANCIAL

You can take classes in financial areas in an MBA program while you are in school or after you have graduated. Look for courses in finance, managerial accounting, financial accounting, budgeting, macroeconomics, microeconomics, forecasting, and financial analysis. Even if you will not be directly responsible for running the numbers in your role as an administrator, understanding what the numbers mean and how they work can be a tremendous asset.

PERSONNEL AND HUMAN RESOURCES

Most classes in personnel management will be in university business schools in the department of management. Look for courses in human resource management (general), organizational behavior, hiring and promoting employees, recruitment and retention, motivating employee behavior, and directing human resources. Besides signing up for a course, you can go to human resources association meetings to learn more. One of the largest human resource professional organizations is the Society for Human Resource Management (www.shrm.org). You can also find excellent resources for ways to learn more about personnel management on their web site.

PLANNING

While in graduate school or afterwards, you can take classes in strategic planning in an MBA or other business program. Most courses that involve strategy will give you good experience with organizational planning. You can also take courses in change management, organizational development, and operations management. In psychology or social work programs, take a course in program development or organizational planning. If there are no specific courses in these areas, ask a professor whose expertise is closest to these topics for a reading list, and take it upon yourself to do a self-study either for credit or just for your professional development.

SUPERVISION AND LEADERSHIP

You can take continuing education classes and attend workshops and seminars on management, leadership, and supervision at local universities and through professional associations. Some states, such as California, actually require formal course work in supervision before your supervision hours as a trainee can count toward the trainee's licensure. Regardless of your state's requirements, taking courses in supervision can help you determine whether becoming a supervisor is a good match for you, and help you hone your supervisory skills.

Most graduate school programs offer courses in clinical supervision. If yours does not, talk with your academic dean or current supervisor about creating an independent study in this area. You can also take business school classes in managing people in organizations, leadership development, and theories of management and supervision. To gain experience as a leader in the classroom, offer to be a team leader on group projects, practice giving effective feedback to others, and ask your professors and group members for specific feedback on your leadership style and abilities.

PROCESSES

There are many classes that can help you learn more about effective process management in organizations. Classes with subject matter including public policy, hospital administration, quality assurance or continuous improvement, business ethics, professional ethics, and program development can all offer exposure to various topics in organizational policy. If you did not have any policy classes during your undergraduate degree, consider taking an undergraduate-level policy course. At many universities, if you are already enrolled full-time as a graduate student, you can take additional courses at low or no charge. If you are out of school, look into courses at your local community college to give you general education in these areas at a low cost.

COMMUNICATIONS

In the classroom, you can learn the theory behind effective business communications. You can also hone your own skills at oral and written communications by taking classes. I recommend taking a course in oral business communications that requires you to give speeches and presentations. You will receive a great deal of specific feedback on your skills and improve your speaking abilities. When you take this type of course in a business school, there will likely be an emphasis on timed speeches, so you will gain practice with keeping your presentation to a specific amount of time. Because direct and concise communication is such a critical skill for an administrator, these types of course can be very beneficial.

Interview with Indira Paharia, PsyD

Dr. Paharia, a licensed clinical psychologist, is an assistant professor as well as the assistant director of the Institute for Graduate Clinical Psychology at Widener University in Wilmington, Delaware. Her specialty is health psychology.

How did you become interested in mental health care administration?
I have always been interested in leadership. During graduate school, I held several positions: coordinator of the Denver Analytic Society; special assistant to Judith Albino, PhD, president of the University of Colorado; graduate representative to the University of Denver; graduate representative to the American Psychological Association. I was also a graduate teaching assistant during my third year.

After licensure, I accepted a position as the director of the behavioral medicine division and assistant professor at Temple University School of Dentistry. Two years later, I accepted my current position. Therefore, my administrative experience is limited to academic settings. My reasons for pursuing leadership positions include: a passion to improve the status quo, enjoyment in developing initiatives, an outlet for creativity, innate leadership ability, greater influence over systems, increased job security, and a higher salary.

Where do you (ideally) see your career within the next 10 or so years?
I am finishing an MBA in health care administration and an MS in health care finance. Within 5 to 10 years, I expect to be a senior-level health care administrator in a large health care system. I also expect to own my own business in health psychology. I have a personal and professional mission statement that I follow closely, especially when making significant life decisions.

What are some ways that a psychology or social work graduate student can gain experience with administration or the relevant skills for this line of work?

Students should acquire experience as a clinical supervisor because many of the skills applied in supervision are transferable to management, and this is the most available opportunity to students. Students can also run for office within their graduate school or within the American Psychological Association of Graduate Students (APAGS). I also suggest they take advantage of any organizational psychology training opportunities and any business classes open to them during their training. Finally, being selected as a graduate teaching assistant is another good way to learn about management.

PROVIDING PROFESSIONAL SUPERVISION AND CONSULTATION

If you have been supervising trainees and you really enjoy the process of supervision, consider adding supervision or consultation to your list of paid services.

WHOM TO SUPERVISE

When you think of supervision, you probably most commonly think of supervising an unlicensed therapist or a trainee, which is what most clinical supervisors do. In many states, trainees or postdoctoral therapists cannot pay for supervision and still have it count toward licensure because paying a supervisor raises ethical issues, such as the creation of a dual relationship. You can supervise certified or licensed clinicians and charge a reasonable rate. Before pursuing this line of supervision, check your state's ethical and legal guidelines, because states vary widely in their stances toward paid supervision.

To work as a paid supervisor or consultant, it is important that you have a specialized area of expertise. Licensed psychologists, social workers, and marriage and family therapists typically do not need to pay a supervisor for general supervision, but may, for instance, want to hire a supervisor or consultant for specific clinical issues. A licensed therapist is likely to consider paying for supervision when they are looking to develop an area of expertise themselves or when they are working with a new presenting problem or client population and require consultation.

Consultations can be conducted over the telephone, so geography is not an issue and you can work with people anywhere. Of course, it is important to have clients sign release of information forms for the consultation and to document the nature of the supervisory relationship (i.e., regular supervision, case consultation as needed, mentorship, etc.).

Supervisees benefit greatly because they are able to hone their clinical skills, receive expert supervision, and achieve higher credibility and expertise, allowing them to gain more clients and potentially raise their hourly rates. Supervisors enjoy the process of supervision and the act of disseminating effective treatments, thereby helping more clients to overcome clinical disorders. It is also often satisfying for supervisors to learn what other therapists in their communities or fields are doing, to learn from the supervisees, and to diversify their services to keep them energetic and intellectually stimulated. The situation is win-win for the supervisor and supervisee.

If this sounds interesting to you, the first thing you need to do is develop a specialized area of expertise if you do not have one already. Further augment your current knowledge by hiring a supervisor or consultant yourself, taking continuing education courses, attending workshops and trainings, doing additional course work, and seeing as many clients as possible in the area of practice you want to enlarge.

WHAT TO CHARGE

The issue of what to charge for supervision and consultation comes up frequently, and the answer is an individualized one. Many supervisors and consultants choose to charge a fee slightly reduced from their hourly client fees, in order to make the supervision or consultation more affordable to those who want and need it, whereas others charge their standard hourly fee. If you are working as a consultant with a licensed clinician, you may elect to charge your normal hourly rate and then offer to watch a videotape or listen to an audiotape at no additional charge. Some supervising experts charge their hourly fee, but give a full hour instead of the standard 50-minute hour. You can offer a sliding scale like you would for therapy patients, based on the financial situation of the person you will be supervising. If you decide to do this, establish a clear scale and put your sliding scale for supervision and consultation in writing.

You could also consider charging less for a single consultation session to expose more people to the process and increase your conversion rate. On the other hand, you may want to offer a discount on a package of consultations. For example, if someone purchases 5 or 10 consultations, they get 25 percent off. This type of discounting would be a good idea when you know that the therapist and his client will most benefit from ongoing supervision or when you find ongoing supervision to be more rewarding and enjoyable.

In setting your fee, it is important to consider both your purpose for doing the supervision and your financial plan. If you are trying to provide consultations specifically for the purpose of disseminating a treatment or generating interest in workshops or other programs, you may choose to charge less for your supervision hour. If you want to use supervision as a primary means of building your practice, then consider your financial feasibility analysis and practice goals when setting your fees. Also think about the people hiring you and what is financially feasible for them. If you overprice your services, people will not consider it a good enough career investment to spend the money. You do not want to underprice, though, because consultation is an excellent career investment for therapists and it is important that they recognize the value of the service you are offering.

OTHER CAREER POSSIBILITIES IN ADMINISTRATION AND POLICY

This section is designed to get you thinking about some other areas where you could put your administrative interests and experiences to work.

GOVERNMENT AND PUBLIC POLICY

As a psychologist with a background in public policy and/or administration, there are many career opportunities available to you. Several psychologists currently hold upper-level government positions in the senate and other branches of government. A level of expertise in human behavior coupled with strong leadership and policy-making skills can add up to an ideal candidate for politics. Think about how much policy is centered on social and humanistic issues.

Public policy researchers and activists have traditionally come from backgrounds in policy, political science, demography, and sociology.

Surveying this list, it becomes obvious how psychotherapists can greatly contribute. Psychotherapists and mental health professionals can contribute a great deal through influencing policies that are going to affect millions. Looking at the current issues of policy research centers, such as the Public Policy Institute of California (PPIC), reveals that many of the primary issues are psychological in nature. For instance, PPIC lists psychological and social issues as their primary policy areas, including children and family, education, immigration, health care, and social issues (www.ppic.org).

THE MILITARY

Psychotherapists interested in the government and military matters are finding excellent clinical and leadership roles in the military. Many mental health professionals who choose to work in the military report that they receive good compensation and interesting job assignments. While working in the military you can learn a great deal, not only about mental health but about leading and managing people. If you choose to leave the military, much of your knowledge about leadership and directing important operations can apply to the civilian world.

CORPORATE AMERICA

Another arena to apply your skills in human behavior and administration is in the private sector, within businesses. Of course you will need to develop your business acumen and experience, but generally speaking, many administrative and leadership skills can cross over very well. Being an administrator in a private hospital, for example, you would have gained a great deal of expertise in managing the finances of an organization, strategic planning, human resources, company policy, supervision, and interdisciplinary communication. You would also have the experience of having many levels of people report to you. You would have honed your leadership skills and begun to feel comfortable in the role of a director. All of these skills, combined with your intricate knowledge of human motivation, emotions, and behavior, can make you highly competitive for an administrative or executive position in a company. A colleague of mine who is a mental health professional recently received a job offer for an upper-level position with one of the major television networks.

Interview with Robert A. Rando, PhD

Dr. Robert Rando is the director of the Center for Psychological Services and an associate professor in the school of professional psychology at Wright State University in Dayton, Ohio. He can be reached via the counseling center's web site, www.wright-counseling.com.

As the director of a counseling center, what are some of your duties?
I am the chief mental health officer at the university and am responsible for the functional and administrative supervision of the center. That is, I have responsibility for oversight of the budget, staffing, professional development programming, quality assurance programming, service offerings, clinical supervision, and research programming. I work to be aware of the national and local college mental health trends and represent these to the university's administration. In my role as chief mental health officer, I serve on a number of university committees dealing with student retention, crisis management, student wellness, and academic success.

What do you enjoy or find challenging about administrative work?
I enjoy being able to impact larger systems. Providing therapy is a very rewarding activity—however, supervising a center that provides 20 hours of therapy to my one hour is more rewarding. There is a wonderful reward inherent in supporting a group of professionals in their provision of such critically important services to a highly valued community.

Are some of the skills that make someone a good therapist the same as what makes them a good administrator?
The ability to listen, empathize, communicate verbally, conceptualize individual and group behavior, and appreciate the impact of systems all support and translate to administration. I believe some skills that administrators have that are not necessarily present for therapists include the ability to multitask, to do long-term visioning/planning, to supervise (administrative and clinical), manage a budget, manage and evaluate personnel, advocate for clients/staff/center, communicate well in writing, present clinical information in understandable language, and understand and manage political systems.

How can psychology students or practicing therapists gain some of the skills that would make them competitive for administrative or directing positions?

There are a number of resources available to those interested. For example, one could take a course or pursue a degree or certificate in a master's of business administration or health systems management program, or attend trainings offered at national conferences such as the American College Personnel Association, American Counseling Association, American Psychological Association, or the National Association of Student Personnel Administrators. The Association for University and College Counseling Center Directors offers an Administrative Institute for aspiring counseling center directors. A number of books and journals also directly address budget management in higher education, counseling center functioning, and theories of college student development.

What are some questions that therapists can ask themselves to determine whether they may be a good fit for working as an administrator or director?

- Do I have a thick skin—that is, can I manage other people's displeasure with me when managing a large system?
- Do I understand and enjoy interacting with political systems?
- Do I enjoy supporting others' professional development?
- Am I willing to work long hours?
- Do I enjoy multitasking?
- Do I enjoy supporting change at a systemic level?
- Am I passionate about the provision of a broad range of services to the college student population?

Interview with Deborah A. King, PhD

Deborah King is an associate professor of psychiatry (psychology) and the director of training in clinical psychology at the University of Rochester Medical Center in Rochester, New York. You can find out more at www.urmc.rochester.edu/smd/psych/educ _train/training/index.cfm.

Why, in your opinion and experience, is administration or directing a program a good career opportunity for therapists?

An excellent question! Therapists are trained to be thoughtful listeners and to understand relationships and systems. These are excellent building blocks for an administrative, leadership position. Most administrators deal with personnel issues, and therapists are uniquely skilled in this arena. As well, in today's changing health care systems, therapists always need to be thinking of their value-add contribution to their agency or institution, or even to third party payers. Those who have the interest and capability to design, evaluate, and lead programs will be able to climb a career ladder and compete for more lucrative positions. Even therapists in private practice must learn business skills for managing their practice and reporting positive, behaviorally oriented outcomes.

What are some of the interesting or exciting aspects of behavioral health care administration or directing a program?

Obviously, one has more of an opportunity to determine the nature and quality of services, and perhaps even shape health care policy, if one is directing and leading programs. In the department of psychiatry where I work, I serve on the budget committee, which functions as the chair's "cabinet" or leadership group. Each year we must determine how to make the most of scarce resources. Since we cannot provide everything to everyone, we make strategic decisions about the populations we will serve (e.g., children, older adults, the seriously and persistently mentally ill). Although at times difficult, this is a stimulating interdisciplinary process that determines the direction and character of our department. Even as training director, I'm aware of how fortunate I am to be helping to shape the next generation of clinicians. Whereas the therapist brings about change one person or family at a time, the clinical administrator or training director has an opportunity to create change on a larger scale by making decisions that affect a larger group or cohort.

Psychologically speaking, I think administrative careers provide an opportunity for therapists to become more familiar and comfortable with their own professional and/or personal authority. This might be especially important for women who still tend to be less comfortable or even familiar with their own power. Psychotherapy training tends to emphasize reflective, empathic listening and to de-emphasize the exercise of overt decision making or authority. A career in administration gives therapists an opportunity to round out their skills and flex different muscles by expressing

304

their own views, directing their own programs, and carrying out their own plans.

What skills do you think are important for therapists who want to become administrators, such as training directors or chairs of committees or departments?

Training directors obviously need good communication skills, an ability to understand systems and work with different disciplines, and a general, broad-based understanding of evidence-based methods of assessment and psychotherapy. What may be less obvious is the need to have strong business skills—for example, to know how to create mission statements and strategic plans, how to conduct needs assessments and program evaluations, and, perhaps most of all, how to put together a business plan.

Whether one moves into a position as training director, clinical program director, or agency head, a strong understanding of systems and their business aspects is imperative. It is getting more and more challenging to justify training expenses in today's competitive health care environment, and training directors need to be comfortable speaking the language of profit and loss. This goes against what many of us wanted to do when we became therapists, but even the most competent therapists won't be able to sustain their programs if they cannot justify their existence in financial terms. It's not rocket science, but it is a necessary science.

How can psychology students, interns, postdocs, or practicing therapists gain some of these skills?

These skills can be acquired in a number of ways if you are willing to engage in the quid pro quo of an apprentice type experience. For example, trainees can volunteer to serve on selection committees and help their programs interview and evaluate candidates for training positions. This allows you to observe the selection process and exercise some important authority in ranking candidates while helping your program out at the same time. It can also work well to team up with a respected faculty member or administrative leader whose actions and values you admire. Volunteer to help with their research or office work (e.g., minutes of meetings, preparing reports) in exchange for some administrative supervision.

Depending on one's interest, time economy, and the nature of local offerings, it is also a good idea to take a course or two at a local business school on strategic planning and other business processes. For those who have the interest and capability, obtaining an MBA or MPH (master's in public health) can be very rewarding professionally. I always recommend to my psychology trainees that they get training beyond the therapist role, in either research, business administration, or public health, to ensure they embody the value-add that I mentioned earlier. After all is said and done, this type of variety is not only the spice of life (it's fun!) but also the source of job security and career advancement.

RESOURCES

BOOKS

Berstein, B.E. & Hartsell, T. L. (2004). *The portable lawyer for mental health professionals: An A-Z guide to protecting your clients, your practice and yourself* (2nd ed.). New York: John Wiley & Sons, Inc.

Dlugacz, Y., Restifo, A., & Greenwood, A. (2004). *The quality handbook for health care organizations: A manager's guide to tools and programs*. San Francisco: Jossey-Bass/AHA.

Dunn, R. T. (2002). *Haimann's health care management* (7th ed.). Chicago, IL: Health Administration Press.

Lombardi, D. N. (2001). *Handbook for the new health care manager* (2nd ed.). San Francisco: Jossey-Bass.

McConnell, C. R. (2003). *The effective health care supervisor* (5th ed.). Sudbury, MA: Jones & Bartlett.

Pozgar, G. (2004). *Legal aspects of health care administration* (9th ed.). Sudbury, MA: Jones and Bartlett.

Reid, W.H., & Silver, S. B. (2002). *Handbook of mental health administration and management*. New York: Brunner-Routledge.

WEB SITES

Society for Human Resource Management:

www.shrm.org

Web site to search for jobs or to post positions if you are hiring:

www.alliedhealthcareers.com

National Council for Community Behavioral Healthcare:
www.nccbh.org/abhm

Catalog of the American Hospital Association Resource Center:
www.aharc.library.net

National Association for Healthcare Quality:
www.nahq.org

The American College Personnel Association (ACPA):
www.myacpa.org

National Association of Student Personnel Administrators:
www.naspa.org

The Association for University and College Counseling Center Directors:
www.aucccd.org

American Enterprise Institute for Public Policy Research:
www.aei.org

Public Policy Institute of California:
www.ppic.org

Terminology

administrator   One who manages or supervises the operations, use, or conduct of an agency, organization, or group of personnel.

budgeting   The act of allocating funds for a budget and requiring adherence to a budget.

business communication   The expression of ideas, objectives, or information effectively in a business setting.

conversion rate   In consulting work, the percentage of people who become ongoing clients after an initial session or consultation.

director   The top administrator in a center, department, agency, or facility who is responsible for the functioning and performance of their organization; may also be referred to as the "chair."

human resources   The department in an organization that consists of a human resources (HR) director, managers, and employees, which manages one of the most important resources in a company: the people. The HR department is typically responsible for recruitment and retention of employees. In different settings, other names for HR may apply. For example, in a university setting, the person who maintains the responsibilities of the HR director may be called the academic dean or the dean of students.

organizational planning   The act of devising or projecting the realization and achievement of programs within an organization.

public policy   The creation of rules, regulations, procedures, and laws that provide direction for various social, economic, and political issues.

training director   The administrative director who oversees some or all aspects of training. In a psychology program, for example, the training director within the university may oversee practicum and internship placements.

CHAPTER 14

Building a Big Business

In a start-up company, you basically throw out all assumptions every three weeks.

Scott McNealy, CEO of Sun Microsystems

As long as you're going to be thinking anyway, think big.

Donald Trump

AN ENTREPRENEURIAL DREAM

When you were younger, did you want to be part of something big? Or, better yet, *start* something big? Did you dream of running a successful company or organization? Did you envision building a business that was directly in line with your vision and what matters most to you?

If you love what you do and want to build a corporation or business out of it, then this chapter is for you. While creating a company is similar to creating a practice, it also differs in many ways, because we are talking about building a business where others are working for and with you, and where you and your services are not the sole commodity, but there are many other services or products available to the clients or consumers. The business is not you, as it is in private practice; instead, the business is all of the services and products that are made available on a local, state, national, or international level.

For this entrepreneurial dream to apply to you, you must *want* it—badly. For it to be most successful, it should be your dream, your fantasy, your life's mission, your career goal. You may not yet have all the skill sets and the business acumen to start a company, but you must have the entrepreneurial spirit—the desire to build a large company or corporation.

The company need not start out big, and it does not have to grow big in terms of volume. You may decide to focus on creating and delivering a smaller number of products or services to ideal clientele at higher prices. One of the most important things to keep in mind regarding the size of the organization you develop is that it will grow as large as your vision. Just as a fish grows in proportion to the size of its bowl, your business will grow to fit the size of your goals for it. Your vision can restrict the business's growth and development or it can allow it to flourish. A big vision will result in a big business.

Continuing with the analogy of a fish, while the vision is absolutely critical and fundamental, it is not enough. You must follow up your vision with execution. The goals that you set and meet are the food and clean water that you give to your fish. Even with a large bowl, your fish will not grow if you fail to feed it consistently. You cannot just feed it once in a while when you have an inspiration, rather; you must feed it over and over again. Being an entrepreneur can present numerous challenges and frustrations on a regular basis. Persistence is one of the keys to being a successful entrepreneur. You cannot let the difficulties and holdups deter you from turning your vision into a reality.

So far in this book I have talked quite a bit about the importance of having a vision. Here is where you really *need* it. Creating a company without having a vision for it is like trying to take a picture without a camera. Of course you could take a mental picture, but the visual memory will fade and become distorted over time. It will never be the same as the crystal clear image in vibrant color that you could capture with your camera.

WHEN YOU DON'T WANT TO DO IT ALONE

When you do not want to build a business on your own, you have many options. You can create and run the company as your business but hire consultants to help out in the areas that are not your greatest strengths. Most successful business owners have scores of consultants and professionals who provide valuable services that save the business time, money, and other valuable resources. You can outsource or bring in professionals in accounting and finance, law, marketing and sales, strategic development, business operations, and human resources.

THE BENEFITS OF A PARTNERSHIP

Another common and often very effective option is creating a partnership. The best business partner is a trusted colleague who shares your vision and has talents and skills in areas that are not your strong points. Following is a discussion of the numerous benefits of business partnerships.

CREATIVITY

Two (or more) minds are often better than one. Having a business partner can help you to develop a more creative, innovative company. When we come up with ideas on our own, we have less incentive and structure to challenge ourselves than when we are accountable to our business partner. Everyone wants to appear intelligent, interesting, and admirable to others, and accountability to a business partner can certainly be effective in pushing us further to think outside the box and develop novel ideas and products. The combination of brainpower can also lead to enhanced innovation.

REDUCED ERROR RATE

A partnership can result in better products because it often serves a checks-and-balances system. Your partner can catch the mistakes or areas for improvement that you did not see. We are all fallible and subject to overlooking both errors and opportunities. Sometimes we even deliberately overlook minor errors because we simply do not want to be bothered with them. Unfortunately, these minor problems can build up and greatly impact your business over time. A partner can push us to work harder to catch errors and can identify and rectify the errors when they do occur. A partnership can assist with the important business goal of continuous improvement.

REDUCED BUSINESS ANXIETY AND STRESS

A business partnership can also serve as a method to decrease your anxiety about running your own company. First, you know that between the two of you, problems will get solved because you will work together until you solve them. It is good to know that you have someone else who is equally invested in getting situations resolved optimally.

Second, when your partner has skills that you lack, you do not have to worry about those areas as much. Let's say that you are an entrepreneurial, creative, intuitive type, and your partner is very practical and strong in accounting and finance. As someone who becomes intimidated by numbers, you are reassured to know that your partner will be taking care of those areas. Of course if you do not have a partnership (or even if you do), you can and should always outsource your weaker areas. The benefit of having a partner with strengths in finance, however, is that you will not watch your bill for financial services increase.

Third, you always have someone with whom to talk. After working with many solo entrepreneurs, I have often heard, "No one really understands what I am going through with my practice/business." This is often true when you are building a business on your own. You do not want to burden friends and family members with constant talk about the stress of starting a business, and they often do not understand anyway. When you have a business partner, however, you have someone to help you cope with the stress, who can truly empathize with the difficulties, and who is constantly there to talk about the business.

The Downsides of a Partnership

Of course there are potential downsides to a partnership as well. Let's explore a few of them.

Personality Incompatibility

One major problem business partners frequently encounter is that after the honeymoon period is over, they realize they either do not get along or do not really like each other. Many partners select one another for their complementary business skills, which is a great idea except that partnerships work much better when personalities are not constantly clashing.

A business partnership is essentially like a marriage: You need to look at it as a partnership for the long term. Do not rush into it without first knowing one another well enough to determine whether you could work together day in and day out. In a business partnership, you do not have to like each other, but it definitely helps. When you enjoy your meetings with your partner and can feel enthusiastic about collaborating and working together, it makes those long hours of work much more bearable.

Some personality incompatibilities can help to balance out a partnership and enhance the business's performance. For instance, if you are laid back and a bit of a procrastinator while your partner is a go-getter and very organized, you can balance each other out quite well. It seems to be a matter of degree—sometimes polar opposites can drive each other nuts. Another important factor in whether you drive each other crazy is how much you respect each other's differences rather than let them bother you.

BUSINESS DISAGREEMENTS

Disagreements may also arise regarding how to run the business, and these disagreements can sometimes stem from personality factors. For instance, if someone is very conservative and cautious while the partner is a risk-taker, conflicts can arise regarding hiring, expansion, or investment decisions. One person may want to save money while the other believes in doing everything at the highest quality and expense.

Some of the operational areas where business partners frequently disagree include:

- Company vision, purpose, and future direction.
- What the target client market is.
- Where to invest marketing dollars.
- Location of business offices.
- Who to hire and when to hire more employees.
- How to gain funding and financing.
- Design and aesthetic decisions for office space and marketing materials.
- Who to hire as contractors or professionals to assist with taxes or legal issues.
- How much to pay yourself from business profits and what benefits to offer.
- Presentational style for sales meetings.
- Business ethical considerations.
- Use of technological resources.

Knowing the business problems that can arise and discussing them ahead of time can significantly reduce the difficulties that come up. Meeting with a consultant or coach before beginning your business can help you work through all of these issues. I recently began consulting with business partners before they create their official partnership agreements to help them gain clarity and understanding of one another's positions.

We put their ideas and agreements in writing so they can refer to them later as disagreements start to arise.

LEGAL AND DISSOLUTION ISSUES

Another potential problem with a partnership is that if you decide to end the business or if one partner decides to leave, it can be more complicated than if you were in business by yourself. If one partner wants to leave the company for personal reasons or to pursue another business opportunity, the partnership will have to be dissolved. This process can be difficult from a business standpoint but can also create a great deal of negative emotions. When partners were colleagues or friends before the business, the friendship can be threatened by business problems. Of course, you would include provisions for company dissolution or partner buyout in your partnership agreement so these factors would be accounted for ahead of time. Nevertheless, disagreements and disputes can occur. The worst-case scenario is that one of the partners contests the provisions in the initial partnership agreement and a long, entangled, expensive legal battle ensues.

WHAT BUSINESS TO BUILD

Some people know they want to be entrepreneurs, but the question is, with what business? Others believe so strongly in their field or craft that they want to spread their ideas to as many people as possible.

Regardless of what type of entrepreneur you are, you will want to create a company that is in line with your personal vision, interests, and entrepreneurial dreams. In working with many entrepreneurs, I have learned that one of the top three factors underlying whether the entrepreneur will succeed is their drive and passion. The other two are start-up capital and persistence.

Being an entrepreneur and beginning a company is hard. The burden is on you to constantly work hard and make the business successful. If you don't make it, you don't eat. As your company grows and you start to hire employees, you begin to feel responsible to them as well, since they are depending on your business for a job to feed themselves and their families. Running your own company can become a 24/7 deal, and you may sometimes feel as though you are literally eating, sleeping, and breathing your business. One client told me, "I feel like I am always working—even when I am asleep, I am dreaming about my business!"

To begin a business, you must first do some research to learn about different opportunities. Unless you already have a clear idea in mind about what company you want to start, look into various areas that may present prospects for you to use your skills. Timmons (in Bygrave & Zacharakis, 2004) recommends the following ways to gather information for potential business ideas:

- Existing businesses — see what is out there that you can emulate.
- Begin or buy a franchise.
- Look into patent brokers that seek viable projects.
- Investigate product licensing and research and development (R&D) within corporations, nonprofits, and universities.
- Go to trade shows, professional conferences, and professional association meetings.
- Survey past or current customers and employees.
- Look at what your competitors are doing.
- Utilize your professional contacts and networks.

It is also important to look at the field and the bigger picture of your local, national, or international community to find growth opportunities. Certain parts of the country may have a much stronger emphasis on certain trends or developments. If you were based, for instance, in Boulder, Colorado, it may be a better idea to begin a business involving organic foods than a business with swimwear. On the other hand, do not fall victim to the idea that because everyone else is doing something, you should too. The market in organic foods in Boulder may already be saturated, and there may be no businesses that sell bathing suits. Many people like to go swimming and sit in hot tubs in the nearby ski resorts, so a swimwear business could do quite well. To come up with a business venture, you want to follow your passion, but do not settle on something until you have done your research.

To get you thinking, here is a list of some business opportunities to which a background in mental health can lend itself very well:

- Wellness centers or holistic health care centers
- Consultation companies
- Learning centers for children or adults
- Parenting centers
- Publications or communications companies
- Training centers in specific areas of mental health

- Spas and resorts
- Health clubs and sports clubs
- Massage therapy and psychotherapy centers
- Physical therapy centers
- Adult education
- Multidisciplinary professional practices
- Spiritual development practices

THE FUNDING TO MAKE IT HAPPEN

Depending on the company you are trying to build, you may need a considerable amount of start-up funding. Lack of capitalization is one of the primary causes of small business failures within the first two years, so the financing of your business is extremely important.

Financing can come from savings or loans. The United States Small Business Administration (SBA) offers SBA loans that may be applicable to your practice or company idea. Their general website, http://www.sba .gov/, is a good source of information for many aspects of starting a business. According to Gatewood (in Bygrave & Zacharakis, 2004), in 1995, 7,000 lenders nationwide each made at least one SBA loan. This number has been on the rise, so there is a great deal of funding through the SBA loans. When working with an SBA-certified lender, the SBA will decide within three days whether to guarantee a bank loan, says Gatewood.

To apply for a loan, go to http://www.sba.gov/financing/basics/apply loan.html. You will need a business plan and a financial plan, including your balance sheets. As discussed in the beginning of this book, a business plan is useful for both loan procurement and corporate planning. The balance sheets are a measure of financial performance, separating out your assets (income) and liabilities (expenses). A nice example of a completed balance sheet is provided at http://www.toolkit.cch.com/tools/downloads /balsheet.xlt.

Another source of funding is through investors. One type of investor is a silent partner who owns a portion of the business but does not want any level of control over the operations of the company. Venture capitalists are another type of investor. These are firms that range in size from individual venture capitalists to very large corporations or investors. Venture capitalists seek out investment potentials that offer a very high potential growth rate. Private practices would typically not be attractive to venture capitalists, whereas other companies that can potentially expand nationally or internationally would be. Individual venture capitalists are sometimes referred to as "angel investors." Keep in mind that selling ownership in the business reduces your level of control over your company.

Do Not Make This Mistake

It is estimated that approximately 80 percent of small businesses fail in their first five years. If you decide to begin a company, you want to do so with the mind-set and activities that predict success and not failure. I think I have made this point several times, but I will make it again to be crystal clear: Do not make the mistake that so many clinicians-turned-entrepreneurs make by thinking that you know how to run a business because you are good at what you do. The quality of your work is extremely important, but there are typically many other aspects of running a business that may not be your strong points. Do not hesitate to hire people who are strong in your areas of relative weakness. You can bring people on as consultants or employees to help you avoid the mistake of so many entrepreneurs when they try to do everything alone.

In Gerber's classic book, *The EMyth Revisited* (1995), he says a "fatal assumption" of entrepreneurs is, "If you understand the technical work of a business, you understand a business that does that technical work" (p. 13). If you understand therapy, that is does not necessarily mean you understand how to run a business that provides therapy services.

Gerber describes phases of a business and states that you know a business is in the infancy stage when "the owner and the business are one and the same thing" (p. 35). If you define the business as the same thing as who you are, the business has already been confined and restricted to an individual person. This is like placing a fish (the business) in a coffee mug (your small vision)—there is very little room for development. In the stage of adolescence, according to Gerber, you begin to get help from others and begin pushing the business beyond its (and your) comfort zone. Finally, in the stage of growth and maturity, the business is operating in full accordance with the entrepreneurial vision. The day-to-day operations are all in line with the vision for the business. This, of course, means that you need to know the overarching vision or purpose of the organization, which requires some planning. Many entrepreneurs don't like to plan, they like to *do*. Remember that failing to plan often means planning to fail.

In short, remember these four takeaway points:

1. Do not try make yourself into the business—that is not sustainable.
2. Do not assume that you know how to turn your craft into a business.
3. Do get help in whatever ways possible if you want to be successful.
4. Do strive to make all of your business decisions in line with your vision.

TO INCORPORATE OR NOT TO INCORPORATE?

In a word: Incorporate. There is really no reason not to incorporate other than the initial incorporation fees, which can range anywhere from $300 to $5000 or more. The least expensive ways to incorporate are by doing it yourself or going through an online incorporation service. The next least expensive option is hiring an accountant to incorporate; you can also hire an attorney to do it. There is no way to get around paying the fees to incorporate. There typically are general incorporation fees, state fees, and city fees. For most types of corporations and limited liability entities, you will also need to have an attorney create an operating agreement and/or other legal documents.

Some of the benefits of incorporating your business include:

- Tax benefits (which vary, based on what type of business entity you create).
- Reduced personal liability and exposure of personal assets.
- Enhanced corporate image for marketing purposes.
- Enhanced corporate image for loan procurement purposes.
- Clear distributions of profits or dividends.

There are many types of corporations that therapists should consider forming when opening a new business, and they are best explained by an attorney. Henry C. Fader, Esq., a corporate and health care partner at Pepper Hamilton LLP, Attorneys at Law, a national firm based in Philadelphia (faderh@pepperlaw.com), described the different types of corporate entities to me as follows.

Many opt to create professional corporations, which apply to professional service firms. A professional corporation can be an S-corp or a C-corp. An *S-corp* is a business corporation that requires an election by the owner and shareholders. This type of corporation avoids taxation at the corporate level. All the money taxed is considered to be profit.

A *C-corp* is a business corporation that is subject to taxation at both the business and shareholder levels. If you were the employee, you would receive a salary. The corporation pays taxes on the profits for the year. If you're paying out dividends to the owner (yourself), you are then paying taxes again. The advantage is that you can choose your fiscal year and it can be something other than a calendar year. Many professionals do this to shift income from one year to the next, depending on which months are the busiest, so they can stay within certain tax brackets. For instance, if your business is quite slow over the summer, you can shift your calendar year to use the slow period to your advantage.

Other company entities include a *sole proprietorship*, which consists of you as sole business owner and operator. This is a common business entity for many private practices. It is not a corporation. With a sole proprietorship, all of your assets are exposed if you are unmarried. If you have a spouse, you can hold assets jointly or in your spouse's name for asset protection.

A *limited liability corporation (LLC)* has the tax status attributes of an S-corp—no taxation at the LLC level. People like it for its flexibility in determining who gets profits and when. In your operating agreement, you can determine how profits are distributed (for example, 90/10 owners can distribute profits 50/50). Some things are deductible for tax purposes in an LLC that are not deductible with other corporate structures. For instance, with an S-corp, you can't typically deduct health insurance, whereas with an LLC you generally can.

A *limited partnership* is a partnership in which one partner is the general partner and one is the limited partner. The limited partner has limited liability. A creditor cannot sue the limited partner for more than their investment (like a corporation) but the general partner can be sued for more. These structures are not very common in professional situations.

Interview with Kathy Miller, MA, LCPC

Kathy Miller is the founding director and president of OASIS: The Center for Mental Health, in Annapolis, Maryland. The center's web site is www.oasismentalhealth.com, and Kathy can be reached at (410) 268-8590.

You have built a very interesting and successful organization, OASIS: The Center for Mental Health. Give us some background on what you have created.

In 11 months, we have served over 800 new patients and provided over 3,000 patient services. We have five social workers, two to three psychiatrists, two full-time administrative staff, two part-time administrative staff, a CFO, and a vice president. I am president and executive director of the organization. We have clients primarily from Anne Arundel County (our target market) and patients who travel from as far away as northern Virginia and Delaware. This is primarily due to the length of time it takes to obtain an appointment with a psychiatrist and, to some degree, a therapist.

How did you formulate the idea behind your company?

I have been a therapist for 29 years and have had the opportunity to work in many different settings. I worked in an emergency room for four years, as well as in clinics, before I went into private practice 20 years ago. It was primarily during my work in clinics and in the emergency room that I recognized how limited services are for the mentally ill and that in a crisis, the situation was exacerbated. I strongly think that the mentally ill are accustomed to limited services and poorly trained professionals. They are ill equipped to disagree or argue with the system. As a result, I envisioned a clinic, similar to an ambulatory walk-in clinic, where people are seen within 24 hours. I was confident that with well-trained professionals and prompt treatment, we could treat people successfully in the community and return them to pre-crisis level.

At OASIS, we have found this to be true. One of our big accomplishments is our availability to see patients as promptly and frequently as needed, when they seek treatment. In our 11 months with 3000-plus services, we have hospitalized only seven people. Much of this is attributed to providing immediate care. Local emergency rooms (to provide comparison) indicate hospitalization for 50 percent of the mental health patients that present to the ER seeking mental health treatment. The two local ERs have referred 25 percent of our patients to us, which translates into 280 patients of our total 700-plus patient base. If it were not for OASIS, 50 percent of those 280 people from the ERs would likely have been hospitalized. In addition to providing immediate care, the cost savings by alternative treatment to hospitalization is significant.

What type of therapists do you employ?
Currently we have five therapists that are all credentialed as LCSW-C. We also accept PhDs and psychiatric nurses. We usually have three psychiatrists, although we are currently working with only two. All the therapists are required to have a background in emergency treatment and/or have worked in an emergency room setting.

Who did you partner or consult with during the development of the organization? What important advice have you learned?
We worked on the concept of OASIS for over two years with a community group that included clinicians, business professionals, people with a family member or loved one in treatment, and interested community members. I also consulted with the owner of a similar business many times.

The best advice I can give is that it is critical for entrepreneurs in the mental health field to recognize that this is a business and it must operate with the bottom line as a priority. This can create a dissonance when trying to meet the needs of the community while juggling the financial and other challenges of a new business. There must be a financial stream to cover this service. We first conceived OASIS as a nonprofit, but watched as several very good nonprofit mental health businesses failed, as nonprofit revenue streams dried up. We then switched to a for-profit model and pursued contracts with several insurance companies.

Do you have any predictions for future trends in the field?
I think our field is *slowly* overcoming the stigma of "mental illness," and I believe this process will continue. I hope we will see an increase in pencil-and-paper tests to screen patients for depression by primary care physicians, school counselors, pediatricians, and ob/gyns. I hope access to mental health treatment will have fewer barriers in the future. If that happens, you may see large companies increase access to mental health on-site instead of just using employee assistance program (EAP) counselors.

What are some of the entrepreneurial skills that therapists need to run successful companies and how can therapists or graduate students gain them?
The entrepreneur must be willing to do the homework—in other words, create a solid business plan and work with a group of advisers

to provide the skills that he or she does not possess. The entrepreneur must be willing to accept criticism of the program and let go of specific aspects if it is recommended for the good of the program. The entrepreneur/therapist must have a good working knowledge of how to put a start-up business together. On reflection, our business plan was dead-on in many areas, but off on other aspects. An entrepreneur must be flexible and adaptable to process new information and act on it quickly.

The therapist or graduate student would benefit by taking a course in running a business, which can be found at most community colleges. I also received help from our local Entrepreneur's Exchange, and the Anne Arundel Economic Development Committee.

How have you marketed your business and gained referrals and clients?

The efforts must be multidimensional. We found ads in local newspapers to be a positive vehicle, as well as meeting frequently with the main referring sources—primary care physicians, pediatricians, ob-gyns—and teaching them how and when to refer to the urgent care center. We also get referrals from the two emergency rooms and local support groups for mental illness. Word of mouth is wonderful. We have a marketing/public relations firm that has been helpful, too.

What are your top five recommendations for a therapist who wants to start a large company in the mental health field?

1. Be sure there is a need for the service in your community. Do your homework. This includes conducting surveys, focus groups, and other quantitative and qualitative research.
2. Find out if anyone else is doing this service or a similar one.
3. Create a business plan and obtain advice from professionals familiar with start-up companies.
4. Be sure you have the financial backing and know how you are going to pay your service providers.
5. Develop a marketing plan on how you are going to get your clients. We all agree there are people in need in the community for mental health services. But there are also barriers to get around: How do they find out about your service? How do they pay for it? And how do you educate the public about the need for the service?

Interview with Kurt Malkoff, PhD

Kurt Malkoff is the executive director of Matrix Psychological Services in Columbus, Ohio. He can be reached at (800) 886-1171 or via the company web site at www.matrixpsych.com.

What led you to create and expand Matrix?

I have been practicing clinical psychology since 1976. My first few years post doctorate were spent in traditional private practice. It became busy so I then brought in a few associates. At that time I viewed it as an hourly practice, as most private practitioners do. I began to recognize that much of the strength of an advanced degree in psychology is not only in seeing patients and doing psychotherapy, but that a therapist can create a business that solves problems. We (therapists) solve business, community, family, and individual problems. This recognition is the key to creating a service delivery system to address those larger problems.

After the first four or five years of doing clinical work along with my associates, I was approached by a large medical group to apply therapeutic services to an HMO (which at the time was a radical move in Ohio). They initially had 6,000 subscribers and we saw a few hundred new therapy patients a year. As their base of subscribers grew, in a couple years it was 40,000. At this point, I realized that I had a business, not a practice.

If you don't look at mental health service as a business, you won't be doing it very long. If you only went into it as a business, you should not have gone into it in the first place. There is a fragile balance between doing good and doing well.

We began doing some employee assistance program (EAP) work. I had never taken a business course but I grew up in the restaurant business and have always been service oriented. The quality of the service you provide is the bottom line, because people can get a service anywhere. That is probably why we have been so successful. We also try to be different. For example, we staff only doctoral level clinical psychologists. Currently, we have a network of around 6,500 psychologists across the country. Some of our corporate clients are The Limited, Abercrombie & Fitch, Lane Bryant, and Victoria's Secret.

The business vision and entrepreneurial spirit are clearly fundamental in creating a company as you describe. How can

323

psychotherapists foster this type of thinking and begin to think about different methods of service delivery?

The key is to almost remove yourself from a linear psychotherapeutic format and look at a larger model of problem solving. I think it's almost impossible to make a living commensurate with the level of training, education, and experience of a doctoral degree today. If a therapist is making around $100,000 with average overhead of 30 to 35 percent, plus taxes, there is a gross income of $50,000. You can use this type of thought process to inspire you to think of doing things differently. This is one of the values of looking at your career options from a broader business perspective rather than a linear one.

Think about what else you can offer and how you can offer it. For example, we have many divisions within Matrix that cover various services and populations. One of our divisions is Unfinished Business. It covers the consulting and preemployment assessment, executive evaluation, and trainings (for mental health practitioners). This division acts as a business within the business and allows us to leverage our strengths and expand our core services. In the context of traditional psychological work, we have an entire program devoted to the assessment and tracking of bariatric surgery patients.

Every year, I take doctoral students as practicum students and have seen differences in this type of business mind-set. I have talked with graduate students who are already bent to go in this direction and who look at their careers as a business. Many do not look at things in this way and feel limited by external circumstances, such as insurance. I think that insurance companies have encroached on the area of EAPs, which can make it difficult to begin an enterprise like this now.

One of our strengths has been our development of a strong EAP base. You can do interesting things like adding additional services to your existing client base. For us, we have the EAP base and have chosen to then offer different services to the same clients. We spend a lot of time trying to know our customer. This is very important—know your clients and what they want.

What are some of the joys and challenges in running a large corporation?

This is a very energizing venture. There is not a day that I come to work when I do not enjoy what I am doing. That does not mean that I enjoy everything I have to do, but I have people here to do the things I don't like to do. I know what I don't like to do, and I don't do a whole lot of it—that is the goal. Of course, I am the end of the line, so if something needs to be done and there is no one to do it, I will be the one to do it. But that does not happen often. We professionals have an exquisite understanding of human behavior and we can help solve problems. We teach the world how to behave.

There are always financial challenges. The difference between a business and an individual practice is that if you do x million dollars of business one year, you want to do x million plus y percent more the following year. There is a moving finish line. Nothing stays the same and you must constantly do more and better. So if you are the kind of person who wants to feel like you reached the finish line, it would be difficult. Successful businesses are constantly evolving and changing. You need to be somewhat competitive and like the challenges of the changes.

What are some qualities that a therapist needs to have or develop in order to be successful as a business director or entrepreneur?
With most successful businesses, there is a chance point. The entrepreneur will need to take a chance or a risk. I took a chance on our current Easton offices and signed a contract for over $1 million. This was a risk that has paid off because it has positioned us as different. You need to make yourself appear different and then actually be different.

Groups like ours tend to begin making money and then the owner or leader does not stay involved. I have always stayed involved. I see about six or eight direct sessions per week. I went to school to be a psychologist so I keep myself in it. I am also teaching, since you learn what you teach. This is the second year that I am co-teaching a business course on power and influence at the Fisher School of Business. It is the most work I have ever done for $2,500, but it was worth it because I was forced to do my homework and I have learned a great deal. I have read many, many business books.

You need to surround yourself with people who know what you do not know. I have no interest in micromanaging, and I have great people working with me. Our office manager, Charlene, has been here 20 years. Toby, our executive vice president, has worked with Matrix for 15 years. To understand this point, you need to understand yourself. I know that I have a strong work ethic, but deeper down I'm rather lazy—if I can do something in one hour instead of four, I will. I try to find people who will do 85 percent of what I can do. If I tried to do it all, I would have to do it all. People do well here because I empower them and do not micromanage. It can be scary because you are putting the checkbook in others' hands and letting them shape the business's destiny. Sometimes they will drop the ball, but usually not.

You need to know what is important in your life. I'm the poster child for work-life balance. I have skied 40 days a year and am typically out of the office 14 weeks of the year. You can do this if you work well when you are there.

A key to any successful business is to know when to cut your losses. I have had projects that I thought were wonderful but were actually sucking up money and time. You have to invest wisely and use your resources appropriately, and get out when something is not paying off.

Do you think that most therapists typically have the skills that can help them run a business?

Not many do have these skills. It would be like looking at medical school applicants and picking out those who could play basketball for the NBA. Most people who go into mental health professions have a limited view of their services and think small. Most therapists work for clinics and hospitals so they can get there at 9 and leave at 5. There is a reason that a full practice is 22 clients a week—that is how the system has been set up and that is what many want to do. I'm not saying that you need to work *more*, but you may need to think *differently*—it comes from you.

The strength of the system I have developed is that we have no clock-watchers because you earn what you earn. It is an eat-what-you-kill model. You are in control. It is not realistic to think you will work 30 hours a week and make a quarter of a million dollars a year. Most therapists do not have the big-vision mentality. It is like finding highly compassionate business people—uncommon.

(*Author's note: This means that you can have a distinct advantage if you develop your vision and thinking-big mentality*).

How might you know if you do have this quality?

Ask yourself whether you have the ability to take advantage of an opportunity. Business success is about taking a chance and going after opportunities. It usually means investing money and committing yourself, your time, and your resources. The really good businesspeople can take a beating—they often lose what they've gained and have war stories to tell. I've had my losses too. I had some accounts that I no longer have—although we have never lost an account because of the quality of services we provided. We manage thousands of cases and have never had a malpractice suit in the past 30 years, because we have the right systems in place.

Most people who develop businesses realize that instead of going from level 1 to level 2 to 3 to 4, they jump from 1 to 3 to 6 to 8. I immediately had two or three people working within my practice. I got the fact that I loved what I was doing and was not going to be financially successful if it was only me. To be successful in a business model, you need to think in a business model, not an individual one. I have a saying that I never want to make $300 an hour—I would rather have 30 psychologists billing at $125 an hour.

Look at where you are investing your time, and assess your ability to make decisions based on numbers. Eighty percent of therapists are doing their own billing and then forget to count this as time put into their practice. You need to honestly be able to calculate how much your ancillary expenses are costing you and make a decision about the quality of life that you want to have. I love psychology, but my real life is my personal well-being, my relationship with my wife and child, my involvement in the community (I chair a nonprofit community agency and am involved in many organizations in the community). When you do this right, you do have a life. That is the beauty of looking at your career from a business perspective—it opens up doors.

I recommend outsourcing billing and administrative services that are not your strengths and that would take a lot of your time. By myself, I could never have created the tracking software that we developed. The finances are key, since many mental health professionals think small about money, compared with other professions like physicians or lawyers. We should not be small-minded in our vision because we have such an extensive knowledge base. There is nothing we cannot help and there are always business opportunities. Know who you are and build on it to bring your knowledge to others.

Where do you see the mental health field going—what is the next big thing?
I think that pain management is the next big thing in mental health. Insurance companies spend so much money in this area. We are actually working on pain management programs now. Contrary to what a lot of the information out there is saying (in graduate programs, in the field), I think there are huge opportunities in mental health now, particularly as it relates to systems and business. Those opportunities are unlimited.

RESOURCES

BOOKS

Bygrave, W. D., & Zacharakis, A. (Eds.) (2004). *The portable MBA in entrepreneurship* (3rd ed.). New York: John Wiley & Sons, Inc.

Drucker, P. F. (1993). *Innovation and entrepreneurship* (1st ed.). New York: HarperBusiness.

Gerber, M. E. (1995). *The EMyth revisited: Why most small businesses don't work and what to do about it.* New York: HarperBusiness.

Hill, N. (1987). *Think and grow rich* (Reissue ed.). New York: Ballantine Books.

Hansen, M. V., & Allen, R. G. (2002). *The one minute millionaire: The enlightened way to wealth* (1st ed.). New York: Harmony.

Joint Commission/JCAHO (2004). *2004-2005 Accreditation process guide for behavioral health care, Joint Commission on the Accreditation of Healthcare Organizations.* Washington, DC: JCAHO.

Kushell, J. (1999). *The young entrepreneur's edge: Using your ambition, independence, and youth to launch a successful business* (1st ed.) (Princeton Review Series). New York: Random House.

Litman, M., Oman, J., & Allen, R. (2001). *Conversations with millionaires: What millionaires do to get rich, that you never learned about in school!* Reno, NV: Conversations with Millionaires LLC.

Strauss, S. D. (2005). *The small business bible: Everything you need to know to succeed in your small business.* New York: John Wiley & Sons, Inc.

Turner, M. L. (2004). *The unofficial guide to starting a small business* (2nd ed.). New York: John Wiley & Sons, Inc.

WEB SITES

American Entrepreneurs for Economic Growth:

www.aeeg.org

National Venture Capital Association:

www.nvca.org

Independent Business Consultants:

www.iibusa.org

Entrepreneur magazine:

www.entrepreneur.com

Inc. magazine:

www.inc.com

An excellent online entrepreneurship resource:

www.zeromillion.com

Fortune magazine:

www.fortune.com

U.S. Small Business Administration:

www.sba.gov

Association of Small Business Development Centers:

www.asbdc-us.org

Service Corps of Retired Executives:

www.score.org

Many resources for entrepreneurs:

www.entreworld.com

Fast Company magazine and resources:

www.fastcompany.com

TERMINOLOGY

accounts receivable (AR)   An asset on your balance sheet, AR accounts represent money that you will be paid, although you may not have been paid yet.

accounts payable   These are liabilities on your balance sheet because they are the unpaid bills of the business—the money you owe to your suppliers and other creditors.

AEEG   American Entrepreneurs for Economic Growth.

balance sheet   A financial statement that shows your assets and liabilities. It includes assets such as cash and accounts receivable, and liabilities such as debt and accounts payable.

capital   The money that you need to fund your business. It can be secured via loans, investors, savings, or other methods.

corporate structure (also called business structure)   The way in which you legally and operationally structure your business—for example, an S-corp, an LLC, or a limited liability partnership.

entrepreneur   A risk-taker who has the skills and initiative to establish a business.

entrepreneurial spirit   What many people call the essence of entrepreneurship. It often entails a sense of drive, independence, courage, risk-taking, natural business acumen, and creativity.

operating agreement   A legal document that dictates your business's terms of operations, including the roles of people involved with the company, profit sharing, and daily business operations.

outsourcing   Hiring outside consultants or companies to do the work that is outside of your core competency or that of your agency. Nationwide, outsourcing has significantly increased over the past several decades.

NVCA   National Venture Capital Association.

R&D   Research and development department within a company or organization.

service delivery system   The method by which you deliver your psychological or other services. This can be an individual model (like private practice), a group model (like group therapy), or a larger-scale model, such as consulting.

venture capital   Funding that is raised from a type of investor called venture capitalists who seek out investment potentials that offer a very high potential growth rate.

More Tools to Help You Become a Successful Therapist

You have spent your valuable time reading this book and I want it to help you enjoy a rewarding career. Please be in touch with any thoughts or feedback at: larina@PAScoaching.com.

Also visit www.TheSuccessfulTherapist.com to find:

- Many more resources and free tips
- Links to highly recommended business and career books
- E-books on marketing, coaching, professional speaking, and media work
- Free subscriptions to a marketing newsletter or The Successful Therapist List
- Information on the seminar *Be The CEO of Your Career*

Special Bonus: If you are interested in coaching to help you create a lucrative career or business, you can receive 25% off your **total costs** with the purchase of this book. Email: info@PAScoaching.com and say that you have this book.

Index

Need Help Getting Started?

Getting Started in Personal and Executive Coaching offers a go-to reference designed to help build, manage, and sustain a thriving coaching practice. Packed with hundreds of proven strategies and techniques, this nuts-and-bolts guide covers all aspects of the coaching business with step-by-step instructions and real-world illustrations that prepare you for every phase of starting your own coaching business.

This single, reliable book offers straightforward advice and tools for running a successful practice, including:

- Seven secrets of highly successful coaches
- Fifteen strategies for landing paying clients
- Ten marketing mistakes to avoid
- Sample business and marketing plans
- Worksheets for setting rates and managing revenue

Getting Started in Personal and Executive Coaching
Stephen G. Fairley and Chris E. Stout
ISBN 0-471-42624-5
Paper • $24.95 • 356 pp • December 2003

Getting Started in Private Practice provides all the information you need to confidently start and grow your own mental health practice. This book breaks down the ingredients of practice into more manageable and achievable components and will teach you the skills you need to avoid making costly mistakes. Containing dozens of tools that you can use to achieve your goals, this book has specific information that can be applied to your business today, worksheets that will help you calculate the true costs of various expenditures and activities, checklists that might save you from disaster, and lists of resources to investigate. Includes:

- Forms and examples of various practice aspects
- Step-by-step advice on writing a business plan and marketing your business
- Suggestions and ideas intended to help you get your creative juices flowing
- Practical and simple formulas to help calculate rates, revenues, and Return on Investment
- Comprehensive information on licensing procedures and risk management

Getting Started in Private Practice
Chris E. Stout and Laurie Cope Grand
ISBN 0-471-42623-7
Paper • $24.95 • 304 pp • October 2004

WILEY
Now you know.
wiley.com

❑ **Getting Started in Personal and Executive Coaching**
(ISBN 0-471-42624-5, $24.95US)

❑ **Getting Started in Private Practice**
(ISBN 0-471-42623-7, $24.95US)

SHIP TO
Name/Title _____
Organization _____
Address _____
City/State/Zip _____
Telephone _____

METHOD OF PAYMENT
❑ Bill my institution, PO# _____ (please include purchase order)
❑ Payment Enclosed (make all checks payable to John Wiley & Sons)
❑ Visa ❑ Mastercard ❑ American Express

Card Number _____Exp. Date _____
Signature _____

Credit card orders invalid if not signed. Add $5 shipping for first book, $3 for each additional book. Please add your local sales tax to all orders; be sure to add shipping and handling charges before calculating sales tax.

TO ORDER BY PHONE CALL TOLL FREE: 1-877-762-2974

MAIL TO: John Wiley & Sons, Inc., Attn: J. Knott,
111 River Street, Hoboken, NJ 07030

Grow Your Mental Health Practice

This essential resource provides crucial advice on how to build and run a mental health practice while serving clients and coping with the seemingly endless series of adjustments, documentation requirements, and ethical dilemmas that confront the profession today.

How to Build and Market Your Mental Health Practice also shows you how to:

• Market your services effectively and ethically
• Enhance your professional reputation
• Build a steady client referral base either inside or outside the managed care system
• Position yourself to serve client and community needs, while building the kind of practice you want

Supplemented with dozens of sample brochures, business plans, marketing plans, and self-assessment exercises, this accessible guidebook is what beleaguered therapists and counselors have been waiting for.

How to Build and Market
Your Mental Health Practice
Linda L. Lawless
ISBN 0-471-14760-5
Paper • $49.95 • 224 pp

How to Get Referrals provides step-by-step guidelines to get referrals by building and leveraging relationships with other professionals, community leaders, and the media.

You'll find out how to develop three primary skills that are essential to weaving a sustainable practice:

• How to interact with and relate to the local community and region
• How to work with managed care organizations and professional associations
• How to network with the World Wide Web community

How to Get Referrals is an excellent guide for getting the referrals necessary for a successful practice. With its concrete, practical advice on building networks and securing client recommendations, this book is a must for any healthcare professional.

How to Get Referrals:
The Mental Health Professional's
Guide to Strategic Marketing
Linda L. Lawless
and G. Jean Wright
ISBN 0-471-29791-7
Paper • $49.95 • 336 pp

WILEY
Now you know.
wiley.com